Gentlemen Collectors

Gentlemen Collectors
A History of Taxidermy in Norfolk (1820-1920) and the
Wild Bird Protection Acts

Ian Valentine

Poppyland Publishing

Copyright © Ian Valentine.

This edition 2024 published by Poppyland Publishing, Lowestoft, NR32 3BB.

www.poppyland.co.uk

ISBN 978 1 869831 37 0

All rights reserved. No part of this publication may be reproduced, stored in a retrieval system or transmitted by any means, mechanical, photocopying, recording or otherwise, without the written permission of the publishers.

Designed and typeset in 10.5 on 13.5 pt Gilgamesh Pro by Lewis Frederick Weller.

Picture credits can be found in the captions for each image.

Front cover: 'H.N. Pashley' by Lydia B. Mathews, watercolour on paper. The inscription reads 'A sketch from life in October 1924'.
Norfolk Museums Service, Norwich Museum and Art Gallery, NWHCM: 1926.55

Back cover: Taxidermy study of a ringed plover by Walter Lowne (1853-1915).
Steve Norris Photography.

Contents

Acknowledgements	vii
Preface	9
Introduction	13
Taxidermy in the Victorian and Edwardian Eras	24
Bluethroat Morning	31
T.E. Gunn and the Norwich Circle	54
Walter's Whale	70
Bustards, Brawls and Bankruptcy	102
The Wild Bird Protection Acts	125
Norwich Castle Museum and Modern Interpretation	163
Notes for the Collector	170
Appendix	175
Index	178

Acknowledgements

The online resource, *Historical Rare Birds*,[1] lists twenty-two taxidermists working in Norfolk. *Historical Rare Birds* is a group supported by British Birds Rarities Committee and set up to share knowledge about historical rare bird records prior to 1950. A few examples of rare birds that were preserved in Norfolk are referenced in this book with kind permission of Mark Pollitt and Keith Naylor who run the website. Where a species is marked 'rejected' this refers to the bird either being incorrectly identified or having been found outside of Norfolk or brought in from foreign parts. To illustrate all of the species that came into the taxidermist's hands would require volumes and might suggest glorification in the number of birds that were killed by the gunners. Instead I have focused on a selection of birds in seven case studies: Pallas's sandgrouse, the bluethroat, the kingfisher and the green woodpecker (the millinery trade), the little auk, the stone-curlew, the great bustard and the red kite.

The majority of the referenced books on ornithology and natural history were written within the one hundred year period of research. Any work on antique British taxidermy owes its debt to Christopher Frost and Pat Morris. Two works call for immediate mention: Frost's prized limited edition *A History of British Taxidermy* written in 1987 and Morris's detailed article that appeared in *Transactions of the Norfolk & Norwich Naturalists' Society*, Volume 28, Part 1, August 1988, entitled 'The work of Walter Lowne, Taxidermist of Great Yarmouth,' in which Morris examines the ledgers and record book of the taxidermist.

Founded in March 1869, the Norfolk and Norwich Naturalists' Society is dedicated to conserving the county's wildlife. Their annual publication, *Transactions of the Norfolk & Norwich Naturalists' Society*, is available to view online. For ease and brevity, the publication is referred to in the text and referenced in the endnotes as '*Transactions*.' Published books by the naturalist Arthur Paterson also provide an insight into the era in which the taxidermist thrived, especially his friend, Walter Lowne. Patterson also describes some of the other tough and unscrupulous characters near Breydon Water, an area which became increasingly popular with the Victorian and Edwardian gunners and collectors. Other reference books appear in the bibliography.

With thanks to: Graham Austen, Felicity Bolton, Natural History Conservator at the Royal Oak Foundation, Oliver Bone, Curator at Norwich Museums Service, Paul Doyle and Gergely Batta-Pajor, Robin and James Ellis, Christopher Frost, Louise Green, Collections and House Manager at Felbrigg Hall, Julie Griffith, Property Curator at Calke Abbey, Susanne Gronnow, Property Curator at Erddig House, Richard Jefferson, Dr Tony Leech, Chair of the Norfolk and

Norwich Naturalists' Society, Steve Norris, Sam Owen, Elizabeth Savory, Jamie Watson and the custodians at Ancient House, Museum of Thetford Life.

Notes

1. https://www.historicalrarebirds.info (accessed 12 September 2024).

Preface

Taxidermy resists modern rationale, caught as it is between Victorian science and aesthetic delight. The late 19th century Wild Bird Protection Acts provided a message of hope to the naturalists who knew things had to change if the specimens they had collected in glass cases could still be seen alive in the natural world. This book is as much about those who eventually sought to conserve birds as those that 'preserved' them.

My interest in Victorian and Edwardian taxidermy is the result of two pastimes colliding: birdwatching and antiques. I've been interested in ornithology as far back as I can remember, a hobby instilled by my father who watched birds all along the North Norfolk coast. As a boy growing up on the Norfolk coast in the late 1970s and early 1980s he took me to the ominously named Dead Man's Wood on the coast near Weybourne. Weybourne station doubled for the station in the fictional seaside resort of Walmington-on-Sea in the BBC Dad's Army episode 'The Royal Train.' My father said that, due to the nature of the tides, Dead Man's Wood got its name from dead mariners washing up there. In the wood, under the tutelage of Moss Taylor, an expert in bird migration, author and regional representative for the British Trust for Ornithology, we would ring storm-driven and migratory birds caught in specially prepared mist nets. Moss, Peter Allard, Don Dorling and the late Michael Seago published *The Birds of Norfolk* in 1999, the most comprehensive book since Bernard Beryl Riviere's *History of the Birds of Norfolk*, published in 1930. Passage and drift migrants were received at the wood, drawn to drink at artificial pools near the nets. I was taught the correct way to hold the birds and ring them: Siskins, Redpolls, Little Buntings, Red-breasted Flycatchers, Dusky Warblers and Linnets. Linnet was the name my father gave to his Enterprise sailing dinghy, the first sailing boat to overwinter at Morston quay near Blakeney.

During winter storms I'd walk the promenade and east beach at Sheringham with my father. The beach had been given back to the birds for the winter and the holiday-makers had long since departed. I remember the Black headed gulls standing in loose groups. Their necks were hunched like they were waiting at a windswept bus stop. Winds built up over the North Sea fetch from hundreds of miles away. The length of fetch affected the severity of the wind and size of the waves, from the Humber, Denmark or the North Pole, over four thousand kilometres away. Waves breaking on the beach could have been generated by storms in mid-ocean. The waves could 'throw' stones that could dislodge clods of material from the cliffs in much the same way as a mallet striking a wall. The tideline variously comprised of old crab pots, cuttlefish, tarred rope, fishing line paternosters and other marine debris. Also, sadly, oiled cormorants and other perished seabirds. Dad sometimes took dead and injured birds to Moss. I recall taking a dead Purple Sandpiper to him. The specimen was put it in his freezer for temporary preservation. Other 'storm finds' and the bird ringing gave me an appreciation of seeing birds up-close and an interest in taxidermy, which came to me later in life.

A side-line trading in antiques lead me to taxidermy. I had a stand at Waterside Antiques Centre in Ely, Cambridgeshire. The stand allowed me to indulge my enjoyment of mise en scène which set out to reflect a lost era. I replicated, in part, a Victorian study, reflecting the pastimes and hobbies of the absentee owner, except that, of course, all the sporting pictures, flags, leather cases, portraits, shotguns and taxidermy cases had price tags on them.

A chance meeting with Graham Austen, an expert with knowledge of birds, taxidermy and repair of specimens, greatly broadened my understanding of the subject. Graham kindly repaired an Edwardian taxidermy study of a White Pheasant which had been vandalised on my stand. Graham's interest in ornithology and natural history began in his early years. In the 1960s Graham had a part-time job in Newson's the Butchers in Ely, Cambridgeshire. Graham borrowed George Newson's .22 rim-fire gun and shot pigeons in Cathedral Park. Understandably, this would now be front-page news for the wrong reasons. Graham recalled the sound of the gun's retort echoing around the cathedral. Tom Lee was one of Ely's characters. He also shot pigeons in the park and used Graham's father's twelve-bore for the task, "Tom Lee of Ely is well known in local shooting circles for his hobby of taxidermy. There are not many such craftsmen left in the country and it is encouraging to find someone who devotes his spare time to the art."[1] At the time of writing a fox prepared by Lee appeared at auction online. His trade label reads, 'Preserved by T. Lee. Taxidermist, 3, Barton Square, Ely Cambs.' The fox was in a poor state and whether it realised the asking price of £75 is doubtful.

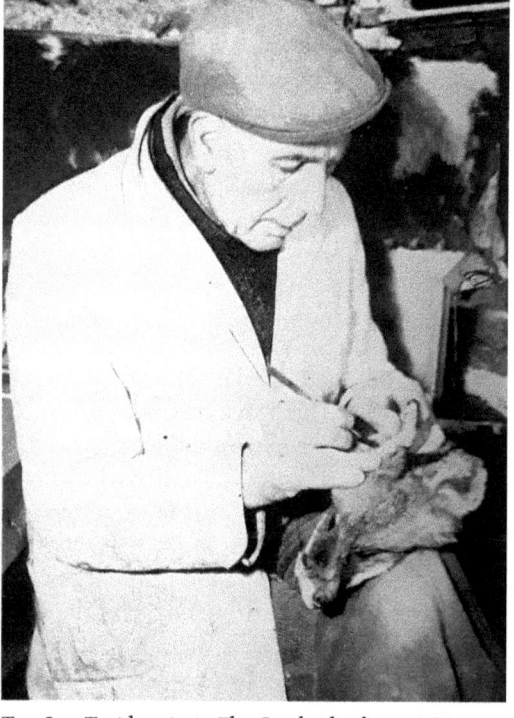

Tom Lee, Taxidermist in Ely, Cambridgeshire, 1960s.
G.R. Prior, Ely.

After school in the early

1960s Graham went to watch Tom work and began to learn from him. Graham described Tom as a taciturn and rough-and-ready Irishman. His wife was completely different, elegantly dressed and prim. Graham was only allowed into the house through the back, 'tradesman's' entrance. She reminded Graham of the actress Elizabeth Spriggs. Although Graham did not take up taxidermy as a profession, he successfully set-up several birds including a woodcock which he purchased from a game dealer in Ely. He began collecting taxidermy so that he could have specimens he could study for his painting, particularly for the texture and structure of feathers. Graham's latest work is a polyptych of the Peregrine Falcons at Ely Cathedral. Graham also applies his artistic talents to painting natural scenes at the back of taxidermy cases to give a three-dimensional element to dioramas, a style going back to Peter Spicer, the renowned taxidermist in Leamington Spa in the late 19th century. This book would not have arisen were it not for Graham's enthusiasm and knowledge.

Ian Valentine
August 2024.

Notes

1. G.R. Prior, unknown source (magazine), c.1973.

Introduction

In the same way that museums have been accused of being complicit with colonialism, taxidermy collections on public display have attracted proscriptive opinions. They have a contentious heritage and have not been free from criticism in recent years. For many people taxidermy is excessive, a reminder of Imperial collecting and pilfering, something that should be resigned to the past, irrelevant in our enlightened age. Victorian natural history specimens are framed by paradox and are perceived by many people as cultural relics. Displays are provocative and unsettling. They ask the question, 'What am I meant to think about this?' The descriptions, 'weird and wonderful,' 'gothic and eccentric' are often used by the casual observer. Individual taxidermy pieces are often seen as objects of buffoonery in popular culture: think Tony Hancock's treasured eagle. In February 2022 I went to see a theatre adaption of *Wish you Were Dead* at the Norwich Playhouse. The set contained taxidermy trophy mounts which were commented on by one of the characters, "They're creepy, and their eyes follow you around the room." Some people are repelled by the uncanny preservation of an animal that was once a sentient creature, a totemic reminder of loss of species and habitat. However, for a moment we have to try to imagine ourselves viewing taxidermy through Victorian eyes, through the vision of another era where 'naturalists' were seen differently to how we perceive them today. Taxidermy was newsworthy. Any fine specimen which could be viewed in a taxidermist's shop window was often reported in a local newspaper. Ornithology was seen as a science where collecting of bird skins was a means by which biology and comparisons between species could be studied. With growing environmental awareness taxidermy needs interpretation as 'natural history' does not quite cover it today. In his 1907 book, *A Bird Collector's Medley*, E.C. Arnold states, "Time was when the possession of a good collection of stuffed birds tended to distinguish a man as a naturalist."[1]

Victorian values attract opprobrium. Modern sensibilities are at odds with what was once viewed as a scientific pursuit. It is difficult to conceive today that collecting bird's eggs was seen as a healthy and educational pastime for the young and featured in publications such as the long-running *Boy's Own Paper* (1879-1967). There is the obvious push to measure yesterday's mores by today's and find the former wanting, leading to presentism. In his introduction to the re-print of *Notes on the Birds of Cley, Norfolk* by H.N. Pashley (taxidermist 1843-1925), Christopher Frost puts it well, "Shooting and collecting were a way of life in Pashley's day. The study of natural history was then at the stage where most knowledge was gained by comparing specimens, and the legacy of taxidermy is still significant in modern zoology especially in the analysis of rare and extinct species. Clearly nobody today would condone the apparent preoccupation with shooting rare birds described in this book, but we cannot be retrospectively critical of behaviour that was both normal and lawful over a hundred years ago merely because it would be unacceptable today."[2] Perhaps natural history museums and country houses in the care of National Trust and English Heritage are the perfect places to untangle and explain this history.

Taxidermists often described themselves as naturalists in the trade directories of the time and also on their trade labels which were glued inside or on the backs of their taxidermy cases. They often contributed to ornithological and natural history publications. Behind the artistic process of taxidermy lay destructive collecting practices, but the progression from shooting and collecting to the Wild Bird Protection Acts is an important story and one that I hope is reflected in this book.

Norfolk is steeped in ornithological history. The county contained ornithologists and naturalists whose knowledge helped in forming the Wild Bird Protection Acts in the late 19th century. Norfolk naturalists also promoted amendments to include species they saw were under threat but not covered in the Acts. The Acts and successive amendments marked a turning point in the popularity of taxidermy and a gradual change in perception of the natural world. Over the last three years in Breckland I've seen marsh harriers, lapwings, flocks of golden plovers and meadow pipits, siskins, ravens and a white-tailed eagle. One wonders how long these birds and other species would have survived in the rapacious years of shooting and collecting if the Acts had not been passed. The Norfolk taxidermist Henry Pashley (1843-1924) recorded, "Not seen [golden plovers] in such large numbers either in spring or autumn as in former years."[3]

Norfolk deserves particular attention as parts of the county were probably the most prolific areas for bird collectors in the British Isles: Breydon Water near Great Yarmouth and Cley-next-Sea on the North Norfolk coast. In his foreword to Henry Pashley's *Notes on the Birds of Cley, Norfolk*, published in 1925, B.B. Riviere reveals the importance of the littoral landscape around Cley, "It is probably a fact that more rare migrants have been obtained by collector within this area than in any other of equal extent in England, or, with the exception of Fair Isle, in Great Britain,"[4] Although the Norfolk coastline is nearly one hundred miles long, it incorporates a relatively short length of cliff. The rest is made up of marshes, dunes and shingle beaches. It's an emergent coastline with shallowing seas, offshore bars, shingle ridges, marshland and mudflats. All provide rich habitats for birdlife, which reflects the fact that bird taxidermy is prominent in Norfolk collections.

There were symbiotic links between Victorian professions and pastimes which included the bird and animal preservers (by the early 1900s trade directories began using the term 'taxidermist' rather than 'animal and bird preserver' or 'bird-stuffer'). Bird dealers, wildfowlers, landowners and collectors, naturalists, farmers, brush makers, butchers, fowl dealers, bird catchers, furriers, hairdressers, hatters (sometimes called 'plumassiers' on account of feather dressing), hide and skin dealers, joiners and carpenters, leather merchants and milliners all had dealings with each other. There were close ties and collaboration between the naturalists and taxidermists, as revealed by the books of Arthur Patterson and the diaries of Maurice Bird. One can say that taxidermists expanded on the techniques of upholsterers, tanners and furriers to reassemble skins. They sometimes looked to the game dealers to source rare specimens. Perhaps the most notorious game dealers in Norfolk were Durrant's in Great Yarmouth. Most of the dealers were concerned with standard fare: hares, pheasants and partridges, rather than anything unusual brought in by a gunner. A number of people could be involved before a specimen arrived in the taxidermist's workshop. In 1878 a pine martin landed in the hands of the famous Norwich taxidermist, T.E. Gunn, "it was trapped by a man named Wilmott in a fir plantation at Hevingham marl pit … Wilmott sold it to Samuel Howard, of the Marsham Arms, who took it to Mr. Gunn."[5] Taxidermists provided a service for collectors, naturalists, anglers and sportsmen but the profession remains mysterious. There was rivalry between taxidermists. The wildfowlers, 'gunners and runners' played one taxidermist against the other to get the best price for a specimen. There are stories of sharp practice and dubious tactics. Many of the minor taxidermists remain in the shadows, where, being a secretive bunch, they would be happy to stay. There are scraps of information and reports including brawls, misdemeanours and debt. There exists ledgers, diaries, letters and workbooks which build up a picture of two important Norfolk taxidermists: Henry Pashley of Cley and Walter Lowne of Great Yarmouth.

The use of arsenic in preserving specimens greatly prolonged the life of the cases but got under the fingernails of careless taxidermists. At the end of *The Record Book of Walter Lowne, bird stuffer of Fuller's Hill* (Great Yarmouth), the naturalist Arthur Patterson writes in his own hand about his friend, "In these last years, [1911-1913] poor old Lowne was frequently ill. He used arsenic for preservatives rather carelessly and probably his illnesses were due to this and his entire collapse."[6] There is no direct proof that the use of arsenic shortened the lives of taxidermists but the preservative mixture used was a heady combination of camphor, powdered arsenic, white soap, salts of Tartar and powdered lime. The use of arsenic might in part explain the longevity of certain taxidermist's work like Gunn's and Lowne's. There are no surviving cases, at least in circulation, of many of the taxidermists mentioned in this book. For instance, Thomas Knights of Norwich gave up using arsenic which might account for the rarity of his cases. One can say that it is now rare to find a case in good condition that predates the 1830s. Insects, or their grubs and eggs, may also have played a part in the destruction of cased taxidermy. They may have been present in prepared specimens when the wooden case was created and sealed, or a badly put together case might cause re-infestation through cracks.

The history of taxidermy in Norfolk can only be thoroughly explained by the relationship between the taxidermists, naturalists and ornithologists. Their interactions were generally congenial but occasionally frosty. Their writing and various articles reveals the curious position the taxidermist had within the world of the naturalist, who naturally wished to preserve species and habitats but at the same time used taxidermy as a conduit to study and learning as well as building up their own private collections. This seems a familiar and even inevitable situation in the years preceding the Protection Acts before the progress in photography and film which allowed close-up study without use of the gun.

It is worth expanding on the backgrounds of a certain number of naturalists as they are intrinsically linked to the taxidermists and their research and are referenced throughout the book. Many were collectors of taxidermy and some of them began creating lists of species when they were children. John Henry Gurney Jr., Henry Stevenson, Arthur Patterson, Thomas Southwell and the Reverend Richard Lubbock are key figures. Gurney wrote the first in a series of natural history publications in 1840 when he was 21 years old. All went on to be passionate founders and members of the Norfolk and Norwich Naturalists' Society in 1869. Taxidermists including Thomas Gunn, Henry Pashley, Walter Lowne and John Cole contributed to the annual *Transactions* of the Society. They also contributed to *Ornithological Notes from Norfolk* which Gurney and Riviere (upon Gurney's death) compiled into annual reports. The information they gave often revealed where a bird was shot, the stomach contents noted before preservation, previous sightings in Norfolk and its perceived rarity. Anything pertinent to gaining more understanding and knowledge. By the 1880s recorders and contributors to Norfolk publications included Lord Lilford, Lord Montagu, E.T. Booth, Maurice Bird, George E. Lodge and the taxidermist Howard Saunders. The taxidermists Walter Lowne and Henry Pashley also continued to contribute sightings and anything they deemed of interest up until their deaths. The Reverend Maurice Charles Hilton Bird, often simply known as 'MCH' (1857-1924) was the rector of Brunstead on the Norfolk Broads. A keen naturalist, he kept a diary of his sightings for over 50 years. Bird's diaries reveal correspondence and friendship with J.H. Gurney Jr., Dr Sydney Long, Arthur Patterson, the photographer Emma Turner and the taxidermists Walter Lowne and Edward Charles Saunders. James Parry has written a biography of Bird entitled *Maurice Bird. The Gilbert White of the Broads* which is published by the Norfolk and Norwich Naturalists' Society.

By the end of the First World War natural history and the burgeoning concept of conservation merged, giving rise to keen advocates including B.B. Riviere (1880-1953) and the third Earl of Leicester at Holkham Hall. A passage from the 1919 *Transactions* reads, "We are fairly entitled to consider the strides which British Ornithology has made since the inauguration of the Norfolk and Norwich Naturalists' Society as largely due to the enterprise of men like Henry Stevenson, Southwell, the two Newtons,[7] and others who belonged to it. The friends of Henry Stevenson have passed away to another land, but there still remain plenty of staunch men, and in saying this no doubt there will come before your minds the well-known names of Arthur H. Patterson, H. N. Pashley, E. C. Saunders, B. Dye, W. G. Clarke, T. E. Gunn, J. Vincent, M. C. Bird, Miss E. L. Turner, C. Ticehurst, S. H. Long, B. B. Riviere, R. Gurney, Sir T. D. Pigott, N. Tracy, W. H. Trick, H. Wormald, C. Borrer, and several others."[8]

John Henry Gurney Jr. (1848-1922) was from an old established Norfolk family. He was one of the original members of the Norfolk and Norwich Naturalists' Society, serving four times as its president. He was an avid collector of taxidermy including the excellent work of John Cole. He lived at Keswick Hall near Norwich where he had amassed a large natural history collection. His ornithological interest extended to foreign climes, as the Reverend J Crompton states in the forwarding address of the *Transactions* of the Norfolk and Norwich Naturalists' Society, 1870-71, "We have to thank heartily Mr. J. H. Gurney, jun. for his paper giving some of the results of his journey in Spain and Algeria, a district rarely visited by ornithologists, as also to rejoice in finding him following with such ardour and scientific accuracy, the steps of his father, to whom this [Norwich Castle] Museum owes such a large debt for his celebrated collection."[9] The influence of his father is revealed by Thomas Southwell in his obituary to Gurney Sr. in *Transactions* of the year:

> In 1838 Mr. Gurney began to keep a Natural History Journal, in conjunction with J. G. Barclay, T. F. Buxton, and the late Charles Buxton: this volume is full of interesting notes, and none more so than his own, which are chiefly about birds. Perhaps the most important is one on the last Norfolk Bustard (killed near Swaffham in 1838) which he saw in the flesh when it was sent up to Norwich. Although his father was too strict a Quaker to allow him to handle a gun, he used to get Bright, the Earlham gardener, to shoot for him, and formed a collection of flat bird-skins, which were sewn into a large book with canvas leaves. His son, Mr. J. H. Gurney, tells me he has never seen this ornithological relic, but believes that not many years ago it was in existence. He also commenced a natural history collection when he was about ten years of age; and a list drawn up by himself, soon afterwards, enumerates sixty-one specimens at Earlham. This boy's collection was stuffed for him by Butcher, Hall, and Hunt, professionals, all of whom, except the last, have now sunk into oblivion. It consisted of Stoats, Owls, Thrushes, &c., but there were some rare birds, as three Smews, a Fulmar Petrel, and a Red-necked Phalarope, the latter shot at Weybourne by his uncle Sir Fowell Buxton.[10]

Gurney's last work, *Early Annals of Ornithology* was published in 1921. By the early 19th century Gurney's letters and articles reveal a drive to protect rare birds from the gunners and egg collectors, reflecting an evolving attitude of 'naturalist collectors.' Previous and successive generations of Gurneys are in the forefront of natural history in Norfolk, including Robert Gurney (1879-1950), J.H. Gurney's nephew, who lived at Ingham Old Hall near Hickling. Robert set up the world's first-ever freshwater laboratory on Sutton Broad to research the ecology of the broad and wider Broads ecosystems.[11] A glass case called 'The Great Gurneys' in Norwich Castle Museum is dedicated to the influential family.

The task of publishing an informative inventory of the birds of Norfolk began with Henry Stevenson's three-volume work, *The Birds of Norfolk, with Remarks on their Habits, Migration and Local Distribution*. Stevenson (1833-1888) published the first volume in 1866 and the second in 1870. The third volume was

John Henry Gurney, Jr. Gurney was one of Norfolk's most respected ornithologists. He was elected a fellow of the Zoological Society in 1868 and a fellow of the Linnean Society in 1885.

Reproduced with permission of the Norfolk and Norwich Naturalists' Society.

completed by Thomas Southwell and published in 1890 after Stevenson's death. The first editions of Stevenson's work contain nine splendid illustrations, five hand-coloured plates and four tinted lithographs. The work remains the most comprehensive 19th century study of the biology, behaviour and distribution of Norfolk birds. Stevenson is keen to acknowledge all his sources, which include most of the prominent taxidermists working in Norfolk during his lengthy research.

Thomas Southwell (1831-1909) was born in Kings Lynn. He contributed to various publications and was honourable secretary to the Norfolk and Norwich Naturalists' Society and president both in 1879 and 1893. He was a founding member of the society and remained an active member up until his death. He contributed one hundred papers and articles in their publications. He also wrote for the Society for the Protection of Birds and was elected a fellow of the Zoological Society in 1872. He was a voracious reader, compiler and knowledgeable on a variety of subjects. The following passage is taken from the Norfolk and Norwich Naturalists' Society, *Transactions* for 1909:

> This well-remembered member died in 1909, in the seventy-ninth year of his age, to the great loss of our Society, which never possessed a more ardent supporter. His life and labours are the subject of an excellent memoir by Dr Sydney Long, which will be found, together with a good portrait, in the ninth volume of our *Transactions*. Southwell's early life was spent at Kings Lynn, where he made many useful observations on birds. Among the papers president's address consigned to the [Castle] Museum after his death is a long article written in 1851, and apparently intended for publication, entitled "Remarks on the Birds of the County of Norfolk, but more particularly the neighbourhood of Kings Lynn," but it was never printed, and would now be thought out of date. From Lynn with his Quaker friend, Daniel Burlingham, Southwell explored the country-side, and spent his holidays in searching for plants and birds … At all times fond of the country, Southwell generally had something to jot down in his journal about birds. On June 5, 1882, we find him noting that he had driven from Thetford to the Wretham meres, where he had seen with delight plenty of Coots, Grebes, Gulls, Tufted Ducks, Pochards, Shovellers, and Mallard … Southwell's principal works, besides numerous scientific papers—many of them of great value— were the continuation of Stevenson's "Birds of Norfolk," and a most useful and important reprint of Sir Thomas Browne's "Norfolk Natural History," as well as an excellent edition of Lubbock's "Fauna of Norfolk." In these publications he received much help from his friend, Professor Newton, an assistance which he was always ready to acknowledge. In 1885 he attended the sale of the Rising collection at Horsey with the writer, when the Buffle-headed Duck and other good things were secured for the Museum. Mr. Rising gave five pounds for this duck, and thought it dear, but on the present occasion it was knocked down to Southwell, after some spirited bidding, for twenty-six pounds, five shillings. In May, 1896, Southwell delivered a lecture to a large audience, with the

Dean of Norwich in the chair, entitled "Birds, their Enemies and their Protection," a subject in which he had long taken a great interest, for, although no sentimentalist, he had bird-life very much at heart. This address, which was given at the Castle, attracted considerable attention, but although printed in full by the newspapers at the time, it was never republished. He was, however, at all times better known as a writer than as a lecturer, and many a good magazine article emanated from his fruitful pen, several of which are enumerated by Dr Long.[12]

Dr Long refers to Sydney Long (1870-1939), ornithologist, Honourable Secretary of the Norfolk and Norwich Naturalists' Society and founder of the Norfolk Naturalist's Trust which became the Norfolk Wildlife Trust. Long played an important role in wildlife conservation in Norfolk, exploring the county in his open-top car. Long wrote a memoir of Southwell stating, "There is one subject in which Mr. Southwell took especial interest, and it is no exaggeration to say that it was in part owing to his continued perseverance in the matter that legislation finally resulted. We refer to the preservation, during the breeding season, of those species of birds that formerly had nesting haunts in this county, and which, owing to the continuous depredations of egg-dealers and others, were rapidly becoming extinct as breeders. He was a strong supporter of the various Bird Protection Societies that have been formed in the county, such as those at Yarmouth, Wells, Blakeney, etc., and Norfolk will ever owe a debt of gratitude to him for the timely support he gave to this movement."[13]

Richard Lubbock's *Observations on the Fauna of Norfolk*, first published in 1845 is regarded as a classic work on Norfolk natural history. The original book, which by the time of Lubbock's death was out of print, is accessible via the Norfolk Record Office. I am lucky to have an edition from 1879 with Thomas Southwell's introduction. Henry Stevenson and Lubbock were great friends - Stevenson wrote an in-depth memoir of his fellow naturalist in the 1876 *Transactions* (the year in which he died) which also appears in later editions of his book. Stevenson's memoir affords the reader with much information on the life of one of Norfolk's most important naturalists. Lubbock was born in 1798, the eldest of eight children who all died before him. Private tutoring and education at Norwich Grammar School lead to completion of a B.A. and M.A at Pembroke Hall in Cambridge and ordination into the Church in 1825. His uncle was J. Postle of Colney Hall near Norwich. Stevenson states that Postle possessed a collection of stuffed birds which had an attraction to the young ornithologist. Stevenson thought that Lubbock may have contributed specimens to the taxidermy collection at Colney Hall as Lubbock was also keen with the gun. A curacy at Downham led to studying the fauna of the Fen district and the habits of the shore birds that frequented the Wash. Subsequent curacies were situated within a few miles from Norwich. The close vicinity of the Broadland to his vicarages at Rockland and Bramerton enriched Lubbock's knowledge of the fauna of the marshes and Broads, an area of Norfolk he devoted much to in *Observations on* the *Fauna of Norfolk*. William White's *History, Gazetteer, and Directory of Norfolk 1883* reveals that St. Mary's Church in Eccles has a, "stained glass window with three lights ... recently erected by subscription, in memoriam of the later rector, the Rev. Richard Lubbock, M.A." Again, this curacy near Attleborough opened up new areas to study including every Broad on the river Bure and the expanse of Breydon Water ('parson-naturalists' present an interesting wider subject of research). Stevenson's memoir reveals Lubbock devoted much of his life to ornithology and natural history collections, "With the late M. Lombe, of Melton, near Norwich, he was in frequent communication when that gentleman was forming his fine collection of British Birds, which now bear his name in the Norwich Museum."[14] His *Observations on the Fauna of Norfolk* also contains detailed chapters on river fish, mammals, falconry and hawking and a detailed description of the bird decoy and its working, which was regarded as a classic in natural history in the Edwardian era. In 1872 Lubbock was elected an honorary member of the Norfolk and Norwich Naturalists' Society.[15] William Alfred Dutt states, "[Lubbock's] knowledge of the habits of different birds enabled him to give useful information on those that collected them."[16] Like many naturalists and taxidermists of the time Lubbock recorded his bird sightings in the annual report of *Ornithological Notes from Norfolk*. For instance, "On March 7th, Mr. E. Gunn [17] received a White Wood Pigeon from Costessey and on September 12th I saw one at Keswick."[18]

The celebrated Norfolk naturalist Arthur Patterson, gave much colour to the world of natural history, taxidermy, wildfowling and collecting. He is another figure central to the history of taxidermy in Norfolk. Little would be known about the skilful Norfolk taxidermist Walter Lowne had it not been for Patterson saving his workbooks from destruction. Patterson was born in Great Yarmouth in 1857. For naturalists, a love of nature invariably began at an early age and Patterson was no exception. This fervour might be interrupted by life's circumstances, a different career or war service, but it's a passion to which they inevitably return. Although Patterson wrote his first nature notebook at twenty-one years old and contributed an article to a local newspaper, he worked at a variety of jobs to earn a living. Beryl Tooley, his great granddaughter said that he worked, "peddling tea, as an assurance agent, taxidermist, a sewing machine salesman, postman, ticket attendant, zoo-keeper and warehouseman. His first regular employment came in 1892 when he was appointed School Attendance Officer, a post he held for twenty years."[19] At the age of thirty-nine he began writing under the pen-name John Knowlittle. He studied the habits of gulls, wading birds and rare visitors to Great Yarmouth, Breydon Water and the Broads. He hung up his gun in exchange for binoculars, but he still knew the old wildfowler gunners who he befriended as a boy. Arthur H. Smith wrote a description of Patterson in the *Naturalist's Journal* in 1901, "It is easy to picture a wiry, slightly-bowed man, with the profile of an artist of romance, standing where reeds and rushes bow over still waters, intently watching the movements of a rare visitor to Broadland."[20]

He was highly thought of by the Norfolk and Norwich Naturalists' Society and became Honorary Secretary of the Great Yarmouth Section of the Society. He wrote numerous articles for nature journals, natural history publications and newspapers, occasionally supplemented by his sketches. Beryl Tooley states, "In May 1935, he realised his greatest ambition, that of being elected an Associate of the Linnean Society of London, which was restricted to only twenty five associates; his name had been put forward by Her Grace the Duchess of Bedford, twenty nine years earlier in 1906. Arthur Patterson died later that years at the age of 78."[21] Founded in 1788 by Sir James Edward Smith, The Linnean Society of London is the oldest society devoted to natural history. It takes its name from Carl Linnaeus, who devised the Linnaean taxonomy of rank-based classification. In 1883, the famous Norwich taxidermist, T.E. Gunn, was also elected a Fellow. Patterson's varied works include: *Man and Nature on Tidal Waters*, *Wild-fowlers and Poachers*, *From Hayloft to Temple*, *The Story of Primitive Methodism in Yarmouth*, *Wildlife on Norfolk Estuary*, *Through Broadland in a Breydon Punt* and, perhaps incongruously, *Notes on Pet Monkeys and How to Manage Them*. The Duchess of Bedford wrote an introduction to *Wild Life on Norfolk Estuary*. Her Grace was a keen and knowledgeable ornithologist, visiting Henry Pashley's taxidermy shop in Cley on many occasions. Pashley also wrote chapters for *The Book of the Open Air: British Country Life in Spring and Summer*, edited by nature writer and poet Edward Thomas.

It is also worth mentioning Bernard Beryl Riviere (1880-1953). B.B. Riviere was a surgeon, naturalist, ornithologist and writer. His father was the well-known painter Briton Riviere who exhibited at the Royal Academy, devoting much of his time to painting animals, especially dogs. Riviere's most well-known book is *History of the Birds of Norfolk* published in 1930. He was an avid member and supporter of the Norfolk and Norwich Naturalists' Society for forty-five years, serving as Vice President, President (1920-1) and Honourable Treasurer and writing articles on various subjects. He also wrote reports for *British Birds* from 1923 to 1934. He died in Salhouse in December 1953.

Arthur Patterson dictating *Nights and Days with the Old Breydon Fowlers* to the young naturalist Edward (Ted) Ellis. Ted Ellis became a well-known naturalist, broadcaster and writer on East Anglian natural history.

Image courtesy of the Norfolk County Council Library and Information Service at www.picture.norfolk.gov.uk.

The Victorian taxidermists are still recognised as highly skilled and creative craftsmen and good examples of Victorian and Edwardian taxidermy often realise high prices at auction. The trade itself is far from being resigned to the past. A cursory internet search will reveal skilled taxidermists operating in Norfolk today including Howard Bennet, Nicky Secker-Bligh, Richard Brigham, and A.M. Edwards. Modern taxidermy, strictly governed by regulations, exists in a world where animals do not need to be killed for the purposes of its art. Zoos, wild-life parks, farmers and 'roadkill' provide potential specimens.

Notes

1. Christopher Frost, *A History of British Taxidermy*, (Lavenham, The Lavenham Press, 1987), p. 13
2. H.N. Pashley, *Notes on the Birds of Cley, Norfolk* (1925), introduction to the new edition by Christopher Frost, (Lavenham, The Lavenham Press, 1992), vi.
3. Ibid. p. 121.
4. Ibid. (Foreword by B.B. Riviere), p. 4.
5. *Transactions*, Norfolk and Norwich Naturalists' Society (Norwich, Fletcher and Son, 1878), p. 611.
6. *The Record book of Walter Lowne, bird stuffer of Fuller's Hill*, Norfolk Record Office, doc ref. MS 4185.
7. Sir Edward Newton and his brother Alfred Newton, both ornithologists.
8. *Transactions*, Norfolk and Norwich Naturalists' Society, (Norwich, A.E. Soman & Co. 1919), pp. 19-20.
9. Rev. J. Crompton, (address) *Transactions*, Norfolk and Norwich Naturalists' Society, (Norwich, Fletcher and Son, 1870-71), p.3. Shelduck.
10. T. Southwell, Memoir of the late John Henry Gurney, Sr., *Transactions*. Norfolk and Norwich Naturalists' Society, (Norwich, A.E. Soman & Co. 1891), p. 158.
11. J. Parry, *Maurice Bird. The Gilbert White of the Broads*. Norfolk and Norwich Naturalists' Society, (Lavenham, Lavenham Press, 2024), p. 104.
12. *Transactions*, Norfolk and Norwich Naturalists' Society, (Norwich, A.E. Soman & Co. 1919), pp.12-13.
13. Dr S. Long, *Transactions. Obituary Notices*. Norfolk and Norwich Naturalists' Society, (Norwich, A.E. Soman & Co. 1909), pp. 135-7.
14. H. Stevenson, Memoir of the Late Rev. Richard Lubbock, First published in 1845, re-printed in Rev. Richard Lubbock, *Observations on the Fauna of Norfolk and more particularly on the District of the Broads*, (Norwich, Jarrold & Sons, 1897), xiv.
15. Ibid. 12, pp. 19-20.
16. William Alfred Dutt, *The Norfolk Broads*, (London, Macmillan, 1906), p. 87.
17. Son of taxidermist T.E. Gunn.
18. B.B. Riviere, *Ornithological Notes from Norfolk*, 23rd Annual Report (1916). p.234.
19. B. Tooley, B, 'Introduction,' *Scribblings of a Yarmouth Naturalist. An edited selection from the Writings of Arthur Henry Patterson, A.L.S., (John Knowlittle)*, (self-published, 2004), p. iii.
20. Ibid. p. 131.
21. Ibid. iii.

Taxidermy in the Victorian and Edwardian Eras

The Victorian age saw a great period of country house building in Britain. The wealthiest captains of industry and commerce bought estates to enjoy country pursuits including the familiar triumvirate of hunting, shooting and fishing. By the middle of the 19th century the craftsmanship of the taxidermist could be seen in the billiards rooms, morning rooms, drawing rooms and studies of country houses. There were cases of British birds and mammals but also exotic birds with striking plumage and 'trophy mounts' from foreign tours. In the Edwardian era taxidermy cases could be seen in the lobby set against dark holly-green walls, perhaps next to a jardinière or aspidistra.

A marked interest in natural history grew as the British Empire expanded. A display case in Norwich Castle Museum explains the importance of voyages of discovery, "HMS Rattlesnake went to chart the treacherous waters of the Great Barrier Reef. The captain's father, who was the Bishop of Norwich, paid for a crew member to collect specimens for Norwich Museum." Naturalists built up collections of British birds and rarities. Carl Linnaeus, a Swedish schoolmaster and doctor, developed his Linnaean system of nomenclature for plants and animals.[1] Linnaeus cited five graduated categories in *Systema Naturae*: kingdom, class, order, genus and species. Through classification, the natural world could be ordered. Collectors became devoted cataloguers. Egg and butterfly collections were exhibited in purpose-built museums in private houses and painstakingly catalogued. New specimens were sought where there were gaps 'in the order.' Some of these collections were eventually given or bequeathed to museums or for scientific research. The philosophers and evolutionary scientists that naturalists were familiar with at the Victorian *fin de siècle*, loom large in a linen-bound notebook of one of my ancestors on my mother's side of the family. The hand-written book is crammed with classification of animals and transcribed passages from Robert Owen, Herbert Spencer, Charles Darwin, Alfred Russel Wallace, August Weismann, Ernst Haeckel and John Lubbock. My great great uncle Reginald meticulously pens classification of mammals and reptiles and transcribes passages from John Lubbock's *Senses of Animals*. Lubbock, first Baron Avebury, Fourth Baronet, was a banker, liberal politician but also a scientist, coining the terms Palaeolithic and Neolithic to denote the Old and New Stone Ages. He was also influential in debates concerning evolutionary theory, corresponding extensively with Charles Darwin who grew up in the same village as him. To indulge in a brief aside regarding my family, Reginald's aunt, Elizabeth 'Bessie' Robertson was in the service of the Lubbock family for most of her life, primarily for Frederick Lubbock, a West India merchant and Baron

Avebury's son. The Pre-Raphaelite painter, Frederick Sandys captured Bessie in a coloured chalk portrait which now hangs on my wall, framed by William Aldous, a Norwich gilder and art dealer. Bessie moved with the Lubbock family around the country for the rest of her life, her last residence in 1891 being *The Rookery* in Downe, Kent, adjacent to Downe House, the residency of Charles Darwin from 1842, with whom Lubbock was on friendly terms.[2] Darwin's *Origin of the Species*, published in 1859, classified species in an evolutionary context and museums became much more scientific in the collection of taxidermy and the information relevant to them.

The expansion of the Empire and the development of travel brought access to whole new worlds of flora and fauna. Naturalists, both amateur and professional, toured the globe in the scientific search for new species. If our own age is that of the conservationist with the technology to film animals in their natural habitat, the 19th century was the period of the zoological collector, whose passion for finding out about the lives of animals was inseparable from the urge to shoot them or preserve them in collections, as one nonchalant entry in my ancestor Reginald's 1909 diary from Nigeria reveals: "Jackdaw steam launch left at 8.30. Telegraph[ed] for prisoners. Shot crocodile. Had lunch."

As the proficiency and reliability of guns improved from the 1820s the numbers of birds and mammals that could be killed and in all weathers increased. The flintlock was gradually disappearing to be replaced by the percussion system. Locks improved and rain-proof pans were introduced. A light, 'dust shot' also helped prevent the bird's destruction if a specimen was being shot for mounting. A collector of taxidermy in Norfolk today said that cartridges were sometimes filled with sand for short-range dispatch. What sand did to the inside of the barrels is another matter. Other gunners were not so careful. Norfolk taxidermist H.N. Pashley writes in his diary on 1 October 1894, "The first Yellow-browed Warbler for Norfolk was taken on this date. This bird was shot with a 10-bore gun and very large shot. Its head was nearly severed and the rump and intestines almost entirely shot away, so the sex could not be determined. I have known several good and rare birds shot in the same way as this. The man who shot it fired off his battered old muzzle loader at the first bird he saw rather than take it home loaded. It was such a weapon as few people would care to fire off. This bird is in Mr. Connop's Museum."[3] Indeed, Billy Bishop, warden of Cley marshes, stated that at least five per cent of guns used by local fowlers were unserviceable—one wildfowler was killed due to a faulty trigger-guard.[4]

The most lauded and nationally recognised gunsmith firm of the period was John Manton, which changed to John Manton & Son until they ceased trading in 1877. There were a few gunsmiths local to Norfolk and they are worth listing for the sake of historical reference: William Brewster (c.1835), who had a shop at Long Stratton, made percussion sporting rifles, W. Davey (c.1835) general gunsmith in Norwich, H. Harcourt (c.1840) who had a shop in Norwich, W.

Havers (c.1835) general gunsmith in Norwich, Jeffries (c.1865) of Norwich, 'general gunsmithing,' James Manning (c.1830) who had a shop in North Walsham, Marrison of Norwich (1830-1850) who made five-cylinder percussion pepperboxes, Mayer (c.1850) general gunsmith in Norwich, J. Mazor (c.1830) a gunsmith in Great Yarmouth, William Morter (c.1830) who had a shop in North Walsham, a Nidzer (c.1830) trading in Norwich, W. Parsons (c.1850) a general gunsmith in Swaffham, Porter (c.1800) a general gunsmith in Norwich, a Reed (c.1800) who had a shop in Aylsham (a specialist in flintlock holster pistols), William Reeve (c.1830) a general gunsmith in Great Yarmouth, D. Scarlet (c.1830) a general gunsmith with a shop in Swaffham, a Spencer (c.1800) who had a shop in Kings Lynn,[5] Richard Jefferson mentions a J. Potter, 'Gun, rifle and Pistol manufacturer, at 52, High Street, [Kings] Lynn.[6] Billy Bishop in his book, *Cley Marsh and its Birds*, mentions a Norwich gunsmith called Rosson delivering a thousand cartridges for the 'gentlemen gunners.'[7] It is also worth noting the London gunsmith, Henry Atkin (1862-1877) who made large bore, wild fowl percussion swivel guns for boats.[8]

The apparent preoccupation with shooting anything that moved, irrespective of scientific study, risks painting an impression of the Victorian and early Edwardian eras in broad brush-strokes. The seemingly blasé notion of 'sport' to mean shooting at any unfortunate bird that came in range was not without contemporary mention and disapproval. Some historians remind us that wildlife in the British Isles was more abundant than it is now but through modern eyes shooting wildlife then in 'the dark days of collecting' can be seen at the very least as excessive. Take Charles Kingsley's wearisome description in *Glaucus; Or, The Wonders of the Shore* (1854-5), "a purposeless fine-weather sail in a yacht, accompanied by many ineffectual attempts to catch a mackerel, and the consumption of many cigars; while your boys deafen your ears, and endanger your personal safety, by blazing away at innocent gulls and willocks,[9] who go off to die slowly; a sport which you feel to be wanton, and cowardly, and cruel, and yet cannot find in your heart to stop, because the lads have nothing else to do, and at all events it keeps them out of the billiard-room;"[10]

It was generally accepted at the time that only detailed study of dead specimens could reveal scientific information. In his *Treatise on Taxidermy*, the zoologist William Swainson wrote in 1840: "Taxidermy is an art absolutely essential to be known to every naturalist since, without it, he cannot pursue his studies or preserve his own materials." In the days before developments in photography and film, taxidermy was also an important way of showcasing wildlife to a wider audience. Sir Stamford Raffles established the London Zoological Society in 1826. He acquired land in Regent's Park to build the zoo, originally to house exotic animals for the purpose of scientific study. In 1847 the zoo opened to the public and was a popular attraction. Visitors could wonder at animals brought from across the globe. The zoo added an aviary, a reptile house and an aquarium. Fascination with taxidermy, that is to say taxidermy as a catalyst to representing the natural world, swung from its position in science to a fashion. The vogue for taxidermy was firmly established by the Great Exhibition at Crystal Palace, London in 1851. John Gould, taxidermist to the Zoological Society and publisher of natural history books, exhibited cases containing 1,500 stuffed Hummingbirds displayed at Regent's Park Zoo. They were one of the greatest attractions at the exhibition, drawing 75,000 visitors including Queen Victoria. A section at the exhibition was devoted to 'furs, feathers and hair,' and various 'oddities' including a preserved pig by M. Smith of Dublin and a collection of stuffed animals by German taxidermist Herman Ploucquet, which included a frog shaving his companion seated in a chair, a diorama admired by Queen Victoria. As a result of these successes famous taxidermy businesses flourished including Kirk in Glasgow, Edmonstone in Edinburgh,[11] Cullingford in Durham, Montague Brown and Betteridge in Birmingham, Hutchinson in Derby, Jeffries in Carmarthen, Sheals and Williams in Dublin, Shopland in Torquay and Gunn in Norwich. London had several taxidermy businesses, the most famous of which was Rowland Ward who became famous for mounting big game trophies. Other firms included Cooper (who specialised in bow-fronted cases of fish), Gardner, Gould and Leadbetter.

Stuffed canaries, parrots and guinea pigs reflects the Victorian desire to preserve pets, loved and lost. Few loving owners today would consider having their dogs and cats stuffed when they die, but the Victorians did and it was not just the gentry that did it. In his book *The Victorian Underworld*, Kellow Chesney quotes Henry Mayhew's description of a tavern that ran a book on dogs killing a number of rats in a certain time, "I entered the room. Sporting pictures hung against the dingy walls. Over the fireplace were square glazed boxes in which were the stuffed forms of dogs famous in their day ... Among the stuffed heads was one of a white bull-dog with tremendous glass eyes sticking out, as if it had died of strangulation. The proprietor's son was kind enough to explain the qualities that had once belonged to his favourite. 'They've spoilt her in the stuffing, sir,' he said." [12] The Victorians held a morbid fascination with death which might explain their enthusiasm towards taxidermy. Rowland Ward, who became one of the most well-known taxidermists worldwide, mounted many pets, mostly cats and dogs, including Rummager, one of Queen Victoria's favourite hounds. The Natural History Museum in Tring includes a collection of taxidermy dogs, including champion greyhound Mick the Miller (1926-38) who won forty-six of his sixty-one races. The craze for taxidermy was not restricted to exotic species. Aside from 'freaks', deformed creatures and different species sewn together, mounted specimens of British wildlife were just as popular. Perhaps due to the accessibility of British migrants and native birds, collectors were able to source both rare and commonplace birds.

As the century progressed taxidermists began producing fascinating tableaux of birds and animals in realistic natural settings, known as 'groundwork,' often excellently created using moss, fern, bracken, sand and rocks, branches and sections of tree trunks, even parts of a fence or coastal breakwater. Painted papier-mâché and dried clay (in which birds' footprints could be impressed) and thick paper over a wooden framework were used to form the solid base. Surfaces could be painted or varnished to appear wet. Birds and mammals could be depicted in their winter environments. Christopher Frost explains, "Artificial snow was usually formed by painting the groundwork with a mixture of plaster of Paris, whiting, size and water, which could be sprinkled with finely ground glass to make it sparkle." [13] Often glycerine was used to preserve the fauna (after dipping into benzoline or turpentine to kill any insects) and grasses and reeds could be painted or dyed after drying. The permutations were endless. Lead-based paint was used to paint the back and sides of box-cases. This was often block-blue or a faded yellow to depict a sunset. Occasionally a watercolour scene was depicted merging with the groundwork in the foreground. This effective impression can be seen in the cases of Peter Spicer of Leamington Spa.

The introduction of the Seabird and Wild Bird Protection Acts in the late 19th century and the founding of nature societies and a general change in public attitude, reduced commercial demand for taxidermy and brought about the closure of some of the smaller taxidermy firms in the 1920s. A closed hunting season also reduced demands on the stuffers. The First World War had a great impact. The young men who worked on estates and farms, who shot or gathered eggs for collectors, were enlisted to fight in France and other theatres of war and many of them would not return home. Soldiers exchanged the woods, thickets, heaths and marshes of Norfolk for the splintered woods of Belgium and France: Trones Wood, High Wood, Château Wood and Oppy Wood. The Army used rural tradecraft to their advantage and soldiers from the countryside became sappers. They caught rats, set traps, laid wire or set surface mines to disperse the German wire. "Following the outbreak of World War One in 1914, the handful of existing female keepers and pheasant rearers, together with keepers' wives and daughters, all rallied round to keep shoots running after many keepers had been conscripted into the armed services. Ladies also undertook earth-stopping duties[14] and in some parts of East Anglia acted as beaters on driven shoots … keeping them 'ticking over' until the menfolk, sadly much reduced in numbers, returned home." [15] If they survived 'going over the top' and walking towards the German guns there is irony in the soldier returning to rural life: setting about planting cover in the estate and walking towards the guns again for the lord of the manor, lifting up the pheasants along with the other beaters on the Sunday shoots. The numbers of dealers and 'field collectors' who made their living supplying the taxidermists were much depleted.

The Army and Navy Co-operative Society Ltd advertised bespoke taxidermy services in the Naturalist Section of their trade catalogue. The taste for displaying taxidermy pieces in the home gradually changed after the First World War, but taxidermy services were still very much a part of the Army and Navy stores business in the 1920s as their 1928-1929 catalogue reveals, "Birds and animals preserved and mounted. Skins cured and mounted as floor rugs, motor rugs, or for wall decoration." Trophy mounts were very much the preserve of the rich. A brass-mounted rhinoceros foot preserved as a tobacco jar was priced at 100/-. Mounting and casing fish was also expensive and time-consuming, "As fish for mounting require a considerable time for drying and 'setting' properly, the execution of an order for even a single specimen usually takes at least three months, and sometimes much longer … Pheasants or other birds (in case, with glass sides and front, wood back and top) from 65/-." The *Army and Navy Cooperative Society* also sold egg collectors' requisites and egg cabinets, 'made in polished stained deal.' A cabinet with 8 drawers and 238 divisions was priced at 56/6.

Taxidermy was used by artists for plate sections in natural history volumes. The ornithologist and artist John James Audubon (1785-1851) practised taxidermy to help him paint his bird illustrations. However, errors occurred when birds were painted after their death. Graham Austen told me that while visiting an aviary, the renowned artist Archibald Thorburn witnessed a tame merlin escape and kill a hawfinch.[16] Thorburn noticed that, on death, the cinnamon coloured iris of the finch changed to a pale grey. It can be assumed that George Edward Lodge's painting of a Hawfinch with grey eyes was based on a dead bird or taxidermy specimen. In his article, 'The Colour of the Iris in the Hawfinch' (1924) R.J. Howard mentions a letter that appeared in *The Zoologist* in 1906. The writer, G. H. Paddock states, "I never saw the irides of a living Hawfinch greyish-white such as one sees in stuffed specimens, and which colour is only assumed at death."[17]

The process of taxidermy and various stages of preserving a specimen required great skill. Tow (hemp fibre) and wood fibre was used for stuffing the internal cavity. (I have also found bits of old cloth, wool and scraps of newspaper in specimens, two of which read, "Oedipus" in French. Mme. Delvair A Fine "Jocasta." And the other; *Rat Starts Fire.—A rat started a fire on Saturday when it attacked Mr. Arnold Thompson, of Meadowfield Road, Stocksfield, Northumberland, causing him to knock over a lamp in an outhouse, and one hundred Angora rabbits were burned to death.* Sadly, there was no date on the cuttings to give the specimens provenance!). The preserved bird or mammal would then be bound and left to dry out, a process which could take weeks. Wires were then employed to keep the natural posture and preservatives applied. The use of arsenic as part of a preservative formula greatly prolonged the life of the specimens. However, taxidermists began to use safer alternatives including Borax. Chemicals used varied. An exhibit in the Museum of Natural History in Funchal, Madeira, shows a large syringe used by naturalist and taxidermist Günther Maul, to inject specimens with formalin.

Photography gradually became a scientific means of cataloguing nature as well as anthropological survey. The first process for producing negatives from gelatine and silver salts was attributed to Peter Mawdsley and sold commercially from 1873. At the end of the 19th century a new flexible photographic medium emerged, cellulose nitrate film, a light material available in a small roll which was easy to transport and allowed several images to be recorded on the same roll, but was highly flammable and easily damaged. The famous Eastman Kodak slogan, "You press the button, we do the rest," applied to the new compact cameras, the 'Pocket Brownies' which emerged in 1892.[18] 1901 saw the Brownie No.2 with an internal 116-roll film. Photography was moving away from the studio *carte de visite* and becoming the principle means for the visual exploration of the world, overcoming the fleeting nature of the gaze by creating a record.

Notes

1. In 1883, the famous Norwich taxidermist, T.E. Gunn, was elected a Fellow of the Linnean Society of London.
2. Private correspondence with Pauline Gilbertson.
3. H.N. Pashley, *Notes on the Birds of Cley, Norfolk* (1925), introduction to the new edition by Christopher Frost, (Lavenham, The Lavenham Press, 1992), p. 31.
4. Bernard Bishop, *Cley Marsh and its Birds*, (Woodbridge, The Boydell Press, 1983), p. 29.
5. A. Merwyn Carey, *English, Irish and Scottish Firearms Makers*, (London, Arms and Armour Press, 1968), pp. 12-91.
6. Richard Jefferson, *A Victorian Gentleman's North Norfolk*, (Hindringham, JJG Publishing, 2013), pp. 123.
7. Ibid. 4, p. 9.
8. Ibid. 5, p. 3.
9. Guillemot.
10. Charles Kingsley, *Glaucus; or, The Wonders of the Shore*, (London, Macmillan and Co., 1890), p.2.
11. John Edmonstone was a slave from Demerara in Guyana. He was granted freedom by his 'owner' and returned to Scotland with him, setting up one of the earliest taxidermy businesses in the British Isles. The firm set about teaching students at Edinburgh University, one of whom was Charles Darwin.
12. K. Chesney, *The Victorian Underworld*, (London, Pelican, 1972), pp. 348-349.
13. Christopher Frost, (1989), *The Ogilvie Bird Collection*, (Lavenham, Lavenham Press, 1989), p. 11.
14. Earth-stoppers were people who went out the night before a hunt to block up fox, rabbit and badger holes in order to prevent a fox going to ground.
15. S.D. Jones, 'Daughters of the Land,' pub. In *Shooting and Conservation*, the BASC Magazine, March/April 2022.
16. Hawfinches were persecuted by farmers. Cley taxidermist H.N. Pashley noted, 'Now and again small flocks visit us and are very destructive to peas etc.'
17. *Transactions*, Norfolk and Norwich Naturalists' Society, (Norwich, A.E. Soman & Co.,1924), pp.80-3.
18. The Brownie camera was inspired by the book *The Brownies, Their Book* based on the elves of Anglo-Saxon folklore, published in 1887 and written by Palmer Cox.

Bluethroat Morning

HENRY PASHLEY AND THE NORTH NORFOLK COAST

The Trade Label of H.N. Pashley
C. Frost.

The North Norfolk coast runs for the best part of twenty five miles from Holme-next-Sea to Kelling. It comprises sandy beaches, pine-forested dunes, marram grass dunes, shingle ridges, fresh grazing marshes, mudflats and creeks, tidal estuaries and cliffs. The coastline is protected by nature reserves and contains designated Areas of Outstanding Beauty (AONB). Its recognition as a 'Heritage Coast' helps protect the natural environment which is of great scientific interest, both nationally and internationally.

From the middle of the 19th century, Norfolk's significance regarding bird populations was revealed in books which included the Reverend Lubbock's *Observations on the Fauna of Norfolk* and Henry Stevenson's *Birds of Norfolk*. In February 1903 in his home town of Holt, the taxidermist Charles Blunderfield Dack conducted a lecture on 'The Migration of the Birds of Norfolk.' A newspaper article reported on the proceedings. Dack described the ornithological importance of the Norfolk coastline, "The geographical position of Norfolk, its projection into the North Sea—enables it to offer a resting place for hosts of birds on their passage, in the spring, from the south of Europe and north of Africa to Scandinavia and Greenland, many rare birds thus find a resting place on the Norfolk coast."[1] A break in the proceedings was filled with Dack's wife and daughter performing a musical interlude. History does not present how well this was received by the audience.

As well as tourists and dinghy sailors, the coast today attracts ornithologists, botanists, geologists and historians. Great effort is maintained in protecting nesting colonies of birds on Blakeney Point and Scolt Head Island. Scolt Head reserve remains relatively undisturbed because of the problems of access. Most of the silted land around Blakeney has been reclaimed as cattle marsh and reserves and the distance to the shallow enclosed harbour at Blakeney known as the 'Pit' and open sea beyond is formed by the tangled veins of creeks, submergent oil-black mud flats covered in samphire and emergent marsh containing salt marsh grass, sea thrift and sea purslane. Invertebrate fauna, lugworms for instance, provide a major food source for the population of wading birds. Blakeney Point is a spit that extends parallel to the coast for over three miles from its mainland connection at Cley-next-Sea, a place simply known as Cley in the Victorian period. The 1,300 acre sand and shingle area was acquired by the National Trust in 1912. My father met Ted Eales a few times while he was birdwatching on the coast. Eales was the warden on Blakeney Point until 1980 as well as being involved in Anglia Television's popular *Countryman* and *Survival* programmes. Dad said that Eales's head was bloodied with cuts where he had been divebombed by terns. Knowing that he had served during the Second World War my father asked him if he still had his tin helmet and, if so, why he didn't wear it. The warden's response was, "It wouldn't be fair on the terns, would it, 'ole partner?" Dr Sydney Long, who proposed the foundation of the Norfolk Naturalists' Trust, had similar views as he watched the terns attack people who got too close to the nests. Long appointed Billy Bishop warden of the Cley nature reserve in 1926. The Norfolk Naturalists' Trust, subsequently renamed the Norfolk Wildlife Trust, started in the same year. The trust ensured that the Cley marshes would be protected in perpetuity. The reserve is one of the oldest nature reserves in Britain and is still owned by the National Trust.

Today, life in the villages along the coast is very different to the Victorian and Edwardian eras when collecting was at its highest. It's worth creating an historical picture of this area of Norfolk which, along with Breydon Water, provided the richest pickings in the county for the collector and busy trade for the taxidermist. The once busy ports of Cley-next-Sea and Blakeney are now silted up and can only be navigated by small craft. The trading wherries must have been a magnificent sight, with their forty-foot mainsails and heavy cargoes of coal, wood, cattle-feed and sugar beet loaded up to the gunwales. An accretion of holiday properties and semi-dormant second homes has changed coastal communities on the North Norfolk Coast. Although Wells-next-the-Sea remains, in part, a working community, Blakeney has the feeling of being shut up in the winter months. To use a phrase first coined by British sociologist Ruth Glass in 1964, the 'gentrification' of coastal properties have reserved much of coastal Norfolk as the playground of the rich. In the 19th century (and up to the 1960s) most of the flint cottages had no inside W.C., no trim, no *cottage orneé*. They were built for seafarers and grafters who needed to be close to the shore. More eggs were collected to eat rather than be 'blown' and preserved as specimens. Lapwing eggs were considered a delicacy and their consumption contributed to their marked decline. Although there was a close season for shooting between 1 March and 1 August from 1880 onwards, their eggs were not protected in Norfolk at this time. The birds themselves were also eaten. Records of taxidermists Henry Pashley and Walter Lowne show that very few geese were preserved. Aside from the fact they would have been cumbersome mounts, this was because geese were for the pot. According to his 'List of Cley Birds,' Pashley stuffed only sixteen geese in his career: twelve greylag geese in twenty-five years and four barnacle geese.

Driving along the coast road today it is easy to forget how poor and hard-working these longshore communities were. Norfolk folk who fell asleep in front of coal fires, woodbines slipping from callused fingers, men who rarely got the salt from their clothes, men surrounded by women who were consumed by worry when their husbands fished when sea was rough. Most Norfolk families, including mine, will find ancestors who were drowned at sea. As for the public houses, there are still hints at their history if you seek them out, but the drive to rename the pubs and strip out artefacts and pictures that had been there for generations, shows scant regard for the past and their rooted cultural significance. Paintings and taxidermy were removed from the Lifeboat Inn in Thornham and the wildfowling guns sold at auction, realising a paltry price and gone forever from the place they belonged. Years ago, a member of staff at the Lifeboat Inn told me that most of the taxidermy cases had been removed, 'for fear of criticism.' Imagine the walls of a dark public bar a hundred and fifty years ago. The walls covered in framed paintings and photographs and taxidermy cases bought at farm sales. There would be a rumble of broad Norfolk accents at the bar: a gamekeeper, game-carrier, taxidermist, wild-fowler, reeder, lugworm-coaxer, whelk-picker, wherryman, pheasant charmer and mole-catcher. Take a gamekeeper working before the First World War. He might have begun his fieldcraft as a keeper's boy before becoming a gamekeeper himself. He would have been taught to cut snare pegs, set gin traps and gate nets and how to 'tickle' trout. He was the perfect boy to hire as he probably knew all the poaching tricks. He learned where the partridges searched for food by looking at the seasonal crop of the birds; the stubble of wheat in September, acorns in October and the first shoots in early spring. He knew the fieldcraft of the marsh, saltings and heath. Shooting snipe above the heather. Thus began his fascination with birds. He got to know the clamour of the Brent geese as they readied themselves for the flight back to the Arctic in April, about the same time as the pheasants began to lay. He familiarised himself with the brown-marbled plumage of the woodcock and how to differentiate the bird from the snipe by its larger size, shorter bill and different grunting call. He studied the birds on the marshes: the godwit, knot, whimbrel and the curlew with its long curved bill and unmistakable call at dusk. He knew the wildfowlers, rich sportsmen and gentlemen collectors who came to shoot.

Birds were often taken to the local taxidermist for preservation. On this part of the North Norfolk coast this taxidermist was Henry Pashley. Pashley had a small workshop on the coast road for the best part of forty years from 1884-1924.[2]

Statements at the bottom of Henry Pashley's trade label indicate that wealthy punters could use him to book their accommodation and attend a variety of activities while they were in the Cley area: 'Boats and attendance for fishing and shooting,' 'Every accommodation, stabling, tennis court, gardens etc.' Pashley's trade label is perhaps the most attractive and imaginative of all the Norfolk taxidermists. A painted scene depicts Cley Mill, the saltmarsh and a wader huddled in the reeds. An article entitled 'Wild Fowling on the Norfolk Coast,' appeared in the *Field* in 1883 and reveals the hospitality of the Pashleys towards their paying guests, "From Holt another five mile drive landed us here at dusk. We are fortunate in securing quarters with Pashley, the well-known taxidermist; his house is stocked, from ground-floor to garret, with fowl of every kind that fly, the Crested Grebe, with mate and family, being seen in curious proximity to a grand case of snowy Ptarmigan, and these in turn give place to a pair of Capercaillie, while a great Whooper Swan dwarfs even these grand birds by his near neighbourhood. And all around ducks, divers, and rarities so dear to the collector's eye are found in profusion. After a good dinner Pashley himself comes in, and when, later, Brett appears,[3] we yarn together far into the night ... we find it hard to sleep, in spite of the comfortable beds which good wife Pashley has provided for us."[4] Photographs reveal Pashley as tall and broad-shouldered, dressed in a tweed country suit with a soft felt cap. He wears thin round spectacles and a full drooping moustache and cigarette stub in mouth accentuates a rather stern and serious expression.

Pashley was born in Holt a few miles inland from Cley in 1843. In the foreword to Pashley's book, B.B. Riviere reveals that although Pashley took up taxidermy as a hobby, it was not until he was over forty years old that he set up as a professional taxidermist. Between 1886 and 1890 Pashley was the licensee of the Fisherman's Arms in Cley. An earlier licensee was John Bastard, a master mariner. Pashley was listed in White's *Norfolk Gazetteer* (1890) as 'Victualler at the Fisherman's Arms, Family and Commercial and Posting House and bird preserver'. Presumably future licensees Hilton Parker Pashley (1933) and Nancie Margaret Everitt Pashley (1947) were relations. Knowledge of his skills soon spread throughout the county and nationally. Riviere states, "A Turnstone in flight, mounted by him, gained one of the five prizes awarded in the bird-stuffing competition arranged by the late Lord Lilford through the columns of *The Field* ... his services were widely and deservedly in demand, and his shop became a favourite rendezvous—a sort of 'Hunters' Club'—for collectors and ornithologists from all parts."[5] A letter in the *Eastern Daily Press* in 1896 describes visiting his shop, "the house of Mr Pashley, which might as well be an off-shoot from the Natural History Museum at South Kensington." Riviere writes sentimentally about the experience of visiting Pashley. It paints a picture of the man and the place reminiscent of Mr. Venus's taxidermy shop in Charles Dickens's *Our Mutual Friend*. (Dickens had his pet raven, Grip, stuffed in 1841). Priviere states:

> If then, Cley may truly be described as the bird collector's 'Mecca' it may with even greater truth be said that no pilgrimage thereto was ever complete which did not included a visit to Mr Pashley. There can be few living ornithologists who have not, perhaps after a September day spent amongst the bushes, stood in that front shop ... or who have not, at Mr. Pashley's invitation, passed through into the warm, cheerful little workshop beyond, with its skinning table and Windsor chair, its cage of Budgerigars, and its countless stuffed birds occupying all the available wall-space from floor to ceiling. A perfect host, perfectly at ease in any company, with a gentle, old-world courtesy peculiarly his own, Mr Pashley knew the magic which could make time fly, and the hours passed all too quickly whilst one listened to his tales of bird-life on this bleak North Norfolk coast. Outside, when at last one left, was the smell of the sea and the call of the migrating birds passing overhead, and the memory of that small, enchanting room, with all its associations, will live long in one's pleasantest dreams.'[6]

Photograph of the Bird-stuffer of Cley, Henry Pashley and his wife, c.1921

Norfolk Record Office, MC 3565/4.

Pashley's workbook was always full. Indeed, his clientele was varied, including motor racing champion Sir Henry R.S 'Tim' Birkin. Pashley wrote to Birkin's father chasing payment. Sir Henry replied, "Many thanks for your letter. I shall be down at Blakeney on Saturday week the 20th so will call in and see you. I am sorry to hear that you have not got your cheque for the other birds but my father is away in France at present but I will do anything I can for you when I see you."[7] Billy Bishop mentions Sir Henry in his book, *Cley Marsh and its Birds*, "Among the many distinguished visitors to the Blakeney area of the Norfolk coast was the late Sir Henry Birkin of motor racing fame, one of the great Bentley drivers of the 'Thirties. He was held in great affection by all the locals to whom he was known as 'Tim' and much respected as a keen and able wildfowler. On one occasion, when he was taking part in a twenty-four-hour endurance race on the famous Brooklands track in Surrey, he arranged for a party of locals to travel by coach to London and from there to Brooklands, to watch the race. For many of the party this was the first time they had been outside Norfolk." [8]

Extracts from Pashley's diary and his lists of Cley birds, comprising *Notes on the Birds of Cley, Norfolk*, posthumously published in 1925, forms an historical account of birds and their migratory patterns spanning thirty seven years. There are a few intriguing entries and also dispiriting revelations regarding the number of birds killed, especially those despatched by the punt-gun. One entry for 31 August 1912 remains a mystery, "A 'sea-serpent' seen by many people on the beach. Two gentlemen described the sight to me. It was, they said, about two miles out, going at great speed—estimated at 60 or 70 miles an hour—and going in an easterly direction. What was it?" [9]

Henry Pashley in his workshop, c.1921
Norfolk Record Office, MC 3565/4.

The writing also offers a valuable insight into the life of a working taxidermist. Although Pashley does not go into great detail compared to Arthur Paterson further along the coast at Yarmouth, it is through Pashley that we get a glimpse of some of the clients and the naturalists that visited his shop, as well as a few of the moneyed 'gentlemen gunners' who visited the area to shoot birds. The gentlemen gunners were collectors (some would only add specimens to their collections that fell to their own gun) who travelled to Cley, primarily to shoot wading birds. Billy Bishop describes the local wildfowlers shooting at first light before going home to get ready for the day's work. The local gunners were soon replaced by the rich sportsmen:

> … the Gentlemen visitors arrived with their boatmen. There were usually five or six groups scattered over the muds. Then the really accurate shooting started. A great many waders were killed. Anything that moved was shot in the hope that it was a rare specimen. My father was henchman to one of those Gentlemen Gunners, a London solicitor named Frank Izod Richards, who employed him for the month of September at the then princely sum of 10s per day … Before the First World War, Mr Richards was perhaps the best known collector and never missed a season on the Norfolk coast. Most Septembers he hired the old fishing smack *Britannia* and anchored her in a favourable position off

Blakeney Point. Many a rare bird has been shot from her decks. [10]

Frank Izod Richards was a keen naturalist from an early age (a familiar trait for most of the naturalists that became well-known). A painting by John Edgar Williams (1846-1883) shows a young Frank with his siblings entitled, 'The Young Microscopists.'

As for his skills as a taxidermist, Christopher Frost describes Pashley's work, " … his best cases are very pleasant, with a charm of their own. He utilised the glass sided variety of case, the backs of which are usually a pale yellow/buff. His birds, which tend naturally to be mostly wading or coastal birds, are normally set on plain wet-looking mudflats, and there is not often a great deal else in décor, except perhaps for a few sea shells or tufts of marsh grass." [11] However, Pashley also set up more exotic birds. A letter to Pashley dated 13 August 1921 enclosed a cheque for ten pounds for a case of hummingbirds "to be packed and despatched to Nottingham." [12]

Pair of Sandwich terns by Cley-next-Sea taxidermist. Henry Pashley, restored by Graham Austen.
Author.

In his 'List of Cley Birds' Pashley writes, 'First [Sandwich Tern] I had was taken August 1, 1891. (None of the gunners here knew the bird.) Since then, seen and taken almost every autumn; occasionally seen in spring. Had one with perfect black head in June 1922, since when they have bred here in increasing numbers.' Michael Seago mentions that in 1943 a colony of Sandwich terns settled on Cley Beach in the centre of a minefield.

Along with other skilled Norfolk taxidermists, Pashley provided mounts for the *Lysaght Collection of Birds*, now residing in Birmingham. William Royse Lysaght (1858-1945) was a wealthy steel manufacturer in the West Midlands. The collection was acquired in 1913 from an earlier collection belonging to E.M. Connop of Wroxham. The printed catalogue in 1913 lists some 680 cases of 400 birds, 1,860 in total. His son, Desmond, offered the collection in 1943 to Birmingham Museum and Art Gallery, which, due to space restrictions was able to take 1,300 specimens representing 325 species. Norfolk specimens account

Case of Sandwich terns by Henry Pashley before restoration.
Author.

for 73% of the original collection, comprising 1,360 birds. One specimen is from further afield: an emperor penguin brought home from South Victoria Land by Captain Robert Falcon Scott's Antarctic Expedition (1912-1913) which was purchased by J.S.H Ormond, a taxidermist in Cardiff.[13] It is of little surprise that many of the birds were collected in Pashley's area of the coast: 90 specimens from Blakeney, 101 specimens from Cley, 12 specimens from Salthouse, 6 specimens from Stiffkey, 5 specimens from Morston, and 1 specimen from Holkham.

The Birmingham Ornithological Collections, Part 2—The W.R. Lysaght Collection of Birds written by Phil Watson provides a fascinating insight into the provenance of specimens in the collection in relation to Norfolk and is a valuable document for research. The paper reveals Pashley's hand in the collection which included two long-tailed ducks (1907), a common scoter, a goldeneye duck (1892), two goosanders, a red-necked grebe, a sooty shearwater (from Flamborough Head in Yorkshire), a Levantine shearwater from Blakeney (1891), a black stork from Salthouse (1888), two gyrfalcons from Greenland (1906 and 1907), a coot from Hickling, an avocet from Stiffkey (1891), a ringed plover from Brancaster (1907), two little stints from Cley (1890), two purple sandpipers from Cley (1895), a broad-billed sandpiper from Cley (1895), a lesser yellowlegs, two grey phalaropes, three black-headed gulls (1898), two glaucous gulls from Cley (1892), a little tern from Blakeney (1907), a noddy, two black larks from Susses and Rye (1907), a golden oriole from Cley (1909), a redwing from Cromer (1907), an aquatic warbler (1913) and a willow warbler (1903). Pashley also preserved many rare birds shot in Norfolk. He preserved 33 Pallas's sandgrouse from the locally well-known 1888 irruption, the 1892 Norfolk great snipe, the two 1911 Norfolk great snipes, the 1912 Norfolk little bustard, the 1912 Norfolk aquatic warbler, the 1913 Norfolk yellow-breasted bunting, the 1921 Norfolk icterine warbler and the 1922 Norfolk arctic warbler.[14]

Sandwich terns before restoration (close-up).

Case Study—Pallas's Sandgrouse, Syrrhaptes paradoxus

Howard Saunders states, "No event in the annals of ornithology has excited more interest than the irruptions of Pallas's Sand-Grouse."[15] Pallas's sandgrouse was named after the German zoologist Peter Simon Pallas in 1773.[16] *Paradoxus* comes from the Greek meaning 'strange.' It has a distinctive stocky build and looks like a cross between a dove and a small grouse or partridge. The bird was classed as an 'irregular invader.' In his list of birds in *Cley Marsh and its Birds*, Billy Bishop describes the bird as 'a wanderer.' The sandgrouse arrived in North Norfolk in 1863 and 1888, and at Winterton on 27 May 1876.[17] The first birds in 1863, thirty in total, were taken at Morston on 30 May. Michael Seago states, "Had these birds been protected as now they could have easily bred."[18] An irruption* took place in 1863 and between the end of May and November, 60 were killed. Two other birds were shot in Waxham. A short article appeared in the *Norwich Mercury* in 1871 and reveals the bird may have been spotted in Norfolk before the first irruption in 1863, "Pallas's Sandgrouse, unknown at Thetford and (with the exception of a single bird killed near Lynn in 1859) unknown in any part of Norfolk till the spring of 1863, and in no instance since that date."[19] *Historical Rare Birds* also cites 1859 as the first time a Pallas's sandgrouse was sighted in Norfolk (and in the British Isles as a whole). The bird was seen at Walpole St. Peter and was eventually displayed at Kings Lynn Museum. Henry Stevenson also records the early sighting which was first recorded by the Reverend F.L. Currie who stated, "we must congratulate ourselves upon our good fortune in securing the bird at all, considering it was shot by a labouring youth wholly unacquainted with its value, and who was quite as likely to have plucked and eaten, or thrown the prize away (the fate of many a valuable specimen), as to have placed it in the hands of the Rev. E. Hankinson, to whom the Lynn museum is indebted for this most interesting specimen, beautifully mounted by Mr. Leadbeater."[20] Stevenson states that the bird had been previously skinned by a local bird-stuffer.

During the 1863 irruption, the Yarmouth naturalist A.H. Patterson noted that the birds were valued in Norfolk and sought after by the collectors, selling for around three guineas each.[21] Specimens from 1863 appear in Norwich Castle Museum (Hunstanton, Horsey and Waxham). In his 1904 book *Notes of an East Coast Naturalist*, Patterson records a Pallas's sandgrouse which was shot on the North Denes near Yarmouth. Curiously the bird was shot "as it resembled a rat" and was sold to a dealer for half a crown.[22] The sale of Robert Rising's collection of birds at Horsey Hall in 1885 included two sandgrouse, one male and one female, shot at Horsey in 1863. The lot realised six guineas.[23] Patterson, in his article 'The Birds of Great Yarmouth' published in *The Zoologist* in 1900, states, "During the invasion of this species in 1863 (when sixty were killed in Norfolk), several were obtained here. The North Denes and sand-hills were most frequented. The first Norfolk bird was found dead in the surf on May 23rd. A gunner named Nudd, on June 6th, shot a male out of a flock of nine.

---

* a sudden increase in an animal population.

He mistook them for Plovers, but described them to me as "running about like Rats."[24] Henry Stevenson took a great interest in the bird, producing a pamphlet entitled, 'Pallas's Sand Grouse in Norfolk and Suffolk.' Stevenson recorded the dates and particulars of each occurrence of the bird in Norfolk (seventy-five birds in total for Norfolk and Suffolk).[25] Stevenson reveals that a Sandgrouse was taken at Elvedon, near Thetford in Suffolk on 6 June 1863, a rare occurrence of the bird appearing so far inland, one other being in Norwich at the beginning of August. In June several of the birds were seen, and some killed, at Wangford Warren, between Brandon and Lakenheath.[26] On 10 July a male was killed at Croxton, near Thetford. Stevenson states, "Mr. Cole, for whom the bird was preserved, has supplied me with the following particulars: 'It was killed on my farm by one of the boys, about the 10th of July last. There were four of them together at the time, feeding on turnip seed; the three remaining ones were seen often afterwards, but could not be shot. Once or twice, when riding, I got within shot, but never when walking. Their flight is peculiar—very sharp and quick, with a humming sound.'" [27]

In May 1888, a second irruption occurred, when over eleven hundred were seen in Norfolk, One hundred and eighty-six were killed.[28] Howard Saunders reveals the passage the birds took, "In 1888, from the end of February onwards, it was noticed that flocks of Sand-Grouse were in movement on the steppes of Orenburg in Eastern Russia; next, flocks were observed passing over Poland, the Austrian Empire, and various parts of Germany; while by May the invasion had reached the British Isles."[29] Henry Pashley states, "First [irruption at Cley] occurred May 30th 1888 (18 in the flock). 33 taken in immediate neighbourhood brought to me. Congregated on a bare, stony 'knoll' in turnip field at Morston, where 75-85 were within view."[30] In his notes, Pashley refers to 1888 as 'the Sandgrouse year.' Martin George states "on each occasion local collectors, and those working for them, exacted a very heavy toll on what was, to them, a new and unfamiliar species."[31] Riviere remarked "that no instance of their having nested is scarcely to be wondered at …. In 1888 the second great invasion took place and between mid-May and 31st October, 1,100 to 1,200 were seen and 186 shot."

There were a couple of instances when it appeared the sandgrouse was attempting to nest in Norfolk, but examples were treated with reservation. Southwell states that the most convincing case was reported by Mr Tolmer of South Pickenham, near Swaffham. Tolmer shot two birds which arose from a nest that contained eggs. Southwell commented that it was unfortunate that no fragment of the eggs were preserved.[32]

Many of the birds were stuffed and cased. Arthur Patterson states, "In the catalogues of sales the Pallas' sand-grouse appear to have been 'spirited away,' probably by private sale or friendly gift, for although almost every collector had them they were not catalogued."[33] Henry Pashley stuffed thirty-three Pallas's sandgrouse. He believed it to be the highest number handled by any taxidermist in the country. J.H. Gurney's response to Pashley's claim was, "not that is anything to your credit."

Billy Bishop states that the first Pallas's sandgrouse that Pashley stuffed was seen by Mr. W. Monement, a landowner in the Cley area. The last sandgrouse was taken in the area on 14 January 1889. Bishop states, "The Sandgrouse were obviously found on the farms more than the free-shooting areas of the marsh and foreshore, as the names of farmers and landowners are mentioned by Pashley more frequently than those of local wildfowlers."[34]

The five specimens of Pallas's sandgrouse in Norwich Castle Museum were obtained in the county during the 1863 and 1888 invasions, including two male shot at Wells.[35] A bird in the museum dated 1889 was shot at Burnham Overy and was set up by Roberts of Thetford. The groundwork depicts a typical coastal habitat of 'sand, shingle, seaweed, grasses and sea holly.' Another 1888 example was set up by Walter Lowne (Lowne stuffed twenty Pallas's in one month alone in May 1888). Other examples are from other parts of the British Isles and from abroad, including the Himalayas. Felbrigg Hall also contains a pair of the birds, located high up in the bird gallery. The museum in Kings Lynn has a specimen mounted on a display box with a 'rare visitors' label. The three examples of Pallas's sandgrouse in the Ogilvie Bird Collection were shot in Suffolk and set up by T.E. Gunn (Ogilvie noted that at least one of the birds were re-stuffed by Gunn in 1888. There are twelve of the species in the Lysaght Collection in Birmingham, all killed in Norfolk 1888-9 at Brancaster, Burgh Castle, Cley, Morston and Waxham). Stevenson's first volume of *The Birds of Norfolk* reveals that some of the sandgrouse shot in Norfolk were preserved by London taxidermists including Leadbeater and Ward. T.E. Gunn's own collection of birds contained a Pallas's sandgrouse which he shot himself at Brancaster on 16 January 1889. Robin Ellis, the great great grandson of Henry Pashley, has a fine trio of Pallas's sandgrouse set up by Gunn. As with the case by Roberts, the groundwork uses *Eryngium maritimum*, sand and stones to depict a coastal habitat. Arthur Patterson stated that the sand-hills near Yarmouth, where many sandgrouse landed, may have greatly resembled "their native barren wastes" with its habitat of marram grass, sand-sedges, sandwort, sea-holly, rest-harrow and hawkweeds.[36]

Ellis thought that there could have been collaboration between Gunn and Pashley in completing the case. However, the Gunn trade label is stamped to verso. Ellis recalls staying with Fred Pashley, his great grandfather, at Carlton House on the High Street in Cley. The house was next to the blacksmiths (now a delicatessen) and he remembers being woken up early in the morning by the sounds of the smithies at work.

It appears that the bird was not seen in large numbers again. Three birds were spotted flying over Thetford in February 1892. In 1906, flocks of ten and twenty

Robin Ellis, aged about twelve years old, being shown the case of Pallas's sandgrouse by his great grandfather, Fred Pashley, son of the Norfolk taxidermist Henry Pashley.
R. Ellis.

Close-up of the case of Pallas's sandgrouse set up by T.E. Gunn of Norwich. The presentation of the case is very similar to the two cases of a sandgrouse set up by Gunn for Fergus Mentieth Ogilvie's collection.
Author with permission from R. Ellis.

in number were at Somerton and Hickling in June and the last record was in 1908 with a flock at Blakeney at the end of May and two at Brancaster on 28 June. There are no authentic cases of nesting. The Sandgrouse Protect Act, 1889, made it an offence to kill, wound, or to expose, or offer for sale any Sandgrouse taken in the United Kingdom. George states that responsibility for persuading Parliament to enact this legislation can be attributed to the Norfolk and Norwich Naturalists' Society. However, the Act came late for the bird as the destruction had already taken place, due to what Howard Saunders euphemistically described as the bird's 'warm reception.' Arthur Patterson ventured, "Few, if any, had patience enough to leave guns at home to study the ways and doings of these birds of the desert."[37] The Sandgrouse Protection Act, 1889 was set out as follows:

> It is an offence, knowingly or with intent between the 1st Feb., 1889, and the 1st Jan., 1892, to kill, wound, or take, or to expose, or offer for sale any sand grouse [sic] killed or taken in the United Kingdom; the penalty for the offence for every such bird so killed, wounded, take, or exposed, or offered for sale is a fine not exceeding £1. This Act has been continued by the Expiring Laws Continuance Acts, up to the 31st Dec., 1897, so that to kill, wound, or take this bird, or to expose it, or offer it for sale if killed or taken in the United Kingdom, is prohibited all year round. The sand grouse was in the Schedule to the Act of 1872, but was omitted from the Schedule to the Act of 1880.[38]

A letter appeared in the Norwich Mercury in 1888 calling for special protection of the bird, with a particular eye on the fox, "An account four or five years ago of an attempt to introduce a new game bird to our woods and fields, 'of a very delicate flavour,' ... exceptional means should be taken for their protection in consideration of the known special fondness of Reynard for those dainty morsels." [39] Writing in 1866, Henry Stevenson records eating sandgrouse. He was not overly impressed by the fare, but concluded that the bird mostly resembled the French Partridge in flavour.

Pallas's Sandgrouse remained newsworthy and sightings were reported across the British Isles as well as in the local press. The legend accompanying the specimens of Pallas's sandgrouse in the Norwich Castle Museum states, 'A flock was last recorded in Blakeney, Norfolk in 1908. The *Thetford and Watton Times* reported an (unconfirmed) sighting in 1915, "A Briston correspondent writes: - Perhaps it would interest some of your readers to hear a Pallas's sandgrouse was seen by one of the postal deliverers on Monday morning when on his round. The bird was in the middle of the road 'basking' and he was not more than ten yards off when it took wing." [40] Pallas's sandgrouse have remained rare visitors to Norfolk. Moss Taylor noted that there were only two occurrences recorded between Weybourne and East Runton in the 1970s and 1980s: one ringed at Dead Man's Wood and one at Weybourne.[41]

ॐ

Henry Pashley contributed to various publications including, *Transactions* of the Norfolk and Norwich Naturalists' Society and *Ornithological Notes from Norfolk*. Notes could be brief but useful in ascertaining patterns of bird behaviour when combined with the sightings of other naturalists and ornithologists. For instance, "October 16/17 (wind NE), Redstarts and Robins in large numbers appeared at Cley (Pashley)."[42] An entry in the *Transactions* for 1922 reveals, "I learn from

Mr Pashley that an immature Iceland gull was killed at Cley on December 9th. This makes the third obtained in Norfolk during the year." [43] Another bird that ended up in his workshop was a honey buzzard, "On June 2nd an adult male was trapped in Bale Wood and brought to Mr Pashley at Cley. It was flushed by a game-keeper from beside the same nest (H.N. Pashley)." [44] His comments sometimes included a snapshot of rural life, "Pashley announced the arrival of four Cranes on their spring migration, which halted near the mouth of the little river Glaven, and remained all the forenoon within 200 yards of a gang of workmen, quietly resting themselves on the side of Wiveton bank. Subsequently Mr. Pashley had a good view of them as they were flying eastwards, and they were next heard of as visiting a piece of water at Weybourne."[45] Pashley, like many of his contemporary taxidermists (especially Gunn of Norwich), passed on information regarding the eating habits of birds by analysing stomach contents before a specimen was stuffed.

Pashley's contributions to natural history were recognised in November 1897 as this piece in *Norfolk News* reveals, "A deserved honour has just been conferred upon an inhabitant of Cley in the person of Mr. H.N. Pashley, who has been elected to a fellowship of the Zoological Society. The choice and varied collection of native birds, and birds and beasts which are not native, formed by Mr. Pashley have been a long and most interesting feature of the neighbourhood." [46]

Pashley died on 30 January 1925. He is buried in St. Margaret's Church, Cley-next-the-Sea. Robin Ellis said that in his later years, Pashley was known as 'the oldest man in Cley.' In August 2022 I went to look for Pashley's grave. I eventually found it residing at an alarming angle, heaving forward in the long grass. Local historian Richard Jefferson[47] asked if I could help him upright the grave to its proper position which we duly managed. The inscription on the gravestone reads, 'In loving memory of Henry Nash Pashley who died January 30th 1925, aged 81 years. Also of Sarah, wife of the above, who died March 1st 1919 aged 75

Henry Pashley, Taxidermist at Cley-next-Sea, c.1921 with his grandchildren.
Norfolk Record Office, 3565/4.

years. In death united.' Richard kindly gave me a tour of Cley one Sunday morning, relaying his knowledge of the history of the region in the eras I was researching and also taking me to Pashley's old workshop on the coast road. In the afternoon he conducted a short walking tour to the public in St. Margaret's churchyard, incorporating the story of one of Cley's most famous residents.

An announcement of the sale of Pashley's natural history collection appeared in the *Norfolk News* in October 1922, "As announced in our advertisement columns, Mr Ernest A. Strangroom is disposing of Mr H.N. Pashley's unique collection of British and foreign birds on Tuesday next in the Town Hall, where the goods have been removed for convenience of sale. This collection, which has been got together by infinite pains and labour, has for long been one of the standard sights of Cley, and many hundreds of visitors have admired the dexterity of the taxidermist and the fidelity to nature expressed by Mr Pashley in his set up of specimens. The collection comprises many rare and valuable birds, and was in fact a veritable museum to the ornithologist."[48]

Author and Richard Jefferson (right) by Henry Pashley's grave in August 2022.
Author.

Richard Jefferson standing outside 'Mariner's Hard' cottage, formerly Henry Pashley's rented shop ('The Fishmonger's Arms'), where he remained until his death. B.B. Riviere paints a sentimental and compelling picture of Pashley's workshop in the 1925 foreword to Pashley's posthumously published book.
Author.

Case Study—The Bluethroat, (Luscinia svecica)

THE BLUETHROAT.

Cyanécula suécia (Linnæus).

Late 19th century engraving of Bluethroats.
Author.

The bluethroat is a rare passage migrant, occasionally seen on the eastern coast of the British Isles, especially in September. Although this small passerine bird was recorded more often than the sandgrouse on the Norfolk coast, the historian Christopher Frost places the bluethroat in the same category of wind-blown rarities, "some years they were not seen at all, whilst other years they were often taken, the record being in 1901, when [Henry] Pashley received twenty-five specimens between the 4th and 27th September."[49] The rarity of the bird and its striking plumage meant that the gunners of the Victorian and Edwardian eras were looking out for a 'Bluethroat Morning,' which Billy Bishop describes as the ideal weather conditions to find rare migratory visitors, "the early collectors learned that an east wind and a mist at autumn migration was the ideal combination." [50] Pashley was particularly interested in the Bluethroat and paid great attention to the occurrences of the bird, blowing in on autumnal easterly gales. A great flight of the birds came in on 20 September 1892, nine were brought in to his workshop. Later in his diary, Pashley noted 1913 to be a "very great Bluethroat year."[51]

Sydney Long described the characteristics of the bluethroat, seen on Scolt

Head in autumn 1930, "It has a very marked white superciliary stripe, and if only a glimpse of the bird is obtained it may even be mistaken for a whinchat. Indeed, in many of its ways, and with its 'tac tac' as its alarm note, it is very chat-like. But it has one very characteristic action and that is, a constant up-flicking of its rather long tail, both when perched and when running on the ground, and at the base of the tail is a conspicuous rufous colouring. In the plumage as we saw the birds the throat was white, and below this was a bluish-brown triangular marking, but there was no "spot" within this."[52] Some of the birds lack the spot and in autumn some of the bright throat colours are replaced by areas of yellowish-white. Long also records a white-spotted sub-species of the bluethroat in the same year, "One in a cottage garden at Salthouse on April 7th and 8th (*British Birds*, Vol. xxiii, p. 339). This is the first record for Norfolk,"[53] (several other of the more common 'red-spotted' bluethroats were recorded at Cley, especially from 11 to 13 September and from 27 to 30 September). In his *Ornithological Notes from Cley-Next-The-Sea, Norfolk, 1880-1881* F.D. Power[54] records observing a juvenile bluethroat, described at the time as a blue-throated warbler, "Whilst watching a number of Redstarts along the sea-wall on the 3rd September last, my brother observed a black-tailed bird which, after following for some time, he secured, finding, to his surprise, a young bird of this species. Owing to its immaturity it is not a very striking specimen, the throat mark being represented by a somewhat triangular yellowish-white blotch, without a trace of colour. The specimen came to me in the flesh ... the legs and form generally were very robin-like; the similarity being also noticed by my brother whilst the bird was alive. The body was unfortunately thrown away before I had examined it for sex."[55] Despite Long's assertion of the white-spotted variant first being seen in Norfolk 1930, a footnote to Power's recordings written by J.H. Gurney in 1891 are worth noting:

> The capture of the Blue-throated Warbler, the second ever killed in Norfolk, is a matter of great interest. Mr. Power having kindly sent it for exhibition, I have been able to compare it very carefully with the plates in Dresser's *Birds of Europe*,[56] from which I make it out to be the white-spotted species (*Cyanecula Wolfi*). The first Norfolk specimen, picked up dead in September, 1841, was the red-spotted species, an adult bird (*Zoologist*, vol. I. p. 180). Mr. Dresser figures *C. Wolfi* in seven plumages on three plates. Mr. Power's specimen agrees fairly with the right-hand figure on plate No. 3 also with the skin of a bird shot in Egypt, which I have always considered to belong to *C. Wolfi*. The breast-spot in Mr. Power's bird is now almost pure white, the slight tinge of yellow having nearly faded. With four exceptions, which have severally occurred in Kent (*Zoologist*, 1853, p. 3945), the Isle of Wight (*Zoologist*, 1866, p. 172), Yorkshire (*Zoologist*, 1876, p. 4956), and the Isle of May (*Zoologist*, 1881, p. 451), all the Blue-throats which have hitherto occurred in Great Britain, have belonged to the red-spotted (*C. suecica*).

It is worthy of remark that the day after Mr. Power shot his bird, another was obtained in Kent (*Zoologist*, 1881, p. 471), but this proved to be the red-spotted (*C. suecica*).'[57]

Presumably Gurney's identification of the white-spotted bluethroat was not officially confirmed and recorded. *Historical Rare Birds* lists a white-spotted bluethroat shot in Sheringham in 1906, now in the collection at the Norwich Castle Museum.[58] The bird was in the possession of the Norwich taxidermist T.E. Gunn. Writing in 1935, B.B Riviere queried the authenticity of the bird, "Mr. F.E Gunn assured me that he remembered this bird being brought in the flesh. In reply to my query as to why it had not been recorded, Mr Gunn told me that during the latter part of his life his father seldom recorded any rarities, more particularly if he thought there was any chance of disposing them to a collector. This I believe to be a fact, though whether, after a period of nearly thirty years, this bird should be accepted as an authentic Norfolk specimen, is perhaps doubtful. The only record for this species for the county is that of a male seen by Mr R.M. Garnett at Salthouse on April 7th and 8th, 1930. The bird made its base in patch of broccoli in a vegetable garden."[59]

In his *Manual of British Birds* (1899) Howard Saunders also maintains that the red-spotted form was the only one which was proved to have visited the country. Saunders distinguished between the sub-species, "There are two, and perhaps three, forms of Bluethroat. The first, which has breeding-grounds in Arctic and sub-Arctic Europe and Asia, exhibits a *red* spot in the centre of the blue gorget of the adult male; the second form, which breeds south of the Baltic, has the spot *white*; in the third and rarer form, the gorget is *unspotted blue*."[60] In January 1884 J.H. Gurney wrote a paper on bluethroats entitled 'On the Occurrence of a Flock of the Arctic Blue-throated Warbler (Erithacus Suecica) in Norfolk.' In the same year F.D. Power records eighty of the birds observed at Cley. Gurney's paper appeared in *Transactions* for 1883-4. 'Arctic' refers to L. svecica, the red-spotted, more common variant on our shores. Erithacus is the genus of passerine birds which today encompasses the robin. In his detailed essay Gurney states that the bluethroat which first occurred in Norfolk in September 1841 was preserved in his father's taxidermy collection. The next time the bird was spotted was in September 1867 when it alighted upon a ship off the Norfolk coast. In September, 1881, a third was shot by Mr. G. E. Power at Cley, "while consorting with Redstarts and Whitethroats"[61] Power presented one of his taxidermy bluethroats to the Norwich Museum, another to Henry Stevenson and two specimens to Gurney.[62] Gurney records unusual numbers of bluethroats appearing in Blakeney in 1882. Gurney states that Blakeney and Cley were 'a tempting locality' for bluethroats and other small birds due to the mud-flats and sand-hills, covered with stunted herbage, and marram-grass, sea-lavender and yellow poppy, reaching for about a mile in a kind of peninsula. Nine birds were shot in Blakeney in 1883. In the same year a solitary bird was shot on Breydon Broad and was preserved in the collection of the classical scholar and naturalist, the Reverend Churchill Babington in Cockfield, Suffolk. Gurney asked the Yarmouth taxidermist Walter Lowne to go out to where the bird was shot but Lowne found no other bluethroats in the area. Gurney examined F.D. Power's ornithological notes from 1883 and concluded that, "From these precise memoranda it would seem that the bluethroats came in just the sort of company they might have been expected in; viz., with Tree Pipits, Wheatears, Yellow Wagtails, and Greater Whitethroats, and this company probably arrived with a light wind from the north."[63]

A few recordings of the bird appeared in *Transactions* from 1900-1930. A brief note in the 1903 edition reveals, "several [bluethroats] were seen and one shot at Cley on 9th September, 1900, and others on the 18th and 31st of the same month."[64] *Transactions* for 1913 records 1910 as a notable year for the birds, "Mr. E. C. Arnold records (*British Birds*, Vol. IV, p. 182) an unusually large influx of bluethroats on the Norfolk coast between Sept. 14th and 19th 1910. Referring to Sept. 14th, he writes:—'The visitation extended over about two miles, and there must have been at least thirty or forty birds in the bushes, scattered about singly, not in parties. From all I could gather, there were nearly as many adults as there were immatures. Mr. Clifford Borrer reports (*British Birds*, Vol. IV, p. 148) that an Arctic bluethroat (*C. suecica*) was obtained on the north coast of Norfolk during the third week in May, 1910. Red-spotted bluethroats usually miss our coast during the spring northern migration, though some are usually reported during the return migration in the autumn."[65] A female bluethroat was noticed during the spring migration on Scolt Head in 1923. Bluethroats at Cley are not mentioned again in *Transactions* until 1927 when several were recorded in September of that year. A committee report on Wild Bird Protection in Norfolk in *Transactions* for 1930, reveals, "The autumn migration on the north Norfolk coast this year will be best remembered, perhaps, for the presence of an unusual number of Bluethroats."[66] The red-spotted bluethroat is included in the 2020 publication, *Norfolk's Wonderful 150*, which celebrates the 150th anniversary of the Norfolk & Norwich Naturalists' Society.

༄༅༅

Unlike the taxidermists working in Great Yarmouth and Norwich, Pashley had very little competition. There were a few other taxidermists working on the North Norfolk coast at the same time as him. They may well have had other incomes, practising their skills as a side-line. This was common in all but few of the taxidermists working in Norfolk. George Alcock, on Westgate Street, Blakeney, traded as 'a bird preserver' (1877).[67] Henry Stevenson mentions Alcock preserving a Pallas's sandgrouse which was shot by Mr. Woods of Morston in June 1863.[68] Robert Clarke traded in Hunstanton before moving to Snettisham. Clarke contributed to the *Lysaght Collection of Birds*, in Birmingham, an example being a red-footed falcon shot in Dersingham Wood, Sandringham in 1908. His advertisement read, 'Taxidermy in all its branches done on the premises, at prices consistent with good workmanship.'[69] In 1890 he was also advertised as a 'dyers agent.'[70] Clarke preserved the 1883 Norfolk Snettisham great snipe and the 1888 Norfolk king eider [duck].[71] Christopher Frost states that Clarke was listed in trade directories from 1888 to 1933, and Lewis Clarke, presumably his father, is listed in 1879. Lewis Clarke placed an advertisement in the *Lynn Advertiser* in 1880 'Bird and Animal Preserver, Snettisham, near Lynn, foreign birds, stuffed and mounted birds and animals re-stuffed, and cases freed from moth &c. Twelve months experience under Roland Ward and Co. Royal Natural History Galleries, London.'[72] With the odd exception, Frost praises his work, 'The settings in his glass-sided cases are particularly attractive, but are dissimilar to those of other Norfolk taxidermists.'[73] John Williams was a bird and animal preserver (1890) in North Creake.[74] Pashley mentions a Tom Overton who was the only boatman at Blakeney (c.1880) employed by 'gentlemen collectors' and a good taxidermist. Pashley mentions that Overton died from consumption at an early age. Further along the coast, a taxidermist named Dorton was working in the village of Burnham (whether B. Thorpe, B. Overy or B. Market is not known). A small article in the *Norwich Mercury* in 1875 reveals, "A very fine specimen of the Fulmar Petrel (*Procellaria glacialis*) was shot at Burnham Overy last week. This bird, though found in number at St. Kilda, is very rarely met with on Norfolk coasts. It was preserved by Mr. J. Dorton, taxidermist, of Burnham, and added to the rare and beautiful specimens of British birds in the possession of Mr. J.W. Richford of this town."[75] Christopher Frost also mentions a 'White of Cromer.'[76] History presents very few examples of specimens of seabirds obtained from the cliff-edged coastline at Weybourne, Sheringham and further along the coast at Cromer, Overstrand and Mundesley. The Lysaght Collection in Birmingham contains a black guillemot shot in Cromer in 1893. One can only assume that the landscape proved to be challenging for even the most avid collectors. A shallow coastal shelf would also hamper large craft getting near the cliffs for devastating battues* that were experienced on the coast off Flamborough.

A curious piece of 'faux taxidermy' resides on display in the delightful Shell Museum in Glandford on the North Norfolk coast, the oldest museum in the county which is home to one of the country's largest collection of sea shells. The museum was founded by Sir Alfred Jodrell (1847-1929), 4th Baronet of Bayfield Hall. Amongst the displays from shells from all over the world can be found a pair of birds of prey in a glass dome complete with groundwork. The birds are made from shells which, cleverly layered, make for effective impression of breast feathers. At a glance the dome looks like it belongs in a Victorian study. The legend in the dome reads, 'Shell Birds presented by Mrs. F. Magness of Kings Lynn—June 1958'.

---

* shooting parties arranged where beaters drive game towards hunters.

Notes

1. *Norfolk News*, 21 February 1903.
2. Billy Bishop reveals that the road was constructed c. 1850. The road was given to the Parish by the Cozens-Hardy family (Bishop, 1983, p. 131).
3. 'One-arm' Brett, wildfowler.
4. *The Field*, (London, 14 February 1893).
5. H.N. Pashley, *Notes on the Birds of Cley, Norfolk*, (Foreword by B.B. Riviere, 1925), new edition by Christopher Frost, (Lavenham, The Lavenham Press, 1992), p. 5.
6. Ibid. p. 6.
7. Letters to Pashley concerning birds and taxidermy. (NRO, Norfolk Record Office MC 3565/2).
8. Bernard Bishop, *Cley Marsh and its Birds*, (Woodbridge, The Boydell Press, 1983), p. 31 (Another eminent visitor to the region after the Second World War was Field Marshal Alan Francis Brooke, 1st Viscount Alanbrooke. Bishop states that he never met a more patient man and praised his photography).
9. Ibid. 5, p. 78.
10. Ibid. 8, p. 11.
11. Christopher Frost, *A History of British Taxidermy*, (Lavenham, The Lavenham Press, 1987), p. 72.
12. Letters to Pashley concerning birds and taxidermy, (NRO, Norfolk Record Office, MC 3565/3).
13. Phil Watson, *The Birmingham Ornithological Collections, Part 2—The W.R. Lysaght Collection of Birds*, (Birmingham Museums and Art Gallery, 2010), p. 43.
14. K.A. Naylor and M.S. Pollitt, *Historical Rare Birds*, (List of Taxidermists), 2021, https://www.historicalrarebirds.info (accessed 12 September 2024).
15. Howard Saunders, *Manual of British Birds*, (London, Gurney and Jackson, 1899), p. 488.
16. Other birds were described by Pallas and his surname is given in the common names of the Pallas's fish-eagle, reed bunting, leaf warbler, rosefinch, grasshopper warbler and cormorant. Seago states that the first British example of Pallas's warbler was shot at Cley on 31 October 1896 (Seago, 1977). Writing in 1983, Billy Bishop states, "I recall [E.C.] Arnold hesitating to shoot one bird because he judged it to be a common species. His helper at that time, was a wildfowler, Ted Ramm, son-in-law of the local taxidermist, no less than H.N. Pashley himself, author of the *Birds of Cley*. Ramm decided to shoot the bird in question himself. It proved to be a Pallas ['s] Warbler." (Bishop, B, 1983). News of Ramm's despatch of the bird spread outside Norfolk. The stuffed specimen was exhibited by a Mr. Dresser at the meeting of the Zoological Society, recorded by Thomas Southwell in the *Zoologist* and Howard Saunder's *Manual of British Birds* (1899).
17. M. George, *Birds in Norfolk and the Law, Past and Present*. Occasional publication No. 6. (Norfolk and Norwich Naturalists' Society, 2000), referring to Seago (1967), p.18. Thomas Southwell states that there were no officially recorded sightings of the bird until the irruption of 1888. However, Southwell states, "I was surprised to learn from Mr. E. J. Boult, of Potter Heigham, that on the 27th May, 1876, he had seen fifteen or twenty of these birds rise from the south sand hills, at Winterton, and go away at a great pace to the northward. Although diligently searched for they were not seen again. I have not the slightest hesitation in accepting Mr. Boult's statement as perfectly

accurate.' (Stevenson and Southwell) *The Birds of Norfolk,* Vol III, p. 392.
18. Ibid. 8, p. 115.
19. *Norwich Mercury,* 29 April 1871.
20. Henry Stevenson, *The Birds of Norfolk, Remarks on their habits, migration and local Distribution,* Vol I, (London, John Van Horst, 1866), pp. 377-8.
21. Christopher Frost, *The Ogilvie Bird Collection,* (Lavenham, Lavenham Press, 1989), p. 112.
22. Arthur H. Patterson, *Notes of an East Coast Naturalist,* (London, Methuen & Co, 1904), p. 46.
23. *Norfolk News,* 3 October 1885.
24. *The Zoologist,* 1900, 4th series, Vol. IV. p. 534.
25. Ibid. 20, p. 384.
26. Ibid.
27. Ibid. p. 389.
28. *The Zoologist* in 1900, 4th series, Vol. IV. p. 534, under 'The Birds of Great Yarmouth.' With thanks to *Historical Rare Birds* website.
29. Ibid. 15, p. 489.
30. Ibid. 5, p. 120.
31. Ibid. 17, p.18.
32. H. Stevenson and T. Southwell, *The Birds of Norfolk, Remarks on their habits, migration and local Distribution,* Vol III, (London John Van Horst, 1890), p. 395.
33. Patterson, A.H., *A Norfolk Naturalist. Observations on Birds, Mammals and Fishes,* (London Methuen & Co., 1930), p. 56.
34. Ibid. 8, p. 14.
35. Michael Seago, *Birds of Norfolk,* (Norwich, Jarrold & Sons, 1977), p. 96.
36. Ibid. 33, p. 54.
37. Ibid. p. 54.
38. J.R.V. Marchant and W. Watkins, (1897), *Wild Birds Protection Acts 1880-1896,* (London, R.H. Porter, 1897), reprinted by Forgotten Books, F.B. & c. Ltd, p. 32.
39. *Norwich Mercury,* 2 August 1888.
40. *Thetford and Watton Times,* 24 July 1915.
41. Moss Taylor, *Birds of Sheringham,* (North Walsham, Poppyland Publishing, 1987), p. 51.
42. B.B. Riviere, *Ornithological Notes from Norfolk. Annual Report.* (1922), p. 255.
43. Ibid. p.260.
44. Ibid. p.234.
45. *Transactions,* 'The Crane (*Grus communis*),' Norfolk and Norwich Naturalists' Society (Norwich, Fletcher and Sons, 1898), p. 510.
46. *Eastern Daily Press,* 6 November 1897.
47. Richard Jefferson played first class cricket for Surrey (1961-66) before teaching at Beeston School, Norfolk. He is the author of *A Victorian Gentleman's North Norfolk,* (JJG Publishing, Hindringham, Norfolk, 2013).
48. *Norfolk News,* 11 October 1922.
49. Ibid. 11, p 71.
50. Ibid. 8, p. 15.
51. Howard Saunders refers to the Bluethroat in Norfolk in his *Manual of British Birds*

(1899), "In September, 1883, considerable numbers were observed on our east coast, especially in Norfolk, where a much larger flock dropped in the same month of 1884. Most of these visitors are immature, and they merely stay to rest themselves after their flight from Scandinavia." (pp. 33-4).

52. *Transactions*, Norfolk and Norwich Naturalists' Society, (March, A.E. Soman & Co., 1929-30) p. 58.
53. Ibid. p. 60.
54. Power was a contributor and member of the Norfolk and Norwich Naturalists' Society. He was author of *Ornithological Notes from a South London Suburb: 1874-1909* and *Ornithological Notes from Cley-next-Sea, 1881*.
55. Ibid. 52, p. 346.
56. Henry Eeles Dresser, *A History of the Birds of Europe* (1871-1896).
57. *Transactions*, Norfolk and Norwich Naturalists' Society, (Norwich, Fletcher and Son, 1891-2) p. 350.
58. In his guide to the Norwich Castle Museum, (pp. 19-20) Thomas Southwell mentions 'the pretty Blue-throat' in a case with blackbirds and thrushes in the museum collection.
59. B.B. Riviere, *British Birds* Vol. XXVIII, (1935), p. 360 (1934 *Norfolk Bird Report*, p. 360.
60. Ibid. 15, p. 35.
61. *Transactions*, Norfolk and Norwich Naturalists' Society. (Norwich, Fletcher and Son, 1881-2), pp. 340, 350.
62. In his preface to Henry Stevenson's second volume of *The Birds of Norfolk*, Thomas Southwell states that the occurrence of the Bluethroat on the Norfolk coast greatly increased since Stevenson completed his first volume.
63. *Transactions*, Norfolk and Norwich Naturalists' Society, (Norwich, Fletcher and Son, 1883).
64. *Transactions*, Norfolk and Norwich Naturalists' Society, (Norwich, A. E. Soman & Co., 1903-04), p. 735.
65. *Transactions*, Norfolk and Norwich Naturalists' Society, (Norwich, A. E. Soman & Co., 1913-14), p. 787.
66. *Transactions*, Norfolk and Norwich Naturalists' Society, (Norwich, A. E. Soman & Co., 1929-30), p. 58.
67. Harrod & Co.'s *Directory of Norfolk and Lowestoft* (1877).
68. Ibid. 20, p. 387.
69. *Eastern Counties of England Trades' Directory, including Norwich and the Counties of Cambridgeshire, Huntingdonshire and Lincolnshire* (1901).
70. W. White, *History, Gazetteer and Directory of Norfolk*, (London, Simpkin, Marshall & Co).
71. Ibid. 14.
72. *Lynn Advertiser*, 2 July 1880.
73. Ibid. 11, p. 72.
74. Ibid. 70.
75. *Norwich Mercury*, 21 August 1875.
76. Ibid. 11, p. 73.

T.E. Gunn and the Norwich Circle

The most renowned Norfolk taxidermist of the era was Thomas Edward Gunn (1844–1923). T.E. Gunn & Son became the most accomplished taxidermist firm in East Anglia. Gunn lived all his life in Norwich where his father had been a carriage builder. Gunn's workshop was 84 and then 84 & 86 St. Giles Street (one directory has him at Regent Street, Norwich (c.1826–1942)). Trade directories in 1877 described him as a naturalist, animal and bird preserver, dealer in birds' eggs and insects.[1] Gunn applied his skill to making rugs, mats, bird screens, feather hats and 'plumes to order.' The company went on to sell stands and glass display domes, known as 'shades.'

Thomas Edward Gunn
Norfolk Museums Service, Norwich Castle Museum and Art Gallery.

Gunn started his career as an apprentice to the taxidermist John Sayer. There were two taxidermists recorded under the name Sayer working in Norwich. Rebecca Sayer of 7, Upper St. Giles Street (1869) advertised as a naturalist, animal and bird preserver, foreign and British birds' eggs and insect dealer.[2] John Sayer (1815–1866) was trading as a 'Dealer in British and Foreign birds' in Elmham in 1854.[3] In 1856 he was trading at Upper St. Giles Street.[4] This would have been about two years before Gunn began his tutelage. Sayer was an accomplished taxidermist, his reputation sealed by setting up birds for E.M. Connop's (Lysaght) collection including two black-necked grebes from Rollesby Broad. In 1885 J.H. Gurney refers to a grey-capped wagtail that was in his father's collection. The bird was said to have been shot in Sheringham in 1842. Gurney states, 'He believes he bought it off the late Mr. Sayer the bird-stuffer, who is always considered to have been a very truthful man, and the bird certainly has the appearance of having been mounted from the flesh'.[5] Thomas Southwell mentions Sayer in a footnote to Richard Lubbock's 1845 work *Observations on the Fauna of Norfolk* in relation to the identification and stuffing of a brown snipe which was subsequently added to Gurney's collection. Sayer preserved many rare birds including the previously rejected 1839 Norfolk spotted sandpiper and the 1865 Norfolk roller.[6] Henry Stevenson was a frequent visitor to Gunn's shop and it was there that some of his best records and notes were acquired. Sayer died in 1866, at the age of fifty-one, and was buried in the Rosary Cemetery.[7] Having already become Sayer's manager, Gunn took over the business when his mentor died.

C.D. Borrer, enthusiastic collector and resident of Cley, wrote on natural history topics under the pseudonym 'Sea-Pie' (Norfolk name for the oyster-catcher). Borrer describes Gunn, "I can remember meeting Mr. Gunn on many occasions, for he often came over to Blakeney to shoot and collect birds when bluethroats and ortolans were arriving. He was an odd-looking man, whom the irreverent designated 'Robinson Crusoe' from the peculiarly shaped hats he sported."[8] I would also add a similarity to 'Old Tom Morris,' the grand old man of golf.

Unlike most of the taxidermists working in Norfolk at the time, Gunn went out to shoot birds as well as buying specimens from dealers. Lowne of Yarmouth had a gun license, but there are no instances in his records where a bird or mammal was stuffed after being shot with his own gun. In his biography of Maurice (MCH) Bird, James Parry records Bird's diary entry for 3 October 1882: "Snow Buntings and Wheatears shot by Gunn at Yarmouth." Parry states, "Thomas (more usually known as T.E.) Gunn was one of the leading taxidermists in Norwich at the time, although MCH seems to have preferred the services of Walter Lowne in Yarmouth."[9]

Victorian interest in shooting and collecting must have increased Gunn's workload and he moved into larger premises opposite Sayer's old place in 1877. Norwich was a thriving city in the mid to late 19th century. It had several major manufacturing industries including clothing and shoes, joinery (Arthur Bell & Sons), the nationally well-known printer and publishers at Jarrolds, a chocolate factory and firms producing drinks and mineral water (including Robertson's Mineral Water, owned by my ancestor). Gunn's trade labels state 'established 1826' which suggests that Sayer, being only eleven at the time, must have taken over the business from someone else, perhaps his father. The business remained at 84-86 St. Giles Street for the next sixty-five years. As his reputation grew, Gunn employed staff to keep on top of the orders. George Herd (1859—1940) was apprenticed to Gunn in 1876 and worked for him on and off for fifty years until his retirement in 1926. Kelly's trade directory has a George Hora, at 30, Havelock Road (1904). One presumes this is a misspelling and refers to Herd. Christopher Frost states that Herd's cases are rare, but all those recorded were indistinguishable from that of Gunn. Frost reveals a little more about Herd.

> George Howard Herd was born in London in 1859, but spent most of his boyhood in Norwich, living with a sister in the Unthank Road district of the city ... He was fond of painting, at which he was self-taught, and

J.H. Gurney apparently used one of his paintings as the frontispiece for one of his books. Herd had a break of a few years from Gunn's employment around 1905, when he was commissioned by Lord Bute to shoot and mount birds for his private museum in Scotland.[10]

By the early 1880s Gunn had already achieved over fifty first-class prizes, including five gold medals at national exhibitions. Gunn participated in the 1881 National Fisheries Exhibition in Norwich, where he displayed 250 specimens of birds, mammals and fish. Frost states, "amongst his cased exhibits was a Pike chasing a shoal of Rudd, a group of Rudd lying on a riverbank, the 'Champion Bream of England' (weighing 11½lbs), an Otter with its young in an old tree stump and a pair of Hooded Crows tracking a wounded Widgeon. He won several gold and silver medals at this exhibition."[11] This ambitious and skilful work must have put him in good stead for tackling larger collections. His reputation increased further at the prestigious Great International Fisheries Exhibition of 1883 in London where he presented nearly 500 specimens, mostly obtained in Norfolk. Gunn won many medals including twenty-one gold and silver medals.[12] The following entry from Gunn's catalogue of the event reveals another one of Gunn's ambitious, structurally complicated and in this case, gruesome, cases. He entitled the scene, 'Struggle for Existence.' The legend read, "This group is an illustration of a singular incident that occurred near Swaffham in Norfolk, a few years hence. A Heron, in striking its prey—an Eel—through the eyes, the victim, in its agony, in turn twisted itself so tightly around the bird's throat as to cause suffocation; both being found dead."[13] The collections at Norwich Castle Museum include an excellent watercolour of Gunn's stand at the exhibition, depicting all 135 cases under two sections: British Sea and Fresh Water Fish and British Fish Eating Birds. Despite his well-known skills in setting up birds, Gunn was equally adept at mounting fish. Gunn put forward 76 cases of fish in the exhibition.

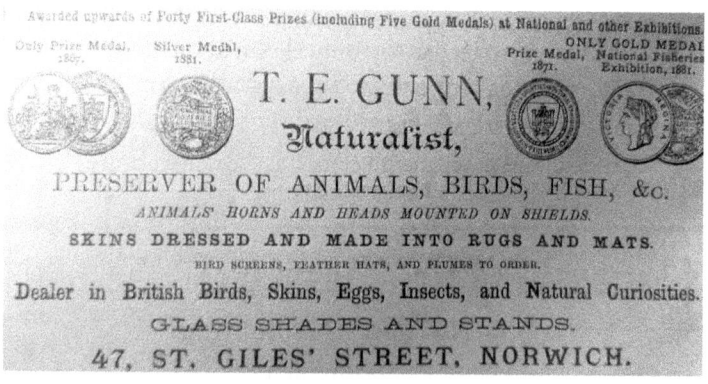

T.E. Gunn's trade label as it appeared in White's History, Gazetteer and Directory of Norfolk, 1883, Simpkin, Marshall & Co.

Gunn contributed to many wildlife publications including *The Naturalist, The East Anglian Handbook*, the *Zoologist, The Naturalists' Circle, Ornithological Notes* and *The Field*. Other specimens in Gunn's hands were brought to the attention of the Norfolk and Norwich Naturalists' Society, especially in their early *Transactions. Transactions* for 1880 reveals the 'more important specimens' (recorded in the *Zoologist* in 1880) which were preserved by Gunn in 1878. It is interesting to note that the birds were recorded across Norfolk (Raveningham, Caister near Great Yarmouth, Breydon Water and Harleston). Gunn also wrote articles for local newspapers, including an article for the *Norwich Mercury* in 1876 entitled 'Taxidermy and Ornithology.' Gunn's reputation was such that clients bypassed other taxidermists on their way to Gunn's door.[14] He gave lectures and presented papers. In 1890 the *Norfolk Chronicle* reports Gunn presenting a paper on 'The Fresh Water Fish of Norfolk' at a special meeting of the 'Science Gossip Club,' held at the Royal Hotel in Norwich. Part of Gunn's paper "contained a long account of the form, habits and life history of the Pike, [Gunn] alluding to it as 'the fresh water shark.'"[15]

Such was the drive for collecting rare birds, *Transactions* of the Norfolk and Norwich Naturalists' Society rarely report instances of mammals prepared by the taxidermists. Exceptions were ermine Stoats, fox-hunting trophies, and domestic and zoo species. stoats, weasels and rabbits were used in a taxidermy case for the quarry of a raptor or owl. In a footnote to the 1879 edition of Lubbock's *Observations on the Fauna of Norfolk*, Thomas Southwell records an instance of a pine martin which came into the possession of Gunn after it was caught trapped in a wood at Heydon.[16] Southwell comments that, "it seems highly improbable that this species would be found here in a state of nature, after having been lost sight of for fifty years." Southwell goes on to state that the marten probably became extinct in Norfolk around 1800. Pat Morris states that the Yarmouth taxidermist Walter Lowne was brought a polecat in 1904, "perhaps one of the last found in Norfolk as this species was extinct there soon after."[17] Southwell relates a tally of a 'list of vermin' killed by a gamekeeper in 1811 on the Suffolk border which included forty-three martens, thirty-one polecats and a staggering four hundred and sixteen stoats and weasels.[18] Today there are projects to re-establish pine martins into areas of Norfolk, one reason being to keep down growing populations of grey squirrels.

A good deal of rare bird species came into Gunn's skilled hands or were shot and recorded by Gunn himself. For instance *Historical Rare Birds* records various examples including the following: recorded and preserved the 1885 Norfolk roller, preserved and recorded the 1887 Orkney pectoral sandpiper, shot and preserved the 1896 Norfolk aquatic warbler, shot the 1901 Norfolk great snipe, killed and preserved the 1902 Norfolk aquatic warbler, preserved the 1907 Norfolk yellow-breasted bunting, preserved and reported three 1913 Norfolk great snipes, preserved the 1920 Norfolk glossy ibis.[19] Most of the contributions that the Norfolk taxidermists made to various publications comprised short descriptions of 'where taken' or the diet of the bird or mammal. Gunn surpassed his contemporaries in providing detailed research and examination which was recognised by his election as a fellow of the Linnean Society. Christopher Frost reveals part of his obituary in the *Transactions* of the Norfolk and Norwich Naturalists' Society, "Since 1864, almost every writer in the country has benefitted from his published records and verbal information readily given." Frost also reveals that in 1912 Gunn presented a paper to the Zoological Society on his discovery of the presence of double ovaries in certain British species, especially falcons.[20]

Collections

The large number of cases produced by Gunn was only made possible by employing several people to work for him. The natural history collection in the 'Raptorial Bird Room' at Norwich Castle Museum contains specimens set up Gunn. He also undertook three decades of work for Fergus Menteith Ogilvie.

Ogilvie was one of the most prolific collectors in East Anglia. His father bought Sizewell House in 1859, renamed Sizewell Hall by his wife in 1886. His land amounted to 6,500 acres, stretching from Minsmere (now a RSPB reserve with woods and wetland) to Thorpeness, including the foreshores and beaches. Along with many Norfolk notables who became prominent naturalists in adulthood, Ogilvie cultivated an interest in the natural world from an early age, having, in effect, his own private reserve to explore where he was able to study birds, especially waders, a group of birds of which he was particularly fond. This hobby progressed to scientific interest, travelling to his father's estate in Argyllshire and all around the country to pursue his research. Henry Balfour, first curator of the Pitt Rivers Museum in Oxford, compiled the biographical book, *Field Observations on British Birds, by a Sportsman Naturalist (the Late Fergus Menteith Ogilvie)*. In the forward to the book, Ogilvie's sister described him as a sportsman-naturalist having equal enthusiasm for both disciplines. Gunn spoke fondly of him. A picture builds up of Ogilvie as a shy, unassuming and reserved man, loyal to his friends. He was meticulous and devoted to his studies of the natural world. After his death in 1918, Ogilvie's widow donated his carefully catalogued collection to the Ipswich Museum where it remains today. The original guide to the collection was published in 1931, comprising twenty-one full page plates.

Christopher Frost has documented the collection in his 1989 limited edition book (250 copies), *The Ogilvie Bird Collection, An Illustrated guide to the F.M. Ogilvie Collection of cased birds prepared by T.E. Gunn of Norwich and presented to Ipswich Museum in 1918*. The book contains excellent photographs and details of 235 birds, all mounted and cased by Gunn. Most of the habitat re-creation for Ogilvie can be attributed to one of Gunn's employees, George Herd. The realism is quite striking. A case of black redstarts depicts the birds having settled on a broken piece of breakwater or camp-shedding. Tawny owls are seen perched on the branches of a tree with an immature bird in a hole in the centre of the trunk. Snow and ice cling to the reeds surrounding three kingfishers and a fourth coming into land above them. Three capercaillies sit on the branches of a pine tree. Ogilvie's collection and that of E.T. Booth in Brighton (1840-90) are celebrated for the very high standard of taxidermy and recreation of habitat in the dioramas. Frost maintains that Ogilvie's collection probably represents the finest single collection of cased birds of their period in the country. Curiously, there are no examples of Gunn's work in E.M. Connop's extensive collection, despite the majority of the birds having been shot in Norfolk. Many of the specimens were mounted by Cole, Pashley and Saunders. It can only be assumed that Connop had his preferred 'bird-stuffers,' which was the want of many naturalists, including Gurney and Stevenson (or that Gunn was busy with his work for other major clients).

Another one of Gunn's clients was Sir Vauncey Harpur Crewe, who had a large natural history collection at Calke Abbey in Derbyshire. Sir Vauncey was one of the most prolific collectors of taxidermy, especially birds, and employed Gunn to set up several cases for him, including a rare example of a stuffed swift, set up by Gunn in 1888. Edward Charles Saunders of Great Yarmouth also set up cases for the collection. Sir Vauncey didn't collect to impress visitors or project his tastes publically, but was pursuing his own passions. Julie Griffith, Property Curator at Calke Abbey states,

> This idea of Vauncey not systematically collecting for purposes of scientific study or for public display can also be inferred in the lack of any form of catalogue or even information list for the collection. There may once have been, but we cannot locate any type of formal cataloguing document either at Calke or the Derbyshire Records Office. Instead, there are small notes peppered in amongst specimens, diaries containing information or the receipts and bills of purchases ... there was a close relationship between Vauncey and both T. E Gunn and his son. In fact, Vauncey made the trip to attend Gunn's funeral in July 1923, just over a year before his own death. It is thought that Gunn taught Vauncey and the Gamekeeper, Agothos Pegg, how to prepare bird specimens. Many of Gunn's work remain, including the Great Bustards."[21]

Calke Abbey and Audley End House in Essex contain the largest collections of taxidermy in country houses that are accessible to the public.

Examples of Gunn's work can be seen at Felbrigg Hall in Norfolk, now under the aegis of the National Trust. Save for an albino woodcock in the Red Bedroom, the taxidermy collection in the Hall resides in the last room encountered on the tour of the house. Now called the Bird Corridor, the room was originally built to shorten the route between kitchen and dining room. The natural history cases have legends stating the species of birds. A free booklet is given to visitors comprising a room-by-room 'tour of the last squire's family home.' The booklet states, "This corridor now houses a collection of birds shot by the squire's grandfather, a keen ornithologist". This refers to Thomas Wyndham Cremer (1834—94). Wyndham Cremer's interests inevitably took him to Blakeney and Salthouse where many of the birds at Felbrigg were killed. Louise Green, Collections and House Manager, kindly gave me more information. The mounts were set up by Gunn and Pratt & Sons of Brighton. Their styles were similar and both firms adopted a pale blue background to their cases, which were generally glass-sided wooden boxes. The boxes, stacked on shelves, some of which are very large, have been in situ for many years. Some of the birds are very faded (especially those of brown and red pigment) and in some cases the plumage has almost faded to white. Exposure to sunlight has been the bane of many collections of taxidermy. Perhaps most noticeable is the collection at Audley End House where there are marked differences in preservation between the specimens on the shaded side of the gallery to those on the opposite side which at one time were in full sunlight.

My last visit to Felbrigg Hall coincided with an excellent tour of the cellar and attic rooms. This was fortuitous, as one of the rooms in the attic contains the taxidermy cases in need of repair, or specimens that had succumbed to insect attack. The guides on the tour, Fiona and Antonia, very kindly allowed me to look inside the room, an opportunity I had taken up years previously. The room has been tidied and organised since then and various cases sit on tables, with plastic boxes underneath containing wings, damaged birds etc. Perhaps the most striking case is the one that contains ten waxwings feeding on rosehips. One cannot avoid the fact that the case illustrates Victorian excessiveness: a single bird for study was often not enough for the collector. Louise Green said that there are no immediate plans for restoring the cases or researching the contents of the boxes. This is understandable due to the obvious pressures on National Trust conservators to maintain a large variety of historical collections and the fabric of the buildings themselves. Other attic rooms contain a large amount of furniture and objects which, as one of our guides said, "Could furnish another house." However, a codicil prevents the sale or removal of anything from the Hall, or indeed, any additions being introduced.

T.E. Gunn's work can also be found at Holkham Hall. Both Gunn and John Cole are the most commonly mentioned taxidermists associated with the collection. Octavius Corder visited the Hall in 1880,

> The Park at Holkham, with its magnificent trees, and splendid lake, abounding in wild-fowl, which breed in great numbers on it, is too well known to need any description of mine. The hall, with its gardens and pictures, and other works of art, many of them of great value, afforded

the visitors great pleasure; the library and stuffed specimens in the museum being of especial interest.[22]

There is little published information about the natural history collection at Holkham. However, there is a late 19th century or early 20th century inventory, copies of which can be provided to the interested for a fee. Much of the collection is displayed in one of the family's personal rooms. A supervised visit can be arranged subject to an associated cost.

Naturalists writing for the *Transactions* of the Norfolk and Norwich Naturalists' Society often recorded their excursions, including this piece of succinct advice for the interested, "Mr. Upcher had a fine collection of stuffed birds at Sheringham Hall, many of them of his own shooting, which he was always pleased to show to anyone interested." Henry Morris Upcher (1839–1921) was born in Sheringham Hall, Upper Sheringham. He was a naturalist and ornithologist and became president of the Norfolk and Norwich Naturalists' Society in 1883. Upcher's warbler was named after him by his friend Henry Baker Tristram, clergyman, naturalist, ornithologist and author of many published works. There is a fine example of the warbler in the natural history collection at the Hall. The current owners have a great interest in the collection. The Hall itself is privately owned but the natural history collection is under the aegis of the National Trust. There are two rooms of natural history, a study and an inventory which contains various mounts by and attributed to Gunn including Icterine warblers, a roller, a Tengmalm's owl, a jack snipe, a greenshank and a badger. There are two interesting glass display domes. One contains a Baillion's crake shot by the Reverend Lubbock at Ranworth in Norfolk, c. 1840.[23] The specimen was acquired by Henry Stevenson in 1879. The other shade contains a stuffed Sabine's snipe, inscribed 'Hockwold August 5th 1889.' The mount was set up by Gunn.

Gunn became ill in 1919 and died on 13 July 1923 at the age of seventy-eight. Active in the trade from 1844, Gunn's firm became the largest taxidermy business in Norfolk and nationally recognised. His son, Frederick Ernest (1869-1950) had worked for his father for several years and continued to run the business after his father died. (Gunn had seven children, three sons and four daughters). Frederick served in the British Red Cross in Russia and

Bittern set up by Frederick Ernest Gunn. The label in the case reads, 'Bittern. Unfortunately shot at Gunton, 25 02 1929'.
Author with permission.

Romania during the First World War and retired from the family business in 1941. Collections at Calke Abbey contain sixty-eight watercolour drawings of birds by F.E. Gunn with pencil descriptions to verso giving the species of bird and where the bird was shot. Many of the birds in the illustrations were reported to be stuffed, put up for future sale or exhibited in the Norwich Castle Museum. Frederick's trade label read, "F.E. Gunn, Established 1826. Pictorial Taxidermist and High Class Furrier." His cases are less common than those of his father and in much the same style. There is an excellent taxidermy bittern by F.E. Gunn in a private collection. The label reads "Preserved by F. Ernest Gunn, St. Giles Street, Norwich." What makes it unusual is the legend in the front of the case, "Bittern. Unfortunately shot at Gunton, 25 2 1929."

Frost states that one of Gunn's other sons, E.W. Gunn (1867–1926) also took up taxidermy. He was buried in a pauper's grave and was by all accounts a bit of a toper and considered less skilful than his father and brother. One of labels gives an address in Ipswich, the other in Bristol.[24]

Fred Ashton (1908-76) was apprenticed to the firm shortly after T.E. Gunn's death in 1924. The inventory of the natural history collection at Sheringham Hall reveals that Ashton stuffed the Upcher family's pet Muscovy duck. The legend at the bottom of the case states,

> Willi: 1950-1959. Pet and friend for 9 years. Willi would answer to his name. He did not mind being handled, or even being held upside down for fun. He did not like to be ignored and would tug at trouser leg until notice was taken.

The duck does not appear to have been stuffed in the hands of an expert taxidermist. Christopher Frost states that Ashton was unlikely to be responsible for any of the Gunn firm's taxidermy, more probably being involved with various preliminary tasks. Frost gives a fascinating account of Ashton's strange personality:

> His own taxidermy was of a quite abysmal standard in later life, and although he may have been a little better in his youth, he was clearly, and sadly, of negligible talent in his chosen field. He was a wildly eccentric character, and everyone who had dealings with him has a story to tell that illustrates his eccentricity. He lived alone at 39, Larkman Lane in the heart of the notoriously rough district of Norwich, and seemed to spend most of his time in the small, uncomfortable and untidy workshop at the back of the house. You had to take great care when entering the building, for immediately inside the door on the right was a cage containing a Crow, which would try, often successfully, to peck you as you went by
> ... Fred owned a field not far from his house, on a part of which he kept pigs. Someone was visiting him one day just as he returned from feeding them. 'Look what one of my old pigs has just done to me,' said Fred in

his Norfolk accent, pulling up his trouser leg to reveal an unpleasant and profusely bleeding deep bite. He would not go to hospital or see a doctor about it, nor had he seemingly any immediate plans to even wash the wound. On another occasion, he opened a parcel containing a supposedly dead poisonous snake—sent over from Ireland, if I remember correctly—only to discover that it was in fact very much alive. It bit him badly, but again he would not seek medical attention. He was extremely ill for several weeks as a result, and was probably lucky not to have died. Fred ate absolutely everything that came in for preservation, and would never waste a carcass after it had been skinned ... rumour had it that Fred had a great deal of money stashed away, and his house was broken into on several occasions. Once he was tied up and beaten, but the intruders did not succeed in finding what they were looking for. Upon his death, the stories proved not to have been entirely apocryphal, for stashed away in countless ingenious and unlikely hiding places were many hundreds of pounds. I was by chance with Fred on the day he died. It was a bitterly cold winter's morning in February, and I remember him complaining that he had for some time been unable to get warm. That afternoon, after I had left, he went out into the garden and dropped down dead. He was 68.[25]

Curiously, in 2020, Lacy Scott & Knight attributed an unlabelled taxidermy case of an otter and cub together with an ermine stoat and weasel to Ashton. The lot was of excellent quality and sold for £230. Examples of Ashton's work, for instance a kingfisher bearing his simple 'H.F Ashton' label are in the collections at Norwich Castle Museum. A cabinet skin of a great bustard is also attributed to him.

The Gunn firm closed in 1950, ending nearly 100 years of trading. Frederick closed the shop, which had been damaged by bombs during the Second World War, presumably in the 1942 'Baedeker' raids. After he retired, Frederick presented his father's bird collection to the British Museum. Frost states that its whereabouts is 'something of a mystery,' and fears that it no longer exists.[26]

OTHER TAXIDERMISTS WORKING IN NORWICH AND ITS DISTRICTS

William White's *History, Gazetteer and Directory of Norfolk*, cites thirteen bird and animal preservers working in the county in 1883. The majority had set up shop in Norwich, with the exceptions of William Wilson of Kings Lynn, John Edwards of Watton and Charles Dack of Holt. The Norwich taxidermists might well have received specimens from the eleven bird and game dealers working in Norwich at the time. The work of Cole and Roberts was in a very similar style to that of Gunn. This triumvirate were the taxidermist's equivalent of the Norwich Circle of painters. John Alexander Cole (1838-1906) contributed to the Lysaght Collection of Birds in Birmingham (two gyrfalcons, one from Iceland and one from Greenland, a short-billed dowitzer and a yellowhammer from Booton in

Norfolk). He also preserved such rarities as the Norfolk night heron, the 1887 Norfolk serin, the 1901 Essex red-footed falcon and the 1905 Norfolk white-tailed eagle.[27] He served his apprenticeship at James Gardner's on Oxford Street, London, prior to setting up business in Norwich in 1864, initially at 11, Davey Place, before moving to Castle Meadow.[28] Christopher Frost states,

> Cole was responsible for the restoration of the Holkham Hall bird collection, a task that took him three years, and he was also entrusted with the job of superintending the removal of E.M. Connop's famous collection from Hertfordshire to Rollesby. Connop, Cole's biggest customer, was probably the most known local collector of his day, and his collection included 336 different species housed in 434 cases.[29]

The majority of the collection was acquired by Birmingham Museum in 1954. His trade label states, "Restored by J.A. Cole, Castle Meadow, Norwich. Prize Medal at the International Fisheries Exhibition." Frost states, "In 1881, Cole and Henry Stevenson together conducted the Duke of Albany around the Norwich Fisheries Exhibition, at which Cole won two bronze medals. (This was the exhibition at which Gunn won most of the major prizes)."[30] The event was well-reported in the Norfolk Press at the time. Cole was, by all accounts, a shy and retiring man with a penchant for collecting paintings of the Norwich School. He was a freeman of the City of Norwich and a keen cricketer. At the age of fifty he was still playing for a county veteran's team. He was also keen on country pursuits as part of his obituary in the *Eastern Daily Press* reveals,

> Angling and shooting also claimed his attention, as did wild fowl shooting, and on several occasions he experienced thrilling adventures when following the latter sport, once, he and two companions having to wade up to their necks to reach the bank when overtaken by the morning tide at Blakeney.[31]

Another obituary for Cole in the *Eastern Daily Press* states, "Birds were undoubtedly the subjects in which he excelled, but he also introduced a new style of mounting fish, which still finds the greatest favour with anglers."[32] Frost presumes that Gunn and Cole continued to work together on occasion, so similar was their work. However, he comments that the work varied in quality, some of the cases being "quite poor and uninteresting."[33] Christopher Stoate states,

> Complications can arise, however, as the more successful taxidermist usually employed others and established a firm involving several people, all working in the style of their employer ... On leaving the firm these former employees invariably continued to work in the style of their mentors so that, for example, the work of John Cole, T. Roberts and G. Herd is barely distinguishable from that of Thomas Gunn, their one-time employer ... examples of his skill as a taxidermist being found in Royal mansions and the homes of peers.[34]

Cole died of a short illness at the age of sixty-eight leaving a widow, a daughter and four sons.

Thomas Roberts, trading at Castle Meadow (and 34, Cattle Market Street), was recorded as having re-stuffed various rare specimens including the 1848 sharp-tailed sandpiper, the 1871 Norfolk purple heron, the 1882 Suffolk purple heron and the 1901 Northants Tengmalm's owl.[35] As Gunn, Cole and Roberts were contemporaries, Frost makes the point that their style and presentation were very similar. Robert's trade label while he was at Cattle Market Street reads, "Roberts & Son, Animal, Bird and Fish Preservers" and "Old collections & specimens cleaned, cured of moth & improved. Animals' skulls and horns cleaned and mounted." His death is mentioned in *Transactions* in 1893,

> I have to lament the loss of two members by death … Mr. T. Roberts, who was a constant attendant at the monthly meetings, and frequently exhibited interesting specimens which came into his hands in the way of business; he was a most skilful taxidermist, very observant, scrupulously exact, and the ready kindness with which he imparted his experience to others will cause his loss long to be felt by working ornithologists.[36]

Other taxidermists were John Beatly in the nearby village of Yelverton, described as a shoemaker, bird preserver and assistant overseer (1877).[37] John Bullock traded on Lower Westwick Street, Norwich and St. Swithin's, Norwich. Christopher Frost states, "John Bullock was in business at Lower Westwick Street in the 1870s and 80s, but by 1890 appears to have moved to Wells [next-Sea] on the north Norfolk coast. I have seen a couple of his cases, one of which bore a label: 'John Bullock, animal and bird preserver, The New Mills, St. Swithin's, Norwich.' Neither was very good."[38] John Elmer of Norwich traded as a "Shoemaker, bird and animal preserver, registrar of birth and deaths, collector of poor rates and assistant surveyor of highways (1854)"[39] William G. Good traded at 49, Stafford Street, Norwich (1890). Christopher Frost mentions a Mr. Hubbard working in Norwich, "described by Stevenson as a "bird stuffer of Norwich" in a reference to a specimen he mounted in 1860."[40] Presumably this specimen refers to a common dipper which was in Hubbard's possession in that year. Frost also reveals that a J. Hunt of 3, Coppins Court, St. Stephens, combined taxidermy with engraving and copper plate printing,

> I have only ever had one case bearing his label, which contained a pair of Bearded Tits with their nest, eggs and a chick in a reedy setting. The date, faintly written in pencil on the back of the case, appeared to be 1855. The earliest reference to him in the county's ornithological literature is in 1826, at which time he lived in Rose Lane.[41]

G. Johnson of Norwich was recorded as having purchased the two 1839 Norfolk Little Bitterns and sold them to J.H. Gurney. He preserved the rejected 1839 Norfolk spotted sandpiper.[42] Gurney refers to Johnson in 1886, "There having been some misapprehension about the 1841 red-breasted snipe, it may here be stated that it never formed part of Stephen Miller's collection; my father heard of its occurrence and requested a bird-stuffer named Johnson to go to Yarmouth and buy it for him, which he did, and brought it back in the flesh, and it is now stuffed and in good preservation at Northrepps Hall."[43] Stevenson also mentions Johnson as having bought two Savi's warblers in the early 19th century. Michael Seago states that the Savi's warbler was a former summer visitor which became extinct about the middle of the 19th century. He cites six known Norfolk examples, three of which are in the Norwich Castle Museum.[44] Thomas Knight was recorded as a bird and animal preserver at King's Street, Norwich in 1856.[45] He was advertised at Upper King's Street in 1854,[46] St. Faith's Lane in 1864[47] and London Street in 1839.[48] Christopher Frost has him at 9, London Road during 1830-70. He preserved the Norfolk sharp-tailed sandpiper, preserved the 1849 little bittern, the 1851 Norfolk caspian tern and the 1860 Norfolk Norton little bustard. He also re-stuffed the 1867 Norfolk rose-coloured starling.[49] Frost states, "the earliest reference to him comes in connection with a Great Bustard he mounted in 1838, the last example taken in Norfolk."[50] The Victorian *Transactions* of the Norfolk and Norwich Naturalists' Society occasionally refers to Knight as "Mr. Gurney's birdstuffer." Henry Stevenson used his services, "Stevenson also employed a bird-stuffer named Knight, whose shop was in King Street, though he afterwards moved to St. George's Street. Knight likewise received many Norfolk killed varieties, and besides working for Stevenson, stuffed many of the birds now in the Museum; but as he gave up using arsenic as a preservative, his specimens have not in all cases withstood moth."[51] Despite his skill as a taxidermist and long career, little is known about him. A small announcement appeared in the *Norwich Mercury* in 1841, "Thomas Knight has on sale a large quantity of British and foreign birds moved from London Street to Rose Corner, King's Street."[52] Many years later in 1882, the following plea appeared in the *Norfolk Chronicle*. "Two pounds reward: to gamekeepers and others: A Barbary falcon having escaped from the collection of J.H. Gurney, Esq, M.P. Any person capturing or shooting the same is requested to deliver it to Mr Knight, bird-stuffer, King Street, Norwich, who will pay two pounds reward on its being delivered to him, either alive, or if dead, then sufficiently fresh for the purpose of stuffing. The above specimen resembles the Peregrine Falcon, but is rather smaller and of a richer colour."[53]

Charles Miles traded in Pulham Market, a village fourteen miles south of Norwich. He was a hairdresser, 'glover' and bird preserver (1850).[54] There was also a John Pear, of All Saints Green, recorded as "Norwich Naturalist and Bird Preserver" (1877).[55] Christopher Frost states, "John Pear of All Saints Green produced cases in a very similar vein to [John] Cole: externally, they are identical. His work is not very common, nor is it always particularly inspiring, although a Herring Gull I have at present is quite nice."[56] A bizarre case involving Pear came to Court in Norwich in 1880, "John Pear of All Saint's Green, was summoned by Harriet Evans, a widow of the same place, for assaulting her on Sunday night, by squeezing her hand. This was a veritable "Tale of a Tub." The parties, who are neighbours, having a dispute as to the possession of a pail of water … the magistrates dismissed the case."[57] William Redgrave was trading on Norfolk Street (1856).[58] Frost also mentions A.J. Rudd (1864-1950), originally a sports outfitter and friend of the naturalist A.H. Patterson. Rudd's birth and death dates rules out any possible confusion with Alfred Nudd, gamekeeper and ornithologist. Frost states that his work is uncommon and he may never have been a full-time taxidermist, which might explain his absence from trade directories.

George Smith, on Cross Street, contributed to the Lysaght Collection of Birds, including a cormorant from Caister, a night-heron from Yarmouth, a tawny pipit from North Denes, Yarmouth in 1897, a dipper from Limekilns, Yarmouth in 1896, a firecrest from Apollo Garden in Yarmouth in 1889. William White's *History, Gazetteer and Directory of Norfolk, 1890*, also has G. Smith & Son trading at 19, Hartl[e]y Road, Great Yarmouth. Thomas Smith was advertised as trading at 4, Gun Lane, Norwich in 1850. Christopher Frost also mentions a John E. Thirkettle working at St. Giles Hill. Jas Yallop traded in the nearby village of Bawburgh, five miles west of Norwich. An advertisement in William White's *History, Gazetteer and Directory of Norfolk, 1886* has him as an "Ornithologist, treatment of all kinds of cage birds." Bird preservation may well have been an additional income (Walter Lowne of Yarmouth greatly profited from his own aviaries, accounting for the number of 'domestic' birds in his ledgers). Thomas Southwell mentions a case of cock-fighting birds in the Norwich Castle Museum that were set up by the Norfolk ornithologist and author John Hunt (1777—1842). Southwell describes Hunt as "formerly a bird stuffer and author." Hunt published a three-volume guide, *British Ornithology*.

Notes

1. Harrod & Co.'s *Directory of Norfolk and Lowestoft* (1877).
2. Ed. E.R. Kelly and Co., *The Post Office Directory of Cambridgeshire, Norfolk and Suffolk* (London, 1869).
3. W. White, *History, Gazetteer and Directory of Norfolk*, (London, Simpkin, Marshall & Co, 1854).
4. *Commercial Directory of the County of Norfolk*, (Craven & Co., 1856).
5. J.H. Gurney and T. Southwell, 'Fauna and Flora of Norfolk,' Part XI. *Birds*. Section I. *Transations of the Norfolk and Norwich Naturalists'. Society* by J. H. Gurney, Jun., F.L.S., and Thomas Southwell, F.Z.S. p. 276. (*Transations*, Norfolk and Norwich Naturalists' Society. vol. ii. p. 226).
6. K.A. Naylor and M.S. Pollitt, M.S. *Historical Rare Birds*, (List of Taxidermists, 2021), https://www.historicalrarebirds.info (accessed 12 September 2024).
7. *Transactions, Norfolk and Norwich Naturalists' Society*, (Norwich, A.E. Soman & Co., 1919), p.21.
8. C. Frost, *The Ogilvie Bird Collection*, (Lavenham, Lavenham Press, 1989), p. 16.

9. J. Parry, *Maurice Bird. The Gilbert White of the Broads*, Norfolk and Norwich Naturalists' Society, (Lavenham, Lavenham Press, 2024).
10. C. Frost *A History of British Taxidermy*, (Lavenham, The Lavenham Press, 1987), pp. 44-5.
11. Ibid. 8, p. 18.
12. Ibid.
13. Ibid.
14. *Transactions*, Norfolk and Norwich Naturalists' Society, (Norwich, Fletcher and Son, 1880), p. 49.
15. *Norfolk Chronicle*, 18 January 1890.
16. A pencil note in the author's copy of the book has 'Heydon' crossed out, replaced with 'Hindringham.'
17. P.A. Morris, 'The work of Walter Lowne, Taxidermist of Great Yarmouth,' *Transactions of the Norfolk & Norwich Naturalists' Society*, Vol. 28, Part 1, (Hunstanton, Wisley Press, August 1988), p. 40.
18. Rev. Richard Lubbock, *Observations on the Fauna of Norfolk and more particularly on the District of the Broads*, First published in 1845, (Norwich, Jarrold & Sons, 1879), footnote by Thomas Southwell, p. 4.
19. Ibid. 6.
20. Ibid. 10, p. 44.
21. Private correspondence with author.
22. *Transactions*, Norfolk and Norwich Naturalists' Society, (Norwich, Jarrold & Sons, 1880), p 156.
23. Baillion's crake is a very rare visitor to Norfolk. James Parry (*Maurice Bird. The Gilbert White of the Broads*, p.62) states that only two county nesting records are known: in 1866 and a nest found in 1889 at Sutton Broad. Sabine's snipe gets its name from Edward Sabine (1788-1883). G.E.H. Barrett-Hamilton writing in *The Irish Naturalist* in 1885 stated that distinguishing Sabine's snipe from common snipe was difficult save for the absence of any white plumage and having only 12 instead of 14 tail-feathers. It is considered one of the rarest of all known birds seen in the British Isles. First seen in Ireland in 1822.
24. Ibid. 8, p. 23.
25. Ibid. 10, p. 50.
26. Ibid. 8, p. 23.
27. Ibid. 6.
28. Ibid. 10, p. 57.
29. Ibid. pp. 57-63.
30. Ibid. p. 63.
31. *Eastern Daily Press*, 5 March 1906.
32. Ibid.
33. Ibid. 10, p. 63.
34. C. Stoate, *Taxidermy. The Revival of a Natural Art*, (London, Sportsman's Press, 1987), p. 33.
35. Ibid. 6.
36. *Transactions*, Norfolk and Norwich Naturalists' Society, (Norwich, Fletcher and Son, 1883), p. 520.
37. *Harrod & Co.'s Directory of Norfolk and Lowestoft* (1877).

38. Ibid. 10, p. 65.
39. White, W., *History, Gazetteer and Directory of Norfolk*, (London, Simpkin, Marshall & Co, 1854).
40. Ibid. 10, p. 65.
41. Ibid.
42. Ibid. 6.
43. *Transactions*, Norfolk and Norwich Naturalists' Society, (Norwich, Fletcher and Son, 1886), p. 404.
44. M. Seago, *Birds of Norfolk*, (Norwich, Jarrold & Sons, 1977), p. 121.
45. *Commercial Directory of the County of Norfolk* (Craven & Co., 1856).
46. W. White, *History, Gazetteer and Directory of Norfolk*, (London, Simpkin, Marshall & Co, 1854).
47. W. White, *History, Gazetteer and Directory of Norfolk*, (London, Simpkin, Marshall & Co, 1864).
48. Pigott's *Directory of Norfolk* (1839).
49. Ibid. 6.
50. Ibid. 10, p. 65.
51. *Transactions*, Norfolk and Norwich Naturalists' Society, (Norwich, A.E. Soman & Co., 1919), p. 21.
52. *Norwich Mercury*, 18 February 1841.
53. *Norfolk Chronicle*, 1 April 1882.
54. Hunt & Co.'s *Directory of East Norfolk and Parts of Suffolk* (1850).
55. Harrod & Co.'s *Directory of Norfolk and Lowestoft* (1877).
56. Ibid. 10, pp. 57-63.
57. *Norfolk News* 3 July 1880.
58. *Commercial Directory of the County of Norfolk* (Craven & Co, 1856).

Walter's Whale

GREAT YARMOUTH AND BREYDON WATER

Born in Martham in 1853, Walter Lowne became the most successful taxidermist working in Great Yarmouth (known in that time as Yarmouth) and the surrounding area. He worked as a taxidermist from the 1870s until his death in 1915. Previously registered at Caister Road, his reputation grew when he began trading at 40, Fuller's Hill in a five room house which was previously a game-dealer's premises. He lived with his wife, Hannah and their domestic helper, Annie Lawn. Lowne supplemented his income based on his skills in taxidermy. In Lowne's case this centred on the increasingly popular sport of golf. In 1883, William White's *History, Gazetteer and Directory of Norfolk* advertises Lowne as a dealer in golf clubs and balls. Featherie golf balls had been introduced to the sport for centuries. The ball comprised a hand-sewn round leather pouch stuffed with goose or chicken feathers. The volume measurement was a gentleman's top hat full of feathers. The feathers were boiled and softened before they were stuffed into the pouch. Making the balls was a tedious and time-consuming business which reflected the expensive price tag. Such balls fetch eye-watering prices at auction today.

Those wishing to enter the taxidermy trade could learn from established taxidermists by dissecting their mounts and disseminating their skills. Pat Morris describes how Lowne took up the art, "In his early twenties Lowne decided to take up taxidermy in his spare time. [Arthur] Patterson gave him a book on the subject and Lowne had a local bird stuffer named Juler set up a cuckoo for him. This was speedily dismantled to reveal its secrets and by 1878, Lowne was selling mounted birds."[1] Patterson reveals more, "In the 1870s Walter Lowne and I were next-door neighbours. Having finished his apprenticeship as a carpenter at Martham, he came to live with an aunt. He had long been contemplating taking up taxidermy, and to that end he built a workshop in the little back garden. We talked about birds over the fence. I set him up with a book, *Gardner's Bird Stuffing*. At that time we both carried twelve-bores. His first experiment was on a starling. Then he obtained a cuckoo and commissioned "Juler," the taxidermist, to "set it up." He did. Lowne carefully went through it, seeing how the wires were fastened, the shape given to the body and so on, learning to stuff it—backwards. The poor starling was a weird bit of work!"[2]

Thanks to the good fortune of Patterson, two important books were saved from destruction. These resources are now available at the Norfolk Record Office and give a detailed picture of the work undertaken by Lowne: *The Ledger of Walter Lowne, 1886-1911*, FX 223/1 and *The Record Book of Walter Lowne, bird stuffer of Fuller's Hill*, MS 4185. In 1988 Pat Morris also describes a small manuscript by Arthur Patterson comprising handwritten reminiscences about Lowne, newspaper cuttings and illustrations. Although a copy is in the hands of Morris, sadly the original belongs to a private collector. In the front pages of his sales record book Patterson writes in his own hand, "Walter and I went in for stuffing together. He at it all night, frequently, after a day's work as a carpenter. I foolishly went courting. We each excelled in our own way. He made a living of stuffing and I got an excellent wife. This book and his ledger I picked up in a rag shop during the [First World] War, saving them from being made into pulp."[3] Unfortunately, no photographs of Lowne exist in public archives. Pat Morris states, "Patterson described Lowne as being of cheerful and optimistic disposition but somewhat dogmatic. He was a large man, above average height and inclined to stoutness."[4]

Norfolk's principal seaport was at its industrial peak at the end of the 19th century. By 1883 'Yare-mouth' was pre-eminent for its herring and mackerel fisheries. The town was nineteen miles from Norwich and connected by two railways. In its heyday there were three railway stations: Vauxhall, Beach and South Town. White's *History, Gazetteer and Directory of Norfolk* reveals the town to "enjoy extensive traffic in coal and timber and corn and is in the great celebrity as a bathing place." There were elegant suburbs, spacious houses and hotels, "The Wellington and Britannia piers, erected for the accommodation of visitors, each extending about 700 feet into the sea, are handsome structures, built in 1854 and 1858, at a cost of nearly £7000 each."[5]

Breydon Water to the west of Great Yarmouth is the gateway to the Broads river system and the UKs largest protected wetland, three miles long and almost a mile wide. In his 1949 book, *Marshland Adventure*, James Wentworth Day describes the expanse, " … the grey wild waste of Breydon opened up. It is a great salt lake, four miles long and a mile wide, an estuary where the tide runs between four and five knots, the mud-flats bare in a few minutes, and only the centre channel is safe for boats of any draft."[6] The Bure, Yare and Waveney rivers drain across flat marshlands to enter the vast tidal basin of Breydon Water. It was a favourite hunting ground for nearly all of the Norfolk taxidermists in the Victorian and Edwardian eras as well as sportsmen and the wildfowlers who made their living from shooting.

Peter and Margaret Clarke state, "In historic times Breydon had an unenviable reputation for the number of birds that were annually shot. These included many rare and beautiful species such as Avocets and Spoonbills and it is a wonder that the latter two species still visit annually."[7] These two species of birds can be used to illustrate the concentration of shooting and collecting in this region of Norfolk, factors all to the benefit of local taxidermists like Lowne. Howard Saunders states, "Prof. Newton has shown (Tr. Norfolk Soc. 1896, p. 158) that in the time of Edward I (1300) the Spoonbill was known, under the name of 'Popeler,' to breed in Norfolk; while up to the days of Willughby and Sir Thomas Browne it used to nest in trees—in company with Herons—in that county and

Suffolk."[8] Arthur Patterson comments "some forty-five spoonbills observed here between 1854 and 1889; of these more than half occurred in May, and one as early as March 20; but at least two-thirds of them are simply dated with the accompanying epitaph—Shot on Breydon."[9] The spoonbill (known in Norfolk in the late 18th century as the 'Banjobill') is included in the 2020 publication, *Norfolk's Wonderful 150*, a collection of species from Norfolk to celebrate the 150th anniversary of the Norfolk & Norwich Naturalists' Society.

Since 1970 the RSPB has the Avocet as its logo, a symbol of conservation and protection. In Patterson's day the approach was very different. Patterson refers to the avocet as having a value attached to its skin like "a halo of conquest." Howard Saunders states, "Reclamation of fen-land gradually circumscribed its haunts, and moreover a large colony at Salthouse appears to have been destroyed in consequence of a demand for Avocet's feathers for dressing artificial flies; while the collection of its eggs also contributed to the decrease of the species, and nesting in England had probably ceased by 1824."[10] Thomas Southwell states, "The Avocet was sometimes called the Shoe-awl probably from the shape of its beak. At the beginning of the present century the poor people of Salthouse made their 'puddings and pancakes' of the eggs of this bird, and 'the gunners to unload their punt guns, would sometimes kill ten or twelve at a shot;' as might be expected, it is now one of the rarest waders. A few returned each spring to their old haunts only to fall victims to the gun, and the last native bred bird having been killed, it can now only be regarded as an irregular migrant. Two were killed on Breydon on the 30th and 31st March, 1876, which not even the mild penalties of the Wild-bird Protection Act could save from being made into 'specimens;' and two others, about the middle of May, 1878, in the same favoured locality, met with a like fate."[11]

Broadland is primarily a man-made habitat, a thread of waterways and expanses of water, or broads, formed from medieval peat diggings. These ancient diggings became flooded from the Middle Ages onwards as sea-levels rose. These shallow broads, numbering about forty, are linked to the Rivers Bure, Yare and Waveney and their tributaries. By the early 1920s rail expansion brought an influx of tourists to

Victorian taxidermy study of an avocet.
Author.

the Broads. Twenty years previously John Payne Jennings had done much to promote Broadland as a rural idyll in photographs commissioned by the Great Eastern Railway Company. Trains brought in the sportsmen and the collectors and allowed the passage of taxidermy cases to the rest of the country (Walter Lowne's ledger shows a clientele spread far and wide). Passage by rail was probably a better way of transporting taxidermy than by road. In 1881, claims were made by a customer against the carrier used by Norwich taxidermist, Roberts. The carrier blamed the damage on the taxidermist as the bird was "not packed to his satisfaction."[12] Railways brought more visitors to other areas of the county. For instance, much earlier in 1862, engineered by John Sutherland Valentine, the Great Eastern built a branch line from Kings Lynn to Hunstanton. Railway expansion in the mid-19th century coincided with the invention of the breech-loading shotgun and sportsmen took advantage of train services which expanded to far-reaching locations including night trains to Scottish moorland for the 'Glorious Twelfth' Grouse shooting season.

By the 1920s The Wild Bird Protection Acts had gradually driven most of the wildfowlers out of business. The shooting of rare specimens and indiscriminate egg collecting had been curtailed by law and overseen by vigilant 'watchmen' put in place by the local protection societies. However, Breydon and Broadland were 'the Badlands' and a difficult area to police by the wardens living on boats on the broads and rivers. Walter Lowne also enjoyed time spent on the water as J. H. Gurney states in 1898, "I once heard of a small flock [bearded titmouse] in a little bay on Fritton Lake,[13] but there are not a great many reeds there, and it is probable they have not bred there for a very long time. Mr. Page, the decoyman, has not seen one in a residence of twenty-eight years, neither has Mr. W. Lowne though often on the Lake."[14]

Arthur Patterson's descriptions in his various books offer a glimpse of some of the people he met along the way, including Lowne and the 'bygone Breydoners.' History also presents insights thanks to the writing of Wentworth Day, (who was Patterson's friend), MCH Bird and to a lesser extent Henry Pashley further along the coast at Cley. The Breydoners were tough, fearless men and women. Mark Cocker writes:

> Just to remind ourselves that Patterson was not just an outstanding naturalist but also a super writer. I want to do two short readings. One of them I suppose is among the most anthologised bits of John Knowlittle.[15] Typically, and it is one of the elements that most distinguishes his writing, it dwells not on nature per se, but on a human community dependent upon nature. More than any bird or fish, a species AP found most captivating and worthy of record, when others did not, was a type of humanity best described as the punt gunner. This community was made up from a very rough tough breed of men who lived on the edge of Breydon and the east Broads (and not forgetting

their equally formidable partners and offspring), who were one part naturalist, one part hunter-gatherer. The notion that they were at all naturalists is one that would have been very strange to most members of the NNNS[16] in Patterson days. But the idea was not at all strange to AP himself. In fact, one of the last of these remarkable characters died in 1902, a man known as Little 'Pintail' Thomas.[17]

Patterson wrote a seven-page obituary for Pintail in *Transactions*, "Of course they relied upon their expertise, not only in tracking and hunting birds and fish, but also in an ability to recognise what they had caught. Part of their business was the sale of rare birds or rare fish and other animals to taxidermists and to a middle-class version of the punt-gunner, an equally rapacious species known as 'the gentleman gunner'. He was often a wealthy collector willing to pay sizeable amount of money for exceptional specimens. So you had to know your wildlife to realise your profits."[18]

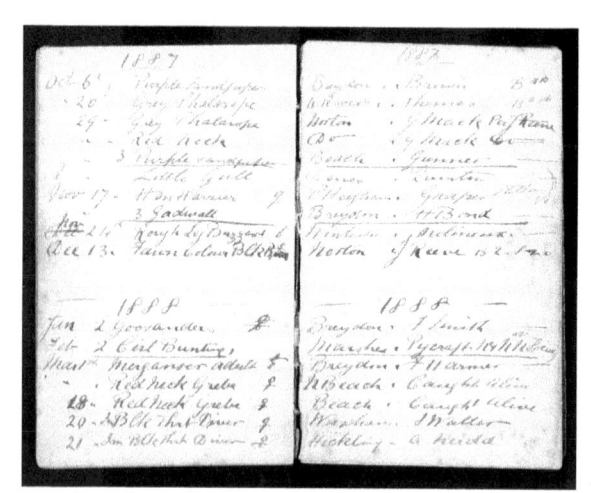

Pages from the workbook of Walter Lowne
Norfolk Records Office, MS 4185.

Lowne's sales ledger records all the work he was paid for over a period of 26 years and is a marvellous record of the diversity of specimens a taxidermist might preserve across their career. By all accounts Lowne appears a hard-working taxidermist and never short of work. Lowne's professional standing reflects the diversity of his trade which, as well as making golf balls, involved preparing mounts for ladies' hats. Reflecting the fashion for exotic birds and animals in the Victorian years there are examples in Lowne's records of the preservation of hummingbirds (1886), a peacock, canaries, a monkey, parrots and guinea pigs loved and lost. Pat Morris spotted

Pages from the Ledger of Walter Lowne
Norfolk Records Office, FX 223/1.

that Lowne also prepared seventy-two decorative fire screens (to hide an empty fireplace in the summer months). They featured herons, bitterns, owls, gulls, kestrels and jays.[19] He also dressed a large number of mole skins, presumably for glove manufacture. His preservation skills also extended to butterflies and bats.

CASE STUDY. THE MILLINERY TRADE. THE KINGFISHER, ALCEDO ATTHIS AND THE GREEN WOODPECKER, PICUS VIRIDIS.

W. Swaysland describes the most brilliantly coloured of British birds, "The plumage may be thus described: from the crown of the head, down the neck, and the whole of the upper part, the wings and tail are of a brilliant green, shading from olive to iridescent emerald and blue; from the beak across the eye is a patch of rufous, which becomes white below the ear-covets; from the base of the beak runs a streak of the above-mentioned glossy green, which meets that upon the wing-covets. The chin and throat are yellowish-white; the breast and under parts are rufous, deepening in colour as it proceeds towards the tail."[20] Swaysland goes on to state, "[the nest] is generally well hidden, and, except for the rats, the Kingfisher, being so beautiful, need fear no foes.[21] It was, however, a favourite 'sport' of some possessed of a gun, some years ago, to kill these beautiful birds; and as they fly straight they are easily marked."[22]

Walter Lowne and other taxidermists sold feathers for millinery work, i.e. a Mr G. Hunt (solicitor and bank manager) received on 5 May 1886, "2 tits for hats," and "Kingfishers for hats." Victorian women valued the brilliantly bright plumage of the kingfisher, green woodpecker and other birds to decorate their hats. In his first volume of *The Birds of Norfolk*, Henry Stevenson clearly states his detestation for this fashion,[23] "Surely it must be a mind of no ordinary insensibility that could contemplate with indifference the wholesale destruction of these living gems … It probably never occurs to the fair owners of those wicked little hats, which mark the present age as one of the most fascinating epochs in the history of female costume, that the adoption of one particular feather, by some reigning beauty, may be the death warrant of a species!"[24] Howard Saunders states (1899), "In few places can [the kingfisher] be considered an abundant species; mainly owing to the fact that it is shot on account of its bright plumage, but partly for its feathers, used in the making of artificial flies."[25] An advertisement by George Diggens & Company at Norfolk House, Norwich in William White's *History, Gazetteer and Directory of Norfolk, 1883*, contained the following, "Our bonnet and millinery department is superintended by experienced ladies, whose taste for embellishing hats, bonnets, and for general millinery is justly celebrated." Pat Morris states, "Contemporary campaigns against the use of birds in the millinery trade, leading to the formation of what became the RSPB, and the popular writings of W.H. Hudson and others, seemed not to have damaged this aspect of [Walter Lowne's] business. Some of his hats seem especially bizarre—three orders were for woodpeckers; pheasant's heads were popular as were terns[26] … It is difficult to understand why one of his customers could wear a parrot on her hat; another ordered a budgerigar for a hat (or maybe supplied her own late companion?)."[27] Green woodpeckers and great-crested grebes (sometimes known as 'loons') were also marked for their plumage.[28] In 1881, an amendment to the Wild Bird Protection Act of 1880 gave special protection to the grebe (a general close season between 1 March and 1 September) and banning collecting of their eggs. Kingfishers were hunted across Norfolk, along rivers, streams, on the Broads and occasionally on marsh dykes and tidal creeks. I occasionally see a pair work a small stream in the Brecks near Litcham, particularly striking when seen against the haw-frosted landscape in the winter of 2022. I'm also assisting in the restoration of a 'kingfisher cliff' to encourage the bird to nest in a carefully constructed plaster face wall with nesting holes. Henry Pashley notes the presence of kingfishers on the coast, "Common. Seen them feeding in the 'creeks' on the marshes, and had them brought to me with their bills plastered with mud. Found on dissection they had been feeding on aquatic insects and ants with their larvae."[29] Kingfishers are known to feed on water-beetles, dragonfly nymphs and small fish including minnows and stickleback. Lowne won 1st, 2nd and 3rd prizes for his reared kingfishers at various exhibitions across the country. At the time kingfishers were kept in aviaries where the main diet was small fish substituting with fresh beef and, as Morris states, hard-boiled eggs. Writing in 1866, Henry Stevenson states, "The young birds, though rather difficult to rear, are extremely amusing when brought up from the nest. Mr. Sayer, a bird-stuffer, in this city, had four alive in the summer of 1862, which were kept in a small aviary where they had ample space to display their natural habits. If a deep basin of water, filled with live minnows, was placed on the floor, they would dart down from their perches one after the other, and with almost unerring aim, secure a victim, which was generally held near to the tail until killed by sundry smart blows against the woodwork; then tossed up with a little jerk and swallowed head downwards."[30]

There are two cases of kingfishers in the Ogilvie collection set up by T.E. Gunn, both of which contain four birds. Seven of the birds are from Suffolk, one was shot by Ogilvie at Cley-next-Sea in

Victorian taxidermy study of a kingfisher.
Author.

October 1900. All seven kingfishers (two adults, five juveniles) in the Lysaght Collection were shot in Norfolk. In an amendment to the Wild Bird Protection Act, kingfishers were protected with a close season, but their eggs were not protected in Norfolk at that time. Arthur Patterson made comment that he knew a man who was not satisfied until he had a dozen kingfishers to put into his case. One of his bird notes written on 23 September 1883 states "50 kingfishers have been shot during August and September. Plenty about." However, writing many years later in 1930, he states, "The gloriously draped kingfisher is another favourite of mine, and I am always sorry I ever levelled a gun at one; but so many are enamoured of its gorgeous attire that they will show you its stuffed skin in a glass-fronted box and solicit you your admiration of it. Even in this time of protective agencies unscrupulous persons cannot resist a shot a passing kingfisher."[31]

Swaysland reveals the names under which the green woodpecker is known, "It is known by a variety of names, most of which, however, are entirely local. Amongst others, it is perhaps most generally known at the Popinjay and Awl Bird; yet it is also known by the names of 'Rain bird' and 'Tongue bird,' whilst in the south it is commonly termed the 'Yaffle' or the 'Gally' bird." Swaysland goes on to state, "it is strictly non-gregarious, and pursues its avocation in a quiet manner, except for the noise made by the beak tapping on the bark."[32] In 1885, Gurney spoke about the excesses of the period, "the green woodpecker is a sadly persecuted species, but, nevertheless, it seems to hold its ground. We visited a birdstuffer's shop together at Thetford, at which there must have been fifty specimens in different stages of preservation. The Norwich birdstuffers have more brought to them than they know how to dispose of. "[33] In 1891 things have not improved. He states, "From the experience of other severe winters I believe the Green Woodpeckers, like the Hawfinches thus sacrificed, are all residents, exposed alike to the privations of such seasons, and from their gay plumage to the observations of a more than usual number of gunners; and such a prize is sure to find its way to the bird-stuffers."[34] Like all birds of striking plumage, including the great spotted and lesser spotted woodpeckers, the feathers of the green woodpecker were prized as adornments for ladies hats. All five green woodpeckers in the Lysaght Collection were shot in Norfolk. Examples by Gunn appear in the Norwich Castle Museum. The Wild Bird Protection Act, 1880, did not include the bird. Amendments to the act included all woodpeckers, but not the protection of their eggs in Norfolk.

ಲಾಡ

Lowne undertook renovation work on established cases. For instance, "45 hours to do large case: in. 3 hr journey to Ormesby altering Eagles, rockwork, varnishing."[35] His travelling charges are seen many times, "sent by train on March 18 to the Roydon [sic] buildings[36] in Gorleston was a gannet for £1, 6 shillings." Griffin & Myhill are occasionally referred to as assistants, the latter evidently helping to build a rock scene for an eagle group in 'Foulsham Case.'[37] In April 1891, The *Eastern Daily Press* wrote about one of Lowne's restoration projects, "Lowne restored, re-mounted and cleaned one of the grandest cases of stuffed birds we have ever set eyes on. Seventeen Ruffs and seven Reeves all killed in Norfolk and purchased at the sale of the Rev. H Temple Frere's collection at Burston Rectory."[38] No doubt Lowne's previous skills as a carpenter helped fashion his good quality wooden cases (Lowne served his apprenticeship in Martham before taking up work as a carpenter in Yarmouth). Morris maintains that Lowne also used ready-made soap or borax boxes for cases and also sold 751 glass domes as separate entities.[39] Borax is a preservative agent still used in taxidermy. It comprises a white soluble salt prepared from boric acid. Borax's safety was in marked contrast to the perniciousness of arsenic and was often used mixed with other ingredients including turpentine, camphor and soap to form a paste. Lowne's use of borax boxes suggests that he possibly moved away from arsenic as preservative techniques changed. The majority of the Lowne cases I have seen are rectangular glass-fronted boxes, painted black with a gilt strip framing the front of the box, inside the glass. Morris describes how Lowne mounted his specimens, "X-rays of extant bird specimens suggested he used a mass of tow, tightly bound with thread to form the body, with a central wire pushed in from the rear and out the top of the head. This and the two leg wires (with sharpened ends, pushed up the legs from the feet) were doubled over and bent into the body. The tail was supported on a separate wire, and the wings (at least in birds up to the size of a teal) were not wired but simply pinned in place."[40] The groundwork, comprising moss and green vegetation is often striking against deep sky blue background. I have seen a pair short-eared owls by Lowne in a private collection which have a mottled pale pink background, presumably to depict a sunset when the owls might be beginning to hunt. Lowne's trade label was fixed to verso and changed a few times over the years he was trading. The most well-known example features two round symbols representing an award given to him at the Fisheries

Two taxidermy cases by Walter Lowne. The black case and distinctive gilt inlay were almost Lowne trademarks. The cases show a stoat on a kit rabbit and a juvenile moorhen.
Author.

Exhibition in Great Yarmouth in 1881.

Between 1890 and 1891 Lowne exhibited caged birds in various classes in national competitions: a kingfisher (Lowne reared five), thrush, starling, hawfinch, bullfinch, linnet, brambling, and shorelark.[41] He won 1st, 2nd and 3rd prizes in shows at Sudbury in Suffolk, Fakenham, Bedford, Great Yarmouth and also the 'All England' shows in Norwich and Cambridge. Lowne hand reared these birds which were taken as nestlings from the wild. The *Norfolk Chronicle* reported on his successes at the Bedford Show, "Mr Lowne, naturalist and taxidermist of this town, was awarded first prize in the Finch Class, for a hawfinch, and for his hand-reared white-throat, an extra second for a wheatear, and a third prize for a hand-reared swallow, at the All England Ornithological Show which was held at Bedford last week."[42]

Frustratingly for owners of Lowne cases, and despite the extensive records, lacunae remain. Lowne is sometimes vague when writing down the exact job in hand. Exact species are not always mentioned, i.e. 'four gulls.' I have a spectacular case of wading birds by Lowne and although the label to verso places it in the Edwardian period, c.1900, precise dating and the client remain a mystery. I have another unlabelled case which displays his typical groundwork. The case has to remain 'attributed.' The coincidence of 'six birds' to a purchaser in Wellingborough, where I picked up the case, has to remain as conjecture. His record book lists in date order the more notable bird specimens that he preserved between the years 1878-1893. Interestingly, the location and collector of each bird are noted as 'where taken' and 'who by.'

Case of wading birds in winter plumage by the Great Yarmouth taxidermist Walter Lowne. Clockwise from bottom left: curlew sandpiper, ringed plover, grey plover, dunlin, reeve, and common sandpiper.

Steve Norris Photography.

Pat Morris gives an excellent insight into how Lowne (and by extension, some of his contemporaries in the trade) sourced specimens, (a) refers to Lowne's ledger, (b) his record book and (c) Patterson's biography in a private collection:

> It is unlikely that Lowne did much collecting himself. He bought a gun license in 1880, but obtained little on his forays, (c) and probably was too busy for much shooting. A substantial proportion of Lowne's work comprised domestic species, including many birds that were presumably from his own aviaries where he also kept and bred various wild species. A lot birds and mammals listed in his ledger were brought to him by members of the public to be mounted (c). These doubtless included shot and trapped specimens, but also birds which he recorded as killed by the newly-erected telephone wires. It is possible that some of his suppliers were less than honest, perhaps wishing to conceal acts of trespass. For example it is difficult to believe the record (b,c) of 15 common buzzards washed up on the beach, though an abundance of little auks in winter 1894-5 and 1900-01 correspond to a note in the logbook (b) 'severe weather' and widespread 'wrecks' of this species noted elsewhere (Fisher & Lockley, 1954). Some specimens were bought from elsewhere (e.g. five bluethroats from Cley, costing 8/1d in 1883) [43] and many skins came from other dealers. He prepared at least seven 'albertross,' [sic] possibly brought to Great Yarmouth by seamen as souvenirs from the Southern Hemisphere.

Many of Lowne's specimens were bought from friends in the country (c) as speculative purchases. Many more came from Durrant's famous game stall in Yarmouth, including a peregrine in 1882 and spotted crake in 1884. Patterson (1904) recorded that Durrant's stall held over 900 birds on 16th December 1899, and was a favourite place to look for unrecognised rarities such as glaucous gulls and Richardson's (arctic) skua, but also, (supposedly), a goshawk and a golden oriole. There was evidently considerable competitiveness and some sharp practice among the buyers and sellers of dead birds, described in several of Patterson's books (Frost, 1987).[44]

Arthur Patterson visiting Durrant's game stall on the market, Great Yarmouth, in 1900.
Image courtesy of the Norfolk County Council Library and Information Service at www.picture.norfolk.gov.uk.

Patterson reveals the somewhat dubious nature of the game stall and its clientele, "The late W. Durrant's game stall in Yarmouth Market has for years been a resort of wildfowlers, sportsmen, and men not wishing to be recognised or known as either, but whose tastes brought them into contact with various creatures, the snaring or shooting of which provides sport without much fear of trouble at the hands of the rural policeman."[45] After Durrant died the game stall was taken over and known as 'Edmond's.'

Pat Morris is keen to express the fact that, "[Lowne] may have been atypical among taxidermists in maintaining an active aviculture enterprise, providing many specimens ... The list of customer's names in his ledger offers no evidence that he was retained by any regular collector, nor that he profited from excessive collecting zeal on the part of any particular individuals ..."[46]

Case Study—The Little Auk, Alle alle

The little auks are oceanic birds, but are forever associated with onshore gales, especially in October and November. In his *Manual of British Birds*, Howard Saunders also refers to the species as Rotch or Rotge, monikers of Scandinavian origin.[47] They appear in great numbers in the Norwegian Sea, but strong northerly or north-westerly winds blow the birds towards the North Sea rather than the Atlantic. Consequently, annual numbers of these passage migrants on the Norfolk coast can vary greatly. Pashley stated that the birds visited Cley every year, sometimes in large numbers. Once near land they were targeted by the gunners, who, as Henry Stevenson states in his first volume of *The Birds of Norfolk* shoot them by "lying up for them behind the banks." Thomas Southwell states that the bird was known to the Blakeney gunners as the "King John."[48] Swaysland states, "Occasionally, during very severe and protracted gales, these birds are compelled to forsake the open sea and take refuge on those parts of the coast where shelter and protection may be found. At these times they are shot with little difficulty."[49] Swaysland

Victorian taxidermy study of a little auk. The specimen was in bad condition and saved by a light varnish. Author.

states that the little auk is a very small bird, scarcely half the weight of a puffin. J. H. Gurney wrote to Arthur Patterson, "The number of Little Auks for Norfolk is verily a big catastrophe to a little species!"[50] Arthur Patterson recorded that, "A local bird stuffer had lately sixteen Little Auks in for preservation." Thomas Southwell reveals a note made by Henry Stevenson which was thought to have been written in 1863, "I find that since 1852 I have seen in the hands of our

Norwich birdstuffers from one to six or eight specimens in each succeeding year, the total number amounting to between thirty-five and forty examples." He goes on to state, "I have known the little auk to occur at North Walsham, Fakenham, Stalham, Stratton Strawless, South Walsham, Scottow, Reymerston, Hevingham, and Buckenham; also at Eaton, Lakenham, and Thorpe, near Norwich, between twenty and thirty miles from the sea, in several instances in the city itself. Many of these birds were alive when first picked up, but, either from previous injury or want of proper food, soon died."[51] The irruptions of auks were recorded in the *Transactions* of the Norfolk and Norwich Naturalists' Society. Arthur Patterson reveals that Hunt (*List of Norfolk Birds*, 1829) describes the auk as rare and "cites but one instance of its occurrence as 'one picked up at North Walsham.'"[52] Gurney recorded the taxidermists who preserved the 285 auks in 1894, "Clarke of Snettisham, Gunn of Norwich (examples in the Norwich Castle Museum), Dack of Holt, Pashley of Cley, Cole of Norwich, Wilson of Lynn, Roberts of Norwich, Lowne of Yarmouth, H. Cole of Northrepps and Howlett of Newmarket."[53] Michael Seago (1977) also mentions the 'Wreck Years' of 1841, 1848, 1861, 1895, 1900, 1910, 1912 and 1955 when a total of 193 little auks were reported. In January 1895 Lowne comments in his workbook, "Weather very severe. 15 Little Auks between 1st and 30th January. Sharp frost, strong winds." Patterson describes the event, with not a little irony, "the delight of those devoted to gunning pursuits."[54] A watercolour illustration of two little auks by F.E. Gunn (one of a collection of sixty-eight drawings) is in the National Trust collections at Calke Abbey in Derbyshire.

ಸಂಐ

Lowne contributed to the *Lysaght Collection of Birds* in Birmingham, including a black redstart (1892) and a pied flycatcher, both birds set up for E.M. Connop. He also preserved many rare species. He owned the 1882 Norfolk white-tailed eagle, preserved the 1883 Norfolk roller,[55] preserved the 1884 Suffolk great snipe, preserved and informed Churchill Babbington about the 1885 Norfolk little bustard. Other species preserved by him include the 1888 little bustard, the 1889 little bittern, the 1890 Caspian plover, the 1891 scops owl, the 1902 little bustard, and the 1904 and 1911 Norfolk serins.[56] Local newspapers often reported a rare bird set up by Lowne. Specimens preserved by other Yarmouth taxidermists were also reported, especially in the *Yarmouth Mercury* and *Yarmouth Independent*, but also the Norwich papers. This must have been good advertising for the taxidermists. Lowne mounted a red-necked phalarope in winter plumage in October 1881, "It is now in the hands of Mr. Lowne, taxidermist, 40, Fuller's Hill, Great Yarmouth, for preservation, and in a few days it will be exhibited in his window."[57] Another report comes from the *Eastern Daily Press* in September 1883, "A very fine specimen of the taxidermist's art is to be seen in the window of Mr. Lowne's, Fuller's Hill, in the shape of a young half-grown female seal which was shot on Breydon."[58] In his biography of Maurice Bird, James Parry reveals that Bird knew Lowne well and often referred to him in his diary, for instance on the 29 June 1885, "Saw in Lowne's shop a male Long tailed Duck in summer plumage which was caught by a boy at Acle this spring in a marsh ditch."[59]

In twenty-six years from 1886 to 1911, (when his health began to fail), Lowne's ledger reveals that he handled 4,784 birds. Morris is keen to point out that many specimens were aviary reared birds,[60] including, presumably, birds from his own aviaries, (over 20% of Lowne's birds and mammals were domestic in origin) but he concedes that 459 owls is an astonishing total.[61] Many of the birds he preserved refer to local and vernacular names. It is interesting to note that the Orders of the Secretary of State in relation to the successive Wild Bird Protection acts also state the local names. For instance, terns are also named as sea swallows, pearls, or dip-ears. Stone-curlews are called Norfolk plovers, or thick-knees. Whereas the Norfolk names for terns are practically obsolete, the monikers for the stone-curlews are still familiar in Breckland today.

A private collector once owned a Montague's harrier set up by Lowne, but traded the specimen in for a rare Victorian Greenland falcon. The collector certainly was keen to get the harrier and he later wondered whether it was the bird described by Jim Vincent in his 1911 diary. Vincent states, "Lowne of Yarmouth showed me a male Montague received from Martham that was shot and sent to him."[62] Vincent shot rare birds and took eggs for local collectors and was a keeper to Edwin Montagu at the White Slea Estate, Hickling. Montagu at that time was Liberal Member of Parliament for West Cambridgeshire. Montagu exemplifies the gradual change in thinking and understanding of the natural world, above and beyond the excessive desire of the collector to possess the next rare bird. Vincent's son, Edwin, states in the introduction to *A Norfolk Diary*, "When Mr Montagu saw Hickling again in 1908, his attitude to the bird life changed, and both he and Lord Lucas (who was also a member of Asquith's government) decided to become conservers of birds rather than collectors. They enjoyed shooting, but confined it to duck, coot, snipe and other more common species. (Ornithologists often decry the shooting man, yet some of the best ornithologists I have met also shot; they at least knew what they were aiming at, and respected the rarer birds that hove in sight)."[63]

Lowne preserved over 500 mammal species as well as mammals used in cases on which a bird is predating or its quarry. Stoats and weasels comprised 15% of the total number of mammals that Lowne stuffed in his career.[64] Stoats were often preserved in their striking white winter 'Ermine' coats. Writing an article on the 'Mammalia of Norfolk, *Mustela erminea* (Linn.). The Ermine Stoat,' Thomas Southwell states, "the mild winter of 1872–3 was remarkable for the number of white, or partially white, Stoats, which found their way to the Norwich birdstuffers. The winter of 1873–4 was also remarkably mild, but quite a number of white stoats were killed, some as late as the month of March. Mr. Gurney states, that in the winter of 1878, he saw at the three principal birdstuffers' in Norwich, six stoats, in which the ermine dress was completely assumed, and twenty-one others in which the change was partial, though in several cases nearly complete. In a birdstuffer's room, at Thetford, in 1882, I counted forty-one white, or nearly white, stoats, not all killed in one year, but he assured me they were only a fair accumulation in the way of his business. The change of colour in this species does not appear to depend upon the severity of the weather to such a degree as is generally believed, and where it does occur in snowless weather the white stoat forms a very conspicuous object, much to its disadvantage."[65]

Weasel in winter coat.
Author.

Morris states that 22% of Lowne's workload involved domestic and zoo species, (including five monkeys), the former reflecting the Victorian sentimentality in preserving a beloved pet. These included 18 cats, five guinea pigs, and 52 dogs, often mounted as heads, a bizarre practise in the modern mind. Wild mammals preserved included otters, red squirrels, weasels, stoats, a few foxes and a few hares. The natural history collection in Norwich Castle Museum contains an otter by Lowne (and many other examples of his work). Morris states that the paucity in numbers of fox-hunting trophies reflects the facts that "the wet pastures of east Norfolk were probably poorly suited to foxes and huntsmen alike."[66] This topography contributes to the fact that there isn't the tradition of fox hunting in that part of Norfolk. Morris highlights some of the more unusual specimens found in Lowne's workbook: a Shetland pony, an alligator, a salamander, lobsters and snakes. Specimens not local or migratory came into his hands, no doubt, due to Yarmouth's links to the continent and other British ports via the North Sea.

Like Gunn of Norwich and Pashley of Cley and to a lesser extent the Thetford taxidermists, Lowne wrote to natural history societies and publishers, informing them of any interesting specimens that came his way. For instance, Lowne writes,

"I have been requested by Mr. Southwell, of Norwich, to inform you, for the benefit of readers of the Zoologist, that I received, for preservation, in August last, a female specimen of the Little Bustard, *Otis tetrax*. It was shot by a boy in a turnip-field at Waxham, Norfolk, and was purchased by a gentleman on board a pleasure-boat, Mr. A. J. Flaxman, of London, for whom I have preserved it. On examination, it was found to have been feeding on clover-leaves and beetles."[67] William Tegetmeier, naturalist and founding member of the Savage Club[68] records in *The Field* the entry by J.H. Gurney in 1889, "I have had forwarded to me by Mr. Arthur Flaxman, a very fine specimen of the Little Bustard (*Otis tetrax*), which was shot on Aug. 10, at Waxham, a small village on the Norfolk coast, between Winterton and [Sea] Palling, in a turnip-field adjoining the sea. It proved to be a female, and it is stated that the ova were 'rather forward,' but their exact size, unfortunately, was not given. The bird has been admirably mounted by Mr. Lowne, well-known as a taxidermist at Great Yarmouth. The food found in the bird consisted of clover leaves and some remains of beetles. The occurrence of the species in this country during August is one of the earliest on record … Neither severe weather nor westerly gales will account for the occurrence of this fine specimen early in August."[69] Lowne received regular visits from naturalists well-known to the Norfolk and Norwich Naturalists' Society. In 1892 Thomas Southwell, then vice-president of the Society, recalls Lowne visiting him with a rare Siberian pectoral sandpiper, a bird that the taxidermist could not identify, "through the vigilance of Mr. Lowne of Yarmouth, I am enabled to record the addition of yet another rare Asiatic straggler to the already long list of Breydon rarities. On the morning of the 30th of August Mr. Lowne called upon me with a small, freshly killed wader, which he said puzzled him, asking me if I could name it for him."[70] In 1883, Lowne allowed John Gurney access to his workshop to study the recent acquisition of an Arctic blue-throated warbler (*Erithacus suecica*).[71]

Kelly's Directory of 1886 mentions Lowne as secretary of East Counties Angler's Society. His passion for angling perhaps crossed over to preserving various species of fish which were predominantly coarse fish from local waters. No doubt his association with anglers was good for business. Lowne also preserved mackerel and various other sea species. His records show that he set up perch, roach, bream, rudd and pike. Pat Morris makes the interesting point that most of the 83 pike specimens that Lowne preserved weighed less than 20lb, "perhaps because Norfolk waters were not a source of larger pike or perhaps because trophy specimens and record fish were customarily sent to a major taxidermist, like Cooper of London, with a reputation for specialising in fish."[72] Of the 402 fish Lowne prepared in 26 years as a taxidermist, 26 specimens were marine fish and set up for private clients, not for museum collections which might be expected at a seaport. These fish included mackerel, herring, a hturgeon, and a flying fish which might have come from foreign waters. In 1891 Arthur Patterson's 'Notes from Yarmouth' reveals a rare large and colourful Opah moonfish which was sold by auction and preserved by Lowne, "A beautiful specimen of this fish was tumbled ashore at Caister on October 17th, 1891, during heavy weather. It was put up at auction on the Fish Wharf, and realised £2. This rare fish had a narrow escape from being thrown on the refuse heap in the garden of the coastguardsman who found it, —and it was only through extreme pressure that he was persuaded by a carrier to let it try its fortunes under the hammer, was afterwards preserved by Mr. Lowne, the taxidermist."[73]

One of the creatures from the ocean that Lowne preserved marks the most extraordinary episode in the history of taxidermy in Norfolk and one of Great Yarmouth's famous attractions. An entry in his ledger for June 1891 matter-of-factly records, "Preserving whale for Mr Cockrill Griffin. Expenses: 38 hours, £20, 4d," £10 short of what the newspapers reported at the time. The end total was £30, the equivalent of £4,500 in current value. Lowne had previously preserved a porpoise which may have given him the experience to tackle the Lesser Rorqual. In any case, he needed help with the task. There were other examples of whales being spotted or stranded on the Norfolk Coast, occasionally recorded in the *Transactions* of the Norfolk and Norwich Naturalists' Society. For instance, this large whale was recorded by Anna Gurney, "1822. March 9th. A whale was entangled among the rocks off Overstrand, and killed by the fishermen. Its dimensions were length, 57 feet; breadth, 13 feet; pectoral fins, 6 feet 6 inches; tongue in length, 9 feet, ditto in breadth, 4 feet. 3."[74] It weighed seven tonnes. Richard Lubbock mentions that Gurney also recorded a twenty-four foot Rorqual entangled and killed off the coast of Runton in 1829. Thomas Southwell records a common Rorqual in 1874, "On the 1st of March, a fine full-grown female of this species was washed on shore at Happisburgh, on the Norfolk coast. I first saw it on the 2nd, but owing to the rough surf that was breaking upon the beach, and the unfavourable position in which it lay, any close examination was impossible."[75]

'Pegotty' recalled the story of Lowne's stuffed whale in the *Great Yarmouth Mercury*, "This unexpected visitor in June 1891 was a 30ft seven-ton lesser rorqual, a pike-headed native of the Arctic oceans far from its usual habitat and unaccustomed to finding itself confined in a river that was not only narrow but also shallow. The creature was unable to manoeuvre to escape from the muddy Yare … Yarmouth taxidermist Walter Lowne was paid the sizeable sum of £30 to undertake his biggest and most unusual assignment—on condition that the boatmen skinned it for him and scraped away the blubber. The boatmen resorted to burning more tar while they tackled the malodorous fat."[76] The whale then went on tour, "Arthur Patterson advised the amateur skinners and, when the last of the summer sightseeing holidaymakers had departed back to their homes, accompanied the stuffed whale to London and other cities and towns for the delectation of the curious paying public, teaching himself to be a circus-type barker. Then it was back home to Yarmouth where its popularity as a holiday attraction endured for years. However, the rigours of time and travel had resulted in wear and tear on the stuffed monster, and running repairs were frequently necessitated and were not always well camouflaged ... Then, although deteriorating into pieces, it came into the ownership of Gorleston publican George Turnrow who ejected the grazing cows from Gosling's Meadow (now Bells Road) to exhibit it, mainly to visitors."[77]

Great Yarmouth Lifeboat Crew with the rorqual whale, 1891.

Image courtesy of the Norfolk County Council Library and Information Service at www.picture.norfolk.gov.uk.

Arthur Patterson recorded the events of the day when the whale washed ashore:

> On June 8th, 1891, a fine female of the Lesser Rorqual Whale (*Balaenoptera rostrata*),[78] "losing its bearings" among the numerous sandbanks of the neighbourhood, eventually found its way into the harbour at Gorleston, where it was speedily attacked by the hardy natives, whom it would have undoubtedly eluded but for an accident which occurred to it when making again for the Roadstead. Coming into contact with the piles it so badly fractured its snout, that it was, for a time, rendered insensible. From loss of blood, and repeated ill-usage at the hands of its unmerciful assailants, it speedily succumbed, and was towed, tail foremost, up the river into the lifeboat house, the boat having been previously launched to make room for it. By means of a winch it was hauled into the building, where for some days it proved a great source of attraction to visitors, and of gain to its possessors. It was afterwards given a public post-mortem, and the skin removed to Yarmouth, and admirably mounted by Mr. Lowne. It has since been exhibited in London[79] and elsewhere. Length, 30 feet; girth, 18 feet; span of tail, 8 feet 2 inches; length of pectoral fins, 4 feet 6 inches; length of jaws, 6 feet 6 inches; baleen running up to 15 inches in length.[80]

Walter Lowne died on 27 January 1915 in Great Yarmouth aged 62 years. He was buried in Belton, Suffolk*, leaving effects valued at £809 13s 9d. He was evidently in poor health. An 'illness' is written into the record book for the year 1897. For 1888, simply 'Crossbills' and 'Kingfishers.' There were no records for 1900 with only one job recorded in 1901. Although Lowne did not concentrate his work on the rarer species of birds there might have been a natural decline in his workload in his later years due to the closed shooting season and also as the Breydon Wild Birds Protection brought wardens to control the area in which

---

*   Belton is now in Norfolk following county boundary changes in 1976.

88   GENTLEMEN COLLECTORS

Arthur Patterson with the rorqual whale (30ft and 7 tonnes) caught in Gorleston Harbour in 1891 and eventually preserved by the Yarmouth taxidermist, Walter Lowne.
Image courtesy of the Norfolk County Council Library and Information Service at www.picture.norfolk.gov.uk.

Lowne worked. Morris writes, "Lowne's death certificate records 'chronic nephritus' as the cause. The last two birds he stuffed were a female Hen Harrier 'from the marsh' on 9 May 1911 and a Glossy Ibis on 28 October 1913. It should be noted that many contemporary taxidermists lived at least 10 years longer than he did, despite similar exposure to arsenic. Patterson also refers to several 'strokes'; the last attack of which was in 1915."[81] Patterson wrote affectionately about his friend in his books. Christopher Frost states that Patterson recalls an evening he spent in the company of Lowne and several others "who made their livings in various ways from wild birds."

OTHER TAXIDERMISTS IN GREAT YARMOUTH

The next well-known taxidermist in Great Yarmouth after Walter Lowne is Edward Charles Saunders (1872-1956) who traded at 10, Church Plain and 98, Arundel Road in 1929. He was trading c.1896-c.1930s. He was undoubtedly influenced by Lowne although his mounts are far less common. As a young man, Saunders would make regular visits to Lowne's taxidermy shop. Saunders also contributed to the *Lysaght Collection of Birds* and for Sir Vauncey Crewe at Calke Abbey. Examples in the Lysaght collection include three red-crested pochards from Breydon (1906), a scaup (1902), a black-throated diver from Yarmouth (1899), a water rail from Horsey (1907), two ringed plovers from Yarmouth (1895), a little stint from Yarmouth (1897), two bar-tailed godwits (1895), a puffin from the Soa Islet in Argyllshire (1909), a skylark from Yarmouth Denes (1900) and two ring ouzels (1898). Saunders also preserved the 1896 great spotted cuckoo, the 1913 Norfolk ortalan bunting, the 1916 white stork and the 1927 Norfolk feffunginous duck.[82] Patterson mentions Saunders in his book *Nature in Eastern Norfolk* (1905) and *Wildlife on a Norfolk Estuary* (1907). In the latter work, Patterson describes an amateur 'puntsman' named Youngs dispatching nine ducks, eight of which were sold to Saunders. Patterson called on the taxidermist and found the ducks to be red-crested pochards and made a water-colour sketch of the best bird. James Parry reveals that Maurice Bird mentions Saunders in his diaries, for instance on 4 July 1905 he writes, "Saunders came from Yarmouth and took away large case of stuffed Scaup, 2 immature Smews, fem., Pintail (Canvey Island) and vary large ad. male Pochard that I killed years ago—a long chance shot out of a flock at the Heigham end of Hickling—it fell near the Pleasure Island. W. Tubby marked it marvellously. Lowne set up this case and 'twas full of moth. Saunders took pair of Marsh and Montagu Harrier to fill it again."[83]

Photographs of taxidermists are rare, even after photography became widespread as a method of recording. One rare exception is a photograph of Saunders taken in 1917 (reproduced from the *British Birds* publication of that year). The photograph shows him seated, looking at the mount of a buff-backed heron on the small table in front of him. Christopher Frost describes the heron as, "Only the second record for Britain—the first having been secured in 1805—was shot on Breydon Water on 17 October 1917 by a local gunner. Saunders set it up, and it was purchased by the collector J.B. Nichols, upon whose death it passed to the Booth Museum in Brighton."[84] Frost goes on to state, "Like Lowne, Saunders kept a record of all the birds he had through his hands, and in 1922 he was persuaded to add a few personal recollections to his diaries. These were never published ... He used the box type of case in the main, and his best cases are more similar to Gunn's in style than to Lowne's. His case backs are usually the normal shade of pale blue, although I have seen a few in which they are a kind of pale buff, a bit like Pashley's ... Some of his later work is really excellent."[85] Saunders also travelled to Henry Pashley's shop in Cley. On 1st September 1891 he helped his fellow taxidermist identify two Levantine shearwaters.[86] In 1913 Saunders began making brief contributions to the *Transactions* of the Norfolk and Norwich Naturalists' Society and was a collector as well as a taxidermist.

Other taxidermists working in Great Yarmouth included J. Carter who preserved the two 1869 Norfolk Richard's pipits, the 1865 Norfolk white stork and the 1869 Norfolk lesser grey shrike.[87] A few of Carter's specimens were reported in the newspapers, for instance a Little Gull, shot on Breydon water, at the end of January 1869. In February 1868, Carter was involved in a sad story of a woman who tried to commit suicide by drowning in the sea. Carter saved her only for the woman to take her own life a few weeks later. John Colby, Jr., traded on Howard Street and Alfred Harvey traded at 42, Row, Charlotte Street in the town, both recorded in 1839. Harvey's advertisement in Hunt & Co.'s *Directory of East Norfolk and Parts of Suffolk* (1850) states, "Preserver of birds and animals in any attitude, retaining the plumage and appearance of life ... all specimens preserved at the above establishment will not be destroyed by moths." A Post Office directory in 1869 reveals him trading as a, "Sworn English and foreign timber measurer and animal preserver at 59, North Quay."[88] He stuffed the rare 1872 Norfolk alpine swift. In this short passage about ortolan buntings in the Great Yarmouth area, J. H. Gurney states, "Last year I bought a specimen of Mr Gunn (a dull-coloured one compared with the plate in Sharpe and Dresser's *Birds of Europe*) which had been netted at Yarmouth in April, 1890, and kept alive two days by a man named Harvey. More recently Mr. Davy, a bird-dealer in Camden Town, who generally has a catcher at Yarmouth, had sent him from that place six, two of which are alive in my brother's possession."[89] Frost states that

Isaac Harvey sent 400 ducks of various kinds to London in one week in 1829, together with 500 snipe and 150 golden plovers all of which were sold by the capital's game dealers.[90] Harvey also sent between 600 and 700 eggs to London on a weekly basis.[91] Christopher Frost reveals a little more about Harvey. His father, Isaac was a bird-preserver and dealer in wildfowl. Frost states, "When the renowned ornithologist John Gould began collecting birds, Isaac Harvey used to send him a basket of Sandpipers and Plovers each week. In 1830 he mounted the first British example of the Pectoral Sandpiper." Frost states:

> Isaac Harvey had a bad reputation amongst sportsmen and collectors, who were never sure whether they would receive back the same bird they had taken him for preservation. Sometimes no bird came back at all, and rare species were especially prone to being 'nibbled by rats' or 'found and eaten by the cat.' Patterson concludes that it was quite likely that Harvey set up the Pine Grosbeak in Stephen Miller's collection, sold at auction in 1853.[92] His son Alfred inherited his father's disposition, and would vociferously curse the mice in their house when customers called in to collect their specimens. He too kept a cat, which was often blamed for a bird's mysterious disappearance. One evening in the 1880s, Alfred Harvey was with a group of his contemporaries when the conversation turned to taxidermists. One of their number, 'Admiral' Gooch, a gentleman gunner who had fallen on hard times, said to Harvey, 'You bird-stuffers are a lot of swindlers. Your cat ate more birds than mice. I know a Purple Sandpiper and a Black-tailed Godwit, not to mention a Little Bittern, which that same cat ate. I'm very much mistaken if I haven't seen the skins of all three in R …'s collection of local birds. No doubt pussy did eat the birds after you'd skinned them. She ate a Glaucous Gull once, didn't she? So I hold that bird-stuffers are all cast in one mould; they'd cheat their own grandmothers.[93]

Nonetheless, Harvey's specimens were reported in newspapers, but the suspicious attitude towards the stuffer make one doubt their authenticity, "Mr Harvey, taxidermist of this town, has now in his possession a fine male Californian Quail which was shot a short time since in North Walsham."[94]

Collecting birds and animals was big business and created competition between collectors and dealers. Unscrupulous dealers offered for sale foreign specimens, primarily birds, with false documentation of when and where the bird was taken, thus enhancing their monetary value as a rarity. This has thrown doubt on some of the scientific publications and literature surrounding old collections. On writing about the collectors and taxidermists in Great Yarmouth, C.B. Plowright states, "In addition to the gunners were dealers and bird-stuffers, notable amongst whom were the two Harveys, and later on Durrant. A fabulous number of birds used to pass through these men's hands, and occasionally something turned up which they were unaccustomed to meet with, and which fetched a good price from the collectors. I regret also to be obliged to add that some of these men were unscrupulous enough to attempt to pass off birds or skins of foreign origin as local productions, and in some cases they were successful in doing so, a thing which I trust never happens with the dealers of the present day."[95] In 1892 Thomas Southwell wrote an article called 'On the Occurrence in Norfolk of the Siberian Pectoral Sandpiper (*Tringa acuminata*)' in which he reveals the dangers of dealing with untrustworthy characters, "On referring to the specimen mentioned by Mr. Stevenson ('Birds of Norfolk,' vol. ii. p. 367) now in the Norwich Museum, it proves to be an undoubted example of the Siberian form. The history of this bird is as follows: In the winter of 1848-9, the late Mr. Gurney purchased of a man named Avilmot, for the sum of £5, a sandpiper which he stated he had killed at Yarmouth in the last week of September, 1848. This transaction, Mr. Reeve, the curator of the Norwich Museum, perfectly recollects, and he informs me that the bird was set up by Mr. Gurney's birdstuffer, Knights. The occurrence is recorded under the heading of 'Pectoral Sandpiper (*Tringa pedoralis*)' in 'The Zoologist,' 1849, p. 2392, the communication being dated 'Feb. 2, 1849.' Subsequently the same man brought to Mr. Gurney two freshly killed specimens of the red-winged starling, which, upon inquiry, proved to be of very doubtful origin and Mr. Gurney was fully convinced that an attempt was being made to deceive him. He therefore, finding the man to be unworthy of trust, sent a second note to 'The Zoologist,' dated August 14th of the same year, and which will be found at page 2568 of that magazine, referring to his previous communication, and concluding with the following remark: "I fear that I was imposed upon with respect to this specimen, and that it is in reality a foreign one." On the 30th March, 1850, Mr. Gurney gave this bird (with others) to the Norwich Museum, instructing Mr. Reeve to place it in the British collection, but without any locality. Everybody who knew Mr. Gurney will be perfectly aware of the extreme caution he exercised in matters of this kind, and will not be surprised at his at once rejecting the bird in question."[96]

Doubt surrounded the authenticity of natural history collections. One such collection was a 'large and miscellaneous collection of birds' owned by Stephen Miller of Yarmouth. Patterson states that the collection was sold off by auction in 1853, but both Henry Stevenson and Richard Lubbock scrutinised the collection, which was in a bad state of preservation. Their attention fell on the rare pine grosbeak in the collection which was seen in numbers on the Yarmouth Denes in 1822. Although the bird appears in Gurney and Southwell's *List of Norfolk Birds* (1885-6), they conclude that the birds were not recently preserved and were probably those taken in 1822, and the bird was 'probably no longer in existence …', Patterson states, "Thus did our earlier naturalists play shuttlecock with records which had a shadow of doubt surrounding them!"[97]

Miles Juler traded at 37, King's Street, Great Yarmouth. He was also listed as a pawnbroker, watch maker and collector of taxes in the town. M. Pycroft of Great Yarmouth is listed as contributing to the *Lysaght Collection of Birds*. He also recorded and preserved the rare 1888 Norfolk dark-breasted barn owl.[98] Christopher Frost describes AG. Smith & Son listed as taxidermists on the Hartley Road in the 1890s. Pat Morris describes G. Smith & Son working at the same time as Lowne.[99] George 'Hoppy' Smith was given the moniker on account of his limp. Later, his sons would become taxidermists, but it appears Smith was a dealer in natural history specimens. Frost records Patterson's thoughts on the man. They give an insight into what Breydon Water was like in the mid-late 19th century:

> He [Smith] raced to and fro among Broadmen, Breydoners, and all the outdoor characters who sported a fowling-piece, or rifled a nest, or pulled over a bird-net. Our energetic ornithologist-dealer collected birds' eggs, and in time became a dealer in birds 'in the flesh'; and in bird skins so prepared as to be amenable to the skilled hand of the taxidermist. For their retention he had many drawers, wherein he displayed them; his walls and tables had much the appearance of a small bird museum. Several Broadsmen prior of the conversion of the broads into bird-sanctuaries, whose forefathers had done much the same before them without let or hindrance, were much addicted to egg-hunting, and the slaying of rare species of birds; they were supplied with these to Smith. Bearded tits, and their young and eggs especially, suffered from these activities, for there was a great demand for them among collectors all over the country; and for this decimation our bird-dealer was described by prominent Norfolk ornithologists as a great bird-vandal. But it was the unscrupulous bird-collector who tempted and forced his hand.[100]

Frost states that many rare birds passed through Smith's hands, including several species that were new to Norfolk, including a tawny pipit, a white wagtail, an Iceland gull, a greater shearwater and a Mediterranean black-headed gull. Frost states the latter was shot on Boxing Day in 1886 and, having purchased the specimen, refused the £100 offered for the gull by J. H. Gurney, gradually raising the price to a grand sum of £300. His greed somewhat back-fired and he ended up selling the bird to Robert Chase, a well-known Birmingham collector for less than Gurney's original pitch. Frost states, "Smith kept a diary for many years which he grandly entitled 'Ornithological Notes', but this, together with many valuable letters from eminent naturalists, was believed to have been burnt after his death. Some of his sons' cases used to reside in the Tolhouse Museum in Yarmouth, as did countless other historic cases by Yarmouth taxidermists, but these were tragically destroyed by an enemy bomb during the Second World War,"[101] The stored natural history collections at Time and Tide Museum, Great Yarmouth, were recently relocated to the North Norfolk Collections Centre due to flood risk.

Pat Morris states that Ed Lighton was listed in Trade Directories (1908–1933)[102] but there were also taxidermists trading who were not necessarily listed in directories. Arthur Patterson mentions a Ben Dye & 'Harvey' working in Yarmouth.[103] Frost reveals that Dye was a baker and self-taught taxidermist. Both Dye and Lowne displayed taxidermy at the 'Good Intent Bird Breeding Society' at Corn Hall in Norwich. The reared birds were judged by Mr J Yallop, a bird-breeder in Norwich. The *Norwich Mercury* describes one of the shows in 1883, "At the west end of the hall were several excellent specimens of the art of taxidermy shown by Mr. Lowne of Fuller's Hill,"[104] and the following year, "excellent displays of stuffed birds, fish and animals, exhibited by Mr. Howard Bunn[105] and Mr. B. Dye, both local amateur taxidermists."[106] Dye became blind later in life, but was able to identify any bird placed in front of him by handling it. Frost states, "Lowne used to prepare George Smith's cabinet skins for him, but Smith became a little disillusioned with Lowne's work, and so took a number of skins along to Ben Dye's one day. Dye delivered them when he had completed the work, and a delighted Smith told him that Lowne had never turned out such work in his life. To show what he thought of his work in comparison, Smith opened a drawer and threw the lot on the fire."[107] Patterson describes George Smith as a bird and egg dealer and bookbinder by profession.

Frost reveals another story. After he had become blind, Dye heard that a cowman had shot a glossy ibis (known locally as a 'black curlew'). Lowne offered five shillings, but the cowman decided that if that was all it was worth he would have it stuffed for himself. The local dealers got to hear about the bird and tried unsuccessfully to persuade the owner to part with it. Dye's later offer of two pounds was accepted, "Dye accompanied the cowman to Lowne's the following day to declare the deal, and asked Lowne to let him know as soon as the bird was ready, and he would then pay for his work. Lowne was incensed, having had high hopes of eventually securing the bird himself, and never forgave his old rival."[108] Arthur Patterson occasionally mentions Dye in his books. In May 1901 Dye missed out on shooting four sleeping spoonbills as a fifth bird was awake, apparently acting as sentry and gave the alarm. Patterson had a tale to tell about Dye and it appears that the old devil had form. Patterson noticed two spotted redshanks in Lowne's workbook after he had rescued it from pulping. One was killed on Breydon Water by 'Watson' on 10 May 1885 and the other killed on Acle marshes on 6 May by a 'marshman.' Both birds were in full summer plumage (Pashley had 27 specimens in 25 years, but never one in full summer plumage). Patterson scribbles the following in the back of Lowne's book, "Two Spotted 'shanks were in the possession of Mrs Palmer, who said for me to choose what I liked of the collection for our museum. These two historic birds were chosen by me. I happened to tell Ben Dye (who was really kind at the time) and the cunning fellow went behind my back, offered her a price for them and got them! They're (1926) still in his possession (the crafty things he's done make very curious reading)."[109] Beryl Tooley, Patterson's great-granddaughter, explains more about the relationship between Dye and Patterson, which goes back to Patterson's youth:

> From a very early age, Arthur wanted a gun … undeterred, Arthur saved enough money to buy a gun but he was too afraid to take it home, for fear of the wrath of his father and stepmother who strongly disapproved of guns. Another friend, Ben Dye, stored it for him in the bake house where he worked. Ben Dye, who became his lifelong companion, and he, went out shooting on the sand dunes, along the river and on Breydon and both had a go at taxidermy to make a little money. Arthur never claimed to be very good at taxidermy, but when times were hard, he was able to supplement his wages with a case or two for a collector. He enjoyed "boxing up" the specimens which turned out well."[110] Patterson's sketches and cartoons reveal a man with a keen sense of humour. An article from the *Yarmouth Independent* in 1908 reports that he was capable of the odd ruse himself, "As a taxidermist, he is a wag as well as adept. On one occasion, being in lack of funds, our friend looked round his room and found upon an old coot that he had shot some time ago before, and in a rather disreputable condition; this he stuffed and painted in such a realistic manner that when finished, it had the appearance of a fine tropical bird; it was forthwith sent to an auction sale-room and sold as the rare Zebra Bird, and found its way to a public rendezvous of music and fashion, where it was placed in a prominent position as a rarity. One evening someone, knowing the history of the bird, related it before the assembled company, when—Tableau![111]

Patterson indicated that J.E. (Ted) Knights worked as an assistant to Lowne in 1895. J.E. Knights was in business on his own account (though not listed in Trade Directories) in 1922. A printed label of that date on a case of sanderlings in Norwich Castle Museum gives his address as 87, Churchill Road and previously 14, Beaconsfield Road, North Denes, Great Yarmouth. However, Frost states that a case from 1922 had 14, Denes Road crossed out to read 87, Church Street. Although not naming him, Patterson refers to Lowne's assistant in a story told by Frost, "Patterson tells the story of the day he left his assistant—whom he does not name, but I assume he refers to Knights—skinning two moorhens as [Lowne] left to catch a train to one of the Norfolk Broads for a fishing match. On his way out, Lowne handed him the bodies of two owls, which he had just skinned to dispose of, "When you've skinned those two Moorhens," he instructed, "take them to the kitchen and ask them to cook them for my supper." Knights in fact handed in the two owl bodies—deliberately one assumes—so it was these that were served up to Lowne when he returned (having won a cup in the fishing competition). He enjoyed his meal, and never found out what he had been eating. (Owls, of course, were not generally regarded as edible)."[112]

Lowne, Saunders and, to a lesser extent Knights, were the best known taxidermists from Great Yarmouth. Frost maintains that the other taxidermists probably struggled to make ends meet, which might account for Ben Dye's sharp practice.

In 1893 the president of the Norfolk and Norwich Naturalists' Society, C.B. Plowright, revealed the private collections in the Yarmouth area brought about by the dealers and taxidermists, answering at length the question, 'And who were the customers to these men?' It makes for interesting reading:

> I have already spoken of Charles Stuart Girdlestone,[113] who seems to have possessed a good collection of birds, which at his death, with his books, and other objects of interest passed to his sister, the wife of Mr. John Baker, a solicitor in Yarmouth, more than once previously mentioned, who subsequently removed to London; but I am not aware what ultimately became of them. One of the birds, a Jack Snipe, killed on the 2nd July, 1825, was given by Mrs. Baker to Lubbock, who in turn gave it to the late Mr. Newcome of Feltwell, with whose collection it still remains in the possession of his son.[114] Many Yarmouth killed birds passed into the collection of Mr. Edward Lombe of Melton, and are now in the Norwich Museum. J. B. P. Dennis of Bury St. Edmunds, also by his own gun, and through his agent, old John Thomas, obtained a large number of Yarmouth rarities, most of which may now be seen at the Bury Museum; Mr. Clark of Saffron Walden also secured many for the Museum of that town, and the Booth Collection, now in the Brighton Museum, contains many East Norfolk rarities, as well as the Gurney collection at Keswick. The collections of Stephen Miller; Rev. C. W. Steward of Caistor; Rev. S. N. Micklethwait of Hickling; Mr. Robert Rising of Horsey; Mr. J. G. Overend of Yarmouth, and Mr. Stevenson have all been dispersed, but of late years, our Chairman, the Rev. C.J. Lucas of Burgh, Mr. W. W. Spolman, and Mr. Connop of Caistor, have each formed large collections, in addition to which many other rarities have gone to enrich collections in all parts of England. I am happy to say that a large number of the rarest specimens which were contained in such of the collections as have been dispersed of recent years, have found a permanent home in the Norwich Museum, where they are open to the study and inspection of all who may be interested in them; and now that a museum has at length been formed at Yarmouth, I trust the first though of those who may become possessed of rare birds and beasts will be to make as perfect a local collection as possible at home, before allowing anything which is a desideratum here, to pass into the hand of strangers. In looking through a list of Norfolk birds, I noted thirty-nine species of extreme rarity, obtained in the Yarmouth district, many of these had been met with only once or twice before they were recognised at Yarmouth, and nine of them, viz., the Caspian Plover, Broad-BilledSandpiper, Pectoral Sandpiper, Siberian Pectoral, White-

winged Black Tern, Mediterranean Black-headed Gull, RedCrested Pochard, Buttie-headed Puck, and Steller's Duck, have all either been met with in no other locality in Great Britain, or were killed in the first instance in the Yarmouth district. I trust I have not been tiresome in my imperfect remarks with regard to the days that are past, but that I may have succeeded in showing how surpassingly rich this eastern sea-board is in at least the section of ornithology, and how brilliant an example has been set us by our predecessors in the field; I would urge, more especially upon the rising generation, the desirability of taking up the systematic, study of some particular branch of natural science; it adds immensely to the pleasures of life to possess some general acquaintance with the whole field of nature, and I would deprecate in the strongest terms anything like exclusiveness or the undervaluing of the work of their fellow-labourers, some reap the corn, some dress it; but if you wish to gain distinction, a very difficult thing to achieve in the present day, and to add to the sum of knowledge, it can only be done by the close study of some particular one out of the many branches into which natural science is divided ... I have said a good deal about collectors and collections, and I may at once state that I am not the one, nor have I the other, fortunately for me I am so circumstanced that, with the assistance of the Norwich Museum, and the great kindness of my many friends, I can always find abundant material for study and comparison, hut a student can hardly pursue his subject without being to some extent a collector, all I wish to impress upon my hearers is that collecting should only be a means to an end, and always be kept subservient.[115]

Sale notices in Norfolk newspapers noted taxidermy collections as particular points of interest, as this notice in the *Norwich Mercury* in 1885 exemplifies, "On Thursday next: valuable furniture for Sitting and Sleeping Rooms, stuffed birds, table services, billiard table, useful black cob, dog cart etc. Smallburgh, Norfolk, will sell at auction in the residence of Mr Robert Cooke ... valuable small collection of stuffed birds, in glazed case, mostly shot in the immediate neighbourhood."[116] Collections were also sold at auction. J.H Gurney reveals a sale in 1876, "At the sale of the late Mr. Doubleday's collection on the 23 August, 1871, I purchased a few Yarmouth rarities, which I am desirous of seeing recorded, viz: a Night heron, two Baillon's Crakes, and a Little Crake. Mr. Borrer, of Cowfold near Horsham, at the same time purchased a Red-crested Pochard, a male in change, marked in the catalogue, "Yarmouth, very rare." I have the following note in Mr. Doubleday's handwriting about it:—"This I also had in the flesh from Mr. Stevens, [of Leadenhall Market], who assured me that it came from Yarmouth, and I have no doubt of the correctness of this statement, as I saw the package in which it came with other sea birds." There were also a pair of Nyroca ducks from Yarmouth, but I have no note of who is now the owner of them. This fine collection fetched £275. There was a large attendance of naturalists to see it dispersed at the Cock Hotel, Epping."[117] Some specimens once owned by Doubleday were purchased by Lysaght for his collection, including a little crake shot in the Great Yarmouth area in around 1871.

Notes

1. Pat Morris, 'The work of Walter Lowne, Taxidermist of Great Yarmouth,' *Transactions*, Norfolk and Norwich Naturalists' Society, Vol. 28, Part 1, (Hunstanton, Witley Press, August 1988), p.35.
2. B. Tooley, '*Introduction*,' *Scribblings of a Yarmouth Naturalist. An edited selection from the Writings of Arthur Henry Patterson, A.L.S., (John Knowlittle)*, (self-published, 2004), pp. 32-3.
3. *The Ledger of Walter Lowne, 1886-1911*, (Norfolk Record Office, FX 223/1).
4. Ibid. 1, p. 36.
5. W. White, *History, Gazetteer and Directory of Norfolk*, (London, Simpkin, Marshall & Co, 1883), p.817.
6. J. Wentworth Day, *Marshland Adventure*, (London, George G. Harrap, 1949), p. 143.
7. P. and M. Clarke, *Where to Watch Birds in East Anglia*, (London, Christopher Helm, 1987) p. 104.
8. H. Saunders, *Manual of British Birds*, (London, Gurney and Jackson, 1899), p. 393.
9. A.H. Patterson, *Wildlife on a Norfolk Estuary*, (London, Methuen, 1907), p. 102.
10. Ibid. 8, p. 561.
11. Rev. Richard Lubbock (footnote: T. Southwell), *Observations on the Fauna of Norfolk and more particularly on the District of the Broads*, (Norwich, Jarrold & Sons. First published in 1845, 1879), p. 90.
12. *Norfolk Chronicle*, 12 March 1881.
13. Fritton Lake or Fritton Decoy is on the border of Norfolk and Suffolk close to Great Yarmouth and Lowestoft. At the time of writing Fritton Lake was chosen as an important thousand-acre re-wilding project.
14. *Transactions*, Norfolk and Norwich Naturalists' Society, (Norwich, Fletcher and Son, 1898), p. 436
15. The pseudonym under which Patterson wrote.
16. Norfolk and Norwich Naturalists' Society.
17. Patterson writes about the exploits of Pintail Thomas on several occasions, see 'Men and Manners' in *Wildlife on a Norfolk Estuary*.
18. M. Cocker, *Transactions*, Norfolk and Norwich Naturalists' Society Transactions, (Lavenham, Lavenham Press, 2008), p. 5.
19. Ibid. 1, p.38.
20. W. Swaysland, *Familiar Wild Birds*, (London, Cassell & Company, 1903), p. 18.
21. The main reason for predators not attacking the bird is that its flesh is repugnant.
22. Ibid. 20, p. 19.
23. Thomas Southwell wrote to the *Norfolk Chronicle* and *Norwich Gazette* in 1898 regarding the extinction of the Great Bustard. He states, "Recently, I grieve to say, I have noticed the feathers of the bustard extensively used as hat plumes, and I fear that, should these become popular, even the wilds of Spain and Central Germany will soon see their last bustard done to death to meet the demands of this hateful trade."
24. H. Stevenson, *The Birds of Norfolk, Remarks on their habits, migration and local*

Distribution, Vol I, (London, John Van Horst, 1866), p. 315.
25. Ibid. 8, p. 279.
26. I have a box which contains original hat adornments worn by my great great grandmother. They include tern wings and the tail feathers of a Lady Amherst's Pheasant.
27. Ibid. 1, p.39.
28. Christopher Frost brings to our attention the plight of many grebes, the bird which Richard Lubbock called "the greatest ornament of the Norfolk Broads." Frost states, "A Mr. Strangeways of London, writing in the *Zoologist* in 1851, said he collected twenty-nine specimens in full summer plumage during April and May of the previous year, all shot in Norfolk. Four of these he preserved, and the rest he made into ladies' boas and muffs, explaining that the breasts of this species had become a fashionable and beautiful substitute for fur. A good specimen, he said, was worth ten shillings." (C. Frost, p. 10).
29. H.N. Pashley, *Notes on the Birds of Cley, Norfolk*, new edition by Christopher Frost, (Lavenham, The Lavenham Press, 1992), p. 112.
30. Ibid. 24, p. 315.
31. A.H. Patterson, *A Norfolk Naturalist. Observations on Birds, Mammals and Fishes*, (London, Methuen & Co., 1930), p. 110.
32. Ibid. 20, pp. 69-71.
33. *Transactions*, Norfolk and Norwich Naturalists' Society, (Norwich, Fletcher and Son, 1885).
34. *Transactions*, Norfolk and Norwich Naturalists' Society (Norwich, Fletcher and Son, 1891), p. 131.
35. W. Lowne, *The Record book of Walter Lowne, bird stuffer of Fuller's Hill*, Norfolk Record Office, doc ref. MS 4185.
36. Presumably Roydon Hall.
37. Ibid. 1, p.41.
38. *Eastern Daily Press*, 7 April 1891.
39. Ibid. 1, p.42.
40. Ibid.
41. Howard Saunders (*Manual of British Birds*, 1899, p. 259), mentions that the shorelark was first noticed as a visitor to England in March 1830 when one was obtained on the coast of Norfolk.
42. *Norfolk Chronicle*, 10 October 1891.
43. In 1977 Michael Seago noted in his *Birds of Norfolk* (p. 121), that single birds of the white-spotted race *cyanecula*, were shot at Sheringham on the 30 April 1906. They are now in the Norwich Castle Museum.
44. Ibid. 1, pp. 40-1.
45. A.H. Patterson, *Notes of an East Coast Naturalist*, (London, Methuen & Co, 1904), p. 100.
46. Ibid. 1, p.43.
47. Ibid. 8, p. 705.
48. H. Stevenson and T. Southwell, T, *The Birds of Norfolk, Remarks on their habits, migration and local Distribution*, Vol III, (London, John Van Horst, 1890), p. 283.
49. Ibid. 20, p. 117.
50. Ibid. 45, pp.182-3.

51. Ibid. 48, pp. 281-2.
52. Ibid, 31, p. 50.
53. *Transactions*, Norfolk and Norwich Naturalists' Society (Norwich, Fletcher and Son, 1894).
54. A.H. Patterson, *Wildlife on a Norfolk Estuary*, (London, Methuen, 1907), p. 19
55. The first record of the occurrence of the Roller in Britain is found in Thomas Browne's *Notes on Certain Birds found in Norfolk*, "On the xiiii of May 1664 a very rare bird was sent mee kild about crostwick wch seemed to be some kind of Jay." (p. 30). The 1865 and 1885 Norfolk roller was preserved by T.E. Gunn. Another 1865 roller was preserved by Sayer of Norwich.
56. K.A. Naylor and M.S. Pollitt, M.S. *Historical Rare Birds*, (List of Taxidermists, 2021), https://www.historicalrarebirds.info (accessed 12 September 2024).
57. *Norwich Mercury*, 8 October, 1881.
58. *Eastern Daily Press*, 2 April, 1883.
59. J. Parry, *Maurice Bird. The Gilbert White of the Broads*. Norfolk and Norwich Naturalists' Society, (Lavenham, Lavenham Press, 2024), p.50.
60. There is one reference to an aviary-bred bird in Lysaght's Collection: a Eurasian eagle owl. The owl was bred in Mr. Edward Fountaine's aviary at Easton, Norfolk. The owl lived in confinement for twenty years and died on 1 January 1888. (P. Watson, 2010, p. 43).
61. Ibid. 1, p. 37.
62. J. Vincent, *A Season of Birds. A Norfolk Diary, 1911*. (London, Weidenfield & Nicholson, 1911), p. 10.
63. Ibid.
64. Ibid. 1, p. 39.
65. T. Southwell, *Transactions*, 'The Mammalia of Norfolk.' Norfolk and Norwich Naturalists' Society, (Norwich, Fletcher and Son, 1883), p. 669.
66. Ibid. 1, p.40.
67. *Zoologist*, 3rd series, (Vol. XIII. 1889), p. 393.
68. The Savage Club, a gentleman's club in London, founded in 1857 and named after the poet Richard Savage, friend of Samuel Johnson.
69. W.B. Tegetmeier, *The Field*, 7 Sep, 1889, Vol. LXXIV. p. 350 J. H. Gurney, jr, *Zoologist*, 1890: p. 57.
70. *Transactions*, Norfolk and Norwich Naturalists' Society, (Norwich, Fletcher and Son, 1892), p. 364
71. *Transactions*, Norfolk and Norwich Naturalists' Society (Norwich, Fletcher and Son, 1893), pp. 599-601.
72. Ibid, 1, p.39.
73. *Transactions*, Norfolk and Norwich Naturalists' Society, (Norwich, Fletcher and Son, 1891), p. 325.
74. 'Extracts from the notebook of the Late Miss Anna Gurney, of Northrepps.' Communicated by J. H. Gurney, 25 August, 1874, *Transactions*, Norfolk & Norwich Naturalists' Society, (Norwich, Fletcher and Son, 1874-75), p. 19.
75. T. Southwell, 'Miscellaneous Notes,' *Transactions*, Norfolk & Norwich Naturalists' Society, (Norwich, Fletcher and Son, 1874-75), p. 62.
76. Peggotty, *Great Yarmouth Mercury* 'Whale's untimely turn in Gorleston river leads to tragic death,' (February 18, 2016).

77. Peggotty, *Great Yarmouth Mercury*,' Army shot at lost whale thinking it was a German submarine,' (May 6, 2016).
78. Name given to the Common Minke whale.
79. At the Royal Aquarium.
80. Ibid. 73, p. 327.
81. Ibid. 1, p.36.
82. Ibid. 56.
83. Ibid. 59, p. 76.
84. C. Frost, *A History of British Taxidermy*, (Lavenham, The Lavenham Press, 1987), p. 69.
85. Ibid.
86. Ibid. 29, p. 23.
87. Ibid. 56.
88. The Post Office *Directory of Cambridgeshire, Norfolk and Suffolk* (London, Ed. E.R. Kelly and Co, 1869).
89. *Transactions*, Norfolk and Norwich Naturalist's Society, miscellaneous notes, (Norwich, Fletcher and Son, 1871-2), p. 61-63. Howard Saunders (*Manual of British Birds*, 1899, p. 213), mentions an immature ortolan, "shot among some Linnets, at Cley, Norfolk, on September 12 1884, another on September 5 1889, and a third on September 15 1892."
90. Ibid. 84, p. 6.
91. Ibid. 11, vii.
92. Ibid. 31, p. 10.
93. Ibid. 84, pp. 69-70.
94. *Norfolk Chronicle*, 15 April 1871.
95. C.B. Plowright, *Transactions, Address at Great Yarmouth*, Norfolk and Norwich Naturalists' Society, (Norwich, Fletcher and Son, 1893), p. 542.
96. *Transactions*, Norfolk and Norwich Naturalists' Society, (Norwich, Fletcher and Son, 1892), pp. 366-7.
97. Ibid. 31, p. 9.
98. Ibid. 56.
99. Ibid. 1, p.36.
100. Ibid. 84, p. 70.
101. Ibid.
102. Ibid. 1, p.36.
103. Ibid, p.37.
104. *Norwich Mercury*, 31 October 1883.
105. Howard Bunn, (1888-1916), taxidermist in Lowestoft.
106. *Yarmouth Mercury*, 1 November 1884.
107. Ibid. 84, pp. 70-1.
108. Ibid, p. 71.
109. Ibid. 35.
110. Ibid. 2, p. 32.
111. *Yarmouth Independent*, 18 February 1908.
112. Ibid. 84, p. 69.
113. Mr. T. Baker, Town Clerk of Yarmouth sold a small collection of birds owned by his

mother. The specimens were taken from the break-up of Girdlestone's collection. Patterson (Ibid. 11, p. 10), noted that the collection was irretrievably lost. Ben Dye purchased a stilt and a petrel was purchased for Yarmouth Museum.
114. The Feltwell Collection went to Gresham's School in Holt, Norfolk
115. Mr. C.B Plowright, president's address, *Transactions*, Norfolk and Norwich Naturalists' Society, (Norwich, Fletcher and Son, 1893), pp. 541-546.
116. *Norwich Mercury*, 3 October 1885.
117. J.H. Gurney, 'Miscellaneous Notes and Observations,' *Transactions*, Norfolk and Norwich Naturalist's Society, (Norwich, Fletcher and Son, 1875-76), p. 225.

Bustards, Brawls and Bankruptcy

North Norfolk

There were acclaimed taxidermists working in other parts of Norfolk. Perhaps most successful were those trading in a part of the county now known as Breckland, especially in the Thetford area. For others there was fleeting acclaim before fading into obscurity or debt, not helped by the gradual change in the wildlife laws brought about by the Wild Bird Protection Acts.

Perhaps the most well-known taxidermist working inland from the Norfolk coast was Charles Blunderfield Dack who traded in Holt for almost forty years. Born in 1848, White's (1883) *History, Gazetteer and Directory of Norfolk,* has Dack trading as a "Bird and Animal Preserver and tobacconist [on] Market Place." Like Walter Lowne, he was a keen breeder and cross-breeder of cage birds, "A village policeman in Norfolk today, who is a descendant of Charles Dack, says that the taxidermist discovered a cure for foot-and-mouth disease. Unfortunately he never imparted it to anyone, and his secret went to his grave with him."[1] Dack was noted for preserving the 1888 Norfolk nutcracker.[2] He is occasionally mentioned in the *Transactions* of the Norfolk and Norwich Naturalists' Society, for instance in 1881 when the taxidermist set up a white albino swallow. Christopher Frost describes Dack as a competent taxidermist, "unlike many of whom taxidermy was not their sole means of support ... His work is represented in the Booth Museum in Brighton in the form of a case containing a pair of sparrowhawks with their nest and eggs."[3] The *Eastern Daily Press* recorded a mighty pike which Dack set-up in September 1896, "Mr George Wheatly, of Melton Constable, fishing in the neighbourhood of Yarmouth on Saturday, landed a grand pike. Its weight was 25lbs and the dimensions 45 inches long ... the fish has been put in the hands of a Mr. Dack, taxidermist, of Holt, for preservation."[4] Dack was evidently a knowledgeable ornithologist. An article in *Norfolk News* on 21 February 1903 reports Dack's lecture on 'Migration of the Birds of Norfolk,' which was held at the Shire Hall, Holt and "warmly applauded." The report describes a crowded attendance and an "excellent set of slides with which the lecture was illustrated." Dack moved onto other areas of research including the "habits and characteristics of the Nightingale" and detailed descriptions "of our rarer visitors, though at one time they were fairly numerous."[5]

Dack suffered financial hardships which were reported in the *Eastern Daily Press* in 1904. The debtor's statement of affairs showed liabilities amounting to over £155—"the causes of failure as alleged by the debtor are falling off of work in the bird-stuffing trade."[6] Five days later another short piece of news occurred in the newspaper regarding the same case, "The debtor stated he started his business with £20 left him by his grandmother. [In] the last six years the bird stuffing had fallen off, the Wild Bird Protection Act causing him to suffer and the mild winters were also against the wild fowl coming over."[7] Another problem for struggling taxidermists was when clients, often wealthy, failed to pay their bills.

F.W. Barnet traded at Greenway House, Fakenham (1896). Also in Fakenham was Edward Drewell who traded on Bridge Street (1890). *Kelly's Directory* (1912) has a Thomas Drewell trading at Holt Road in the town. Although little is known about him, it appears his forays in the countryside brought him in front of the Bench, at this time when he was working as a bricklayer. Drewell was fined for trying to net fish, "Thomas Drewell of Fakenham, bricklayer, was charged by Charles William Horsley, honourable secretary to the River Wensum Preservation Society, with unlawfully taking, otherwise than by angling, in the day time of 30th July, certain fish in the stream belonging to Mr Charles Horsley … Horsley stated that the offence was committed about 3.30am on the morning of Sunday. He saw the defendant throw a net, and when pursued he ran away … repetition of the offence would be more severely punished."[8] W. Lockwood was working in Fakenham in the early 20th century. A cased hobby of Lockwood's sold at auction in 2020 and was redolent of the style of Walter Lowne. His trade label was basic and read, "W. Lockwood. Taxidermist, Fakenham. Cases cleaned and repaired." An online article on the 1913 Sun Precision motorcycle includes a relevant paragraph, "Mr Williams inherited the bike from his mother's cousin, Cora Lockwood, who lived with her family in a confectioner and taxidermist shop. One of a row in Bridge Street … now the site of a municipal carpark."[9]

There were two taxidermists under the name Dale working in Aylsham. Deborah Dale on Red Lion Street traded as a hairdresser, bird preserver, tobacconist and "fancy dealer" (1890).[10] Robert Dale, on Market Place was advertised as a hairdresser, perfumer, stationer, bird and animal preserver years previously (1856).[11] Robert Dale epitomises the diverse services a taxidermist could offer. His sales department offered ornamental hair, combs, brushes, cutlery, jewellery, stationery, walking sticks, fancy goods, foreign and British cigars, periodicals and newspapers. Hairdressing was one of the most common additional trades. It does make one wonder what the creatures were being stuffed with! Another trade was picture framing where the taxidermist used the same skills, tools and materials for picture surrounds as they did in preparing the glass-fronted wooden taxidermy cases. Deborah took over the business after her husband's death in 1877. The business may well have petered out. A farmer, William A. Easton of Cawston, took her to court to recover the price of stuffing an otter that had been uncompleted by her husband. Easton said that the work had not been properly done and he was allowed the fee.[12] Deborah Dale died on the 15 May 1897 aged 59 years.

Other locations in the area saw John Spinks working from The Butchery in North Walsham. He was advertised as a hairdresser and bird preserver (1883). He may have had a long career in the trade as a local newspaper reported a fine stock dove in his hands in October 1847. Thomas Turner worked as a taxidermist in Aylmerton (1904) and Christopher Frost has him working in Attleborough. The *Norfolk Chronicle* lists a taxidermist called Tom Turner working in the town in 1910. Frost states, "I have seen a few cases, not of high quality, by Thomas Turner. He was in business from just before the turn of the century, and died in 1946. He always used peat for his groundwork, a medium usually associated with earlier work."[13] The *Norwich Mercury* (15 February 1902) contained an article on 'a preacher,' Mr. Robert Newstead, native of Swanton Abbot, "now curator of the Grosvenor Museum, Chester." He took up taxidermy at Tatterford near Fakenham.[14] J.H. Gurney mentions a Cole of Northrepps preserving Little Auks in 1894 (at the same time as 'Cole of Norwich' who also helped to preserve the seabirds).

Kings Lynn, Fenland borders and the Wash Coast

Parts of the Wash coast on both sides have been reclaimed for agricultural purposes but the landscape has retained its desolate, flat and often inaccessible topography with little escape from the winter elements. The vast mudflats, saltmarsh, shallow seas and low tides provide one of the most important winter habitats in the country for wading birds including dunlin, grey plover, knot, oyster-catchers, turnstone, curlew, redshank and bar-tailed godwit. The Wash estuary has been designated a Site of Special Scientific Interest (SSSI) and a National Nature Reserve and is regarded as the most important estuarine mudflat in Britain.

Soon after his ordination and curacy at Downham, the Norfolk naturalist Richard Lubbock acquired knowledge of the coastal birds of the Wash in a time before the landscape had been altered by drainage and cultivation.[15] For the Victorian egg collector and wildfowler, the low tides, as today, revealed expansive mudflats which were dangerous to exploit without local knowledge. Northerly or easterly winds could bring winter migrants to the coast, many of which fell to the gun to be set-up by a local taxidermist. Trade publications show that Kings Lynn contained a cadre of taxidermists. The town's maritime history is still very much part of the fabric of the place today. William Fiddy traded at Ferry Lane close to the banks of the river Ouse (1856). He was also recorded as a carpenter, victualler and bird stuffer at the nearby Crown and Mitre.[16] S.P. Saville, traded at 13, Regent's Street, Cambridge and later on the High Street in Kings Lynn. Saville preserved the 1854 Cambridge upland sandpiper. [17] Various Wilsons, presumably a family business passed down, appear in Kings Lynn. William Wilson traded at 29, Broad Street, Kings Lynn. He preserved the 1868 Norfolk sharp-tailed sandpiper. [18] Christopher Frost lists Wilson residing there from 1879-88 and John Wilson, presumably his son, is listed at the same address from 1890-1937, "An albino Redwing is mentioned by Stevenson as having been seen in Wilson's shop in 1863."[19] J.H. Gurney also mentions that Wilson was one of ten taxidermists who helped to preserve dozens of little auks who 'fell to the elements' on the Norfolk coast in 1894. The *Norwich Mercury*, 11 August 1911, details a taxidermist called James Wilson (of Broad Street) being summoned for discharging fireworks in the public street, "The defendant set fire to a "bombshell" in the Passage of the Plumbers' Arms. It exploded in the doorway."[20] He was fined 2s 6d. Another trade directory has him residing on Checker Street. The *Lynn News & County Press* reveals a Herbert Wilson in the town in 1914, but the article is not related to his prowess as a taxidermist, "Herbert Wilson, bird-stuffer, Lynn, was summoned for cycling without lights at Gaywood on January 9, and was fined 1s 6d."[21]

Frost lists a D. Dale as another Kings Lynn taxidermist, 'the museum in the town has an old case label saying: 'D. Dale, hairdresser, perfumer, bird preserver, tobacconist, stationer, jewellery, Berlin wool and fancy goods.' It is unknown whether this is Deborah Dale who traded in Fakenham. Frost also mentions a Salt of Kings Lynn.[22] Salt was working at the turn of the 20th century and lived on Railway Road. He advertised in the *Lynn News and County Press*, in 1906, "Birds and animals preserved and set-up in their natural surroundings." Moving inland, a taxidermist called Baker traded in Downham Market. He preserved the 1860 Norfolk Castle Rising little bustard.[23] William Fox traded in Stoke Ferry (1896) and was previously listed in 1891 as a naturalist and hairdresser. His

Christopher Page, curator of the Bird Department at Lynn Museum and Art Gallery (1902-1931).

Image courtesy of the Norfolk County Council Library and Information Service at www.picture.norfolk.gov.uk.

son took up the trade as a taxidermist when he lived in Wiggenhall St. Germans in 1901.

Taxidermy specimens can be seen on request in Lynn Museum's stored collections. Between 2006 and 2008 Lynn museum merged with the Townhouse and the collection was stored. Many of the specimens were in need of restoration by the conservators at Norwich Castle. There was an understandable move to prioritise the archaeology and social history of the town. However, one of the first exhibits that strikes the visitor to Lynn Museum today is Horace, the Indian tiger shot in Jeypore, India, in 1876 by Edward, Prince of Wales, the future King Edward VII.

Breckland

The Reverend Robert Forby in the first volume of his work, *The Vocabulary of East Anglia. An Attempt to record the Vulgar Tongue of the twin sister counties, Norfolk and Suffolk, 1830* reveals a 'breck' as "a large division of an open cornfield, q. d. break. Ray[24] calls it land ploughed the first year after it has lain fallow. It is certainly not so restricted by us." The 'breck' or 'break' reflected the practice where the heaths were periodically broken, ploughed and planted up with crops. After three years, or when the land was exhausted, the land was allowed to revert back to heath. A common jest is that it may be ploughed with two rabbits and a knife.

The name Breckland was first used in 1894 by the Norfolk naturalist William Clarke. Shirley Toulson states, "According to his son, the late R. Rainbird Clarke, who was director of the Castle Museum in Norwich for many years, he so loved the area that he had named that he was unwilling to spend a night away from it, and regularly shaved with a prehistoric flint implement which he found near Brandon."[25] Kate Sussams reveals the importance of shooting in Breckland, "The improvement in sporting guns in the second half of the eighteenth century led to the growth in popularity of game shooting amongst the gentry and this coincided with the fashion for landscape parks as appropriate surroundings for gentleman's residences. Together these two factors were to have a profound effect on Breckland."[26] Breckland's land-use included gunflint mining in areas to the south of Brandon. In 1925, Clarke commented that Breckland was a changing landscape, falling victim to forestation, road-building and, in a rush for productivity, agricultural expansion. Breckland has seen the greatest change in land use over the last two hundred years. The transformation has been created by farming and forestry, especially the creation of Thetford Forest to provide a reserve of timber lost by the demands of the First World War. The Forestry Commission's reforestation efforts amounted to the largest land change in Britain during the 20th century. Millions of acres of land were planted with conifers to create a timber source for the United Kingdom. Two centuries ago the majority of the topography of 250,000 acres comprised open heathland and short grassland, the favoured habitat of the great bustard and stone-curlew.

CASE STUDY—THE GREAT BUSTARD, OTIS TARDA

A detailed history of the extinction of the great bustard can be found in Henry Stevenson's *Birds of Norfolk*, Volumes II (1866) with an updated appendix on the bird by Thomas Southwell in Volume II (1870). Southwell and others refer to this bird as 'a noble species.' and Norfolk remained the last of the counties in the British Isles to have the bustard as a resident species. Writing in 1870, Stevenson states that few people can remember when the great bustard roamed the land. The birds were thought to have been native in the country since around 1527 (The *Lestrange Household Book* records a bustard killed with a crossbow in that year). Thomas Browne writes about the bird in his *Notes on Certain Birds found in Norfolk* in the late 1600s, "Bistardæ or Bustards are not vnfrequent in the champain & feildie part of this country, a large bird accounted a dayntie dish, obseruable in the strength of the brest bone & short heele layes an egge much larger than a Turkey."[27] In their article, 'Birds in the Stiffkey Hall Accounts,' David and Robert Yaxley reveal the bird species recorded in these 1570 household accounts, including the great bustard. They state that the name given to the bird in 1593, was "Baked Busterd."[28] Thomas Southwell states that in 1849, Richard Lubbock wrote, "Mr Browne, the Rector of Blo' Norton, tells me that in 1793 his grandfather, whilst riding on a Sunday from Eccles to Wretham to perform divine service, passed seven Bustards which were walking about close to the road. They did not retreat or appear much alarmed. Mr. B was fond of coursing, but notorious as a bad hare finder. "To show you how near they were to me," said he, "I could find hare sitting among them."[29]

Taxidermy mount of a great bustard in a private collection in Breckland.
Author.

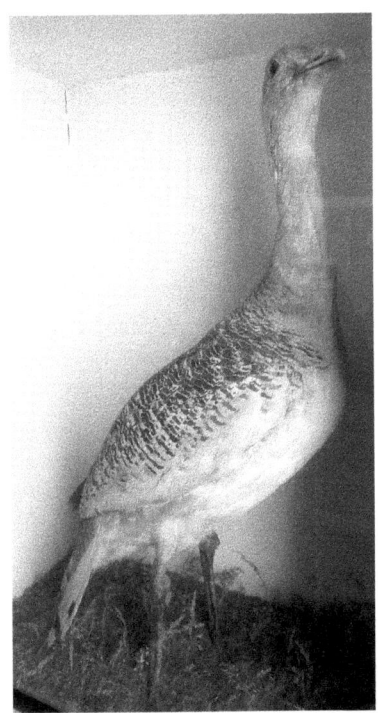

Female great bustard at Ancient House, Museum of Thetford Life.
Author with permission from Norfolk Museums Service.

In his ornithological lecture in Holt in 1903, the taxidermist Charles Dack gave a detailed account of the bird, stating, "From their habit of running when disturbed they have sometimes been called the English Ostrich."[30] Richard Lubbock, however, emphasizes the tameness of the birds, "Mr. 'Daniellin in his *Rural Sports*, notices a similar instance, in which a bustard on Salisbury Plain permitted a sportsman to approach, with no concealment, and kill it with a common fowling piece ... Lord Albemarle informed me that, many years back, his keeper found a bustard sitting upon her nest in a peafield at Eldon, near Thetford. She admitted of a near approach as a pheasant does under similar circumstances; and he thought it possible to take her alive upon her nest by throwing a casting net over her. The feat very nearly succeeded."[31] Lubbock goes on to describe bustards being hunted by greyhounds, and being lured and killed by feeding them up with turnips in hard winters. Such was the want of destruction, it is small wonder the bird ceased to exist in Norfolk. Peter and Margaret Clarke state, "Some 200 and more years ago flocks of Great Bustards used to roam this treeless plain until the species became extinct with the shooting of the last bird in 1838."[32] Among the seven specimens in Norwich Castle Museum is probably the last of the Norfolk race, the female killed at Lexham in 1838. Five years before, three female birds on Great Massingham Heath had their eggs taken. Thomas Knight of Norwich, ('Gurney's bird-stuffer'), has the unenviable honour of having set-up the last Norfolk bustard. The bird was presented to the Museum in 1877 by the Rev. W. A. W. Keppel. Stevenson states that the bustard in question was found to contain an egg "ready for exclusion." In the same year another indigenous bustard was taken in a population that had by now dwindled to small numbers, "In the month of February of that year, a female bustard was brought to the Cambridge market, where it was bought by Mr. Smith, the butler of Pembroke Hall, for Mr. William Borrer, of Cowfold, in Sussex, then an undergraduate of Peterhouse, in whose possession it still remains."[33]

The two main Norfolk 'droves' which inhabited the Brecks were tracts in the Swaffham-West Acre and Thetford districts. Stevenson states that the bustards were most prevalent in Norfolk at West Acre and although there were two distinct tracts that is not to suggest that they did not on occasion mix together. In the summer of 1819, nineteen birds were observed in the Thetford area and the Reverend Robert Hamond[34] of West Acre recalls seeing a whole drove of twenty-seven bustards flying by within fifty or sixty yards. Hamond was also a taxidermist and lived at High House, West Acre until his death in 1831.

Thomas Southwell reveals an occurrence of the bird in 1830, "I find the following note, dated November 30, 1870, in Mr. Stevenson's handwriting, "Mr. Drake, late of Billingford, told me to-day he had recently seen Tom Saul (late coachman to Cremer in Wyndham's time), and talking of bustards, he said, somewhere about 1830 he remembered riding with the late A. Hamond and Mr. Fountaine of Narford, near Walton Bottom, below Westacre Field, where they saw something at a distance he could not make out, but took for sheep troughs.

Mr. Hamond offered to make a bet that the objects were bustards. Saul rode on, the birds rose and fled, and Mr. Hamond remarked, "Did you ever see sheep troughs take wing before." Saul was of age in 1831, and this was about that time .... Mr. Drake says he has somewhere a bustard's egg given to his father by the late Mr. Downes of Gunton, and his father always understood it was found on Beechamwell Common."[35] Stevenson states that another bustard was killed in the year of 1838 at Dersingham near Castle Rising, and another on the coast at Morston about the same time. Stevenson was unable to ascertain whether the bird was eaten or stuffed. It appears that the bird was considered good fare as Stevenson reveals, "The late Mr. Birkbeck informed Mr. J. H. Gurney that he remembered on one occasion a West Norfolk friend sending a young bustard to his father as a present for the table, showing that they were occasionally so used in West Norfolk, as late as the end of the last or beginning of the present century. The late Col. Hamilton, also, in his *Reminiscences of a Sportsman* (vol. i., p. 178), gives an account of a bustard, which he had been invited to dine off some fifty years ago by the late Mr. Hyde, of Lexham Hall. It had been shot, it appears, by a tenant of Mr. Hyde's, who, when riding up a lane with his gun and a terrier dog, saw a large bird fly across about twenty yards before him. He shot at and winged it, but, on recovering itself, the bird ran so fast that but for his terrier which seized and held it till he came up, it must have escaped. "It proved," says the colonel, "an excellent bird, and the breast was of two colours, brown and white." Mr. Newcome says that when Mr. Colquhoun lived at Wretham, it was reported that there was generally a bustard or two hanging up in the larder."[36]

Stevenson thought Robert Hamond and most of his neighbours protected the bustards on their estates (there were instances where birds were caught and successfully domesticated), but inevitably a bird would occasionally fall to the gun. Other estate owners were not so protective. Stevenson mentions swivel guns and batteries of duck guns killing "a very considerable number of Bustards." He states, "Not a thought of the extermination of the species seems to have passed through their minds. Either they were entirely indifferent about the matter, or else they believed that since, as long as they could remember, there had always been bustards on the brecks, therefore bustards there would always be."[37]

Since the extinction of the native race single immigrants have appeared on a few occasions including Roudham Heath in 1840, Larling in 1841, Hockwold in 1876, Stiffkey in 1891 and Costessey in 1894. Robert Hamond described sightings of bustards after 1838 as "migratory stragglers." No others were recorded until 28 March 1863 when a female was found dead after striking overhead wires at South Creake (now in Norwich Castle Museum).[38] One was seen at Horsey Mere in 1867 where it was seen "stalking in the marshes, like an over-grown turkey." H.M. Upcher reported a male at Black Dyke Fen in 1876, "A Great Bustard took up his abode in my fen on the 24 January, 1876, in a piece of coleseed. He seemed to consider this field quite as private property, for I do not think he was ever absent for a whole day till the 24 February.[39] In the same year and shortly before his death, Richard Lubbock replied to his friend Henry Stevenson regarding a sighting of a bustard the previous year at Hockwold near Thetford. J.H. Gurney reported to the *Zoologist* in 1894 regarding a female great bustard, "February 1st. A female Great Bustard was shot at Costessey, near Norwich, by a man named Paul, of which a full account has been given by Mr. T.E. Gunn (*Trans*, Norfolk Nat. Soc., V. p. 656), Its gizzard contained an angular flake of flint (which must have been an awkward morsel to swallow) and three small pieces of pottery, one of a blue colour, recalling to mind New Zealand Moa stones."[40] The specimen was purchased by Sir Vauncey Crewe but was not included in the sale of his collection in 1925 and 1926.[41] Thomas Southwell describes another bustard in the Castle Museum, "At the bottom of the case is a fine Bustard. The beautiful group of these birds in the centre of the room, as already explained, represent the extinct race of Norfolk-bred Bustards, which have vanished never to return, the species now ranking with us as an occasional migrant; of the latter class, the bird above mentioned is a representative, having been shot at Winterton on the coast in the year 1820."[42] The present position of the case of bustards in the Bird Room has changed little since Southwell admired them. Visitors can see the birds as they approach the front desk. James Wentworth Day also writes about seeing the taxidermy specimens of the great bustard in the museum.

Great bustards disappeared from Cambridgeshire, Hertfordshire, Berkshire, and Salisbury Plain about 1810. Stevenson states, "The precise time at which the extinction of the Norfolk bustard took place, like that of the extinction of many other species, is not, perhaps, now to be determined with accuracy. The year 1838 is the last when examples are known with certainty to have been killed, but several persons believe, and with some show of reason that a bird, or even two birds, lingered on in this tract till 1843 or even 1845. This last date, however, is the very latest that can be assigned, and the probability, from the evidence available, is in favour of the extermination having been thoroughly effected seven years earlier namely, in 1838."[43] Wentworth Day states, "A few lingered on the Yorkshire and Lincolnshire Wolds until about 1826, and on the Suffolk heaths until about 1832. The last two big 'droves' in Norfolk haunted the Brecks about Westacre and Icklingham, which is just in Suffolk. Major H.A. Birkbeck has a very fine case of Norfolk bustards at Westacre High House, where the old Hamond collection of birds, got together by former owners of the estate, are still housed in the main hall."[44] John Birkbeck of Litcham Hall, told me, "I well remember the stuffed birds in cases both sides of the Great Staircase." Southwell describes Hamond's collection as a "matchless series of Norfolk Bustards." Norwich Castle Museum has a mounted specimen of a Great Bustard set up by Hamond, "killed from West Acre, Norfolk."

Stevenson reveals more about Hamond's collection, "In Mr. Hamond's collection at Westacre, Highhouse, are a male and female, in one large case, of which the male bird, as Mr. Hamond informs me, came from Spain and the female, as I learn from Mr. Robert Elwes, is the one (before mentioned) shot by his father, Mr. Henry Elwes, at Congham, in 1831, and was stuffed by the Rev. H. Dugmore. In the same house are also four bustard's eggs, of which one is marked "Ash Breck, Westacre, 1836, taken by Richard Hamond." The three others are all believed to have been taken at Westacre at least thirty years ago."[45] Stevenson believed Elwes's collection at Congham House near Kings Lynn to be the finest Norfolk series of five bustards in two cases, all shot in 1820. In his detailed chapter on the bustard, Stevenson lists all known taxidermy specimens and eggs in East Anglia. A few other examples are a female great bustard preserved at Elmham Hall, which originally came from the sale of the collection at Plumstead Hall in 1857, a pair at Weeting Hall and a specimen in the Lombe collection which passed on to Mrs E.P. Clarke at Hillington Hall.[46]

Norwich Castle Museum's unique display of a group of great bustards includes the notorious specimen by Knight and another by Thomas Roberts which was shot at Horsey in 1820. Another one of the birds was shot at Beechamwell. The museum has a cabinet skin, "found dead from farm in South Creake" and preserved by Fred Ashton, T.E. Gunn's assistant.

The single great bustard in the Lysaght Collection was shot on Swaffham Heath in around 1830 and several other migratory examples have been obtained in this county since that date. The two little bustards in the collection are also Norfolk specimens. One was killed at Trunch and the other near Norwich. Both are females. There are also two others, male and female, localities unknown.[47] A stuffed female specimen can be seen at Ancient House, Museum of Thetford Life. The bird was given to the museum by Prince Frederick Duleep Singh, who was the Maharaja's second son. The prince bought Ancient House in 1921 in order to create a new museum for Thetford. According to the curatorial team, the female bustard in residence was thought to have been trapped at Cavenham Heath in Suffolk in 1820 and prepared by B. Corbett of Piccadilly, one of the earliest London taxidermists. However, scraps of newspaper found at the bottom of the case suggest it may have died earlier in 1817. The bird was originally acquired by a Mr Johnson for £46 as part of the sale of the Sir Thomas Thornhill collection at Riddlesworth Hall.

In summing up his ornithological notes for 1870, Southwell writes:

> I cannot do better than conclude with quoting the words of Professor Newton when speaking of the Great Bustard (in a letter to the writer), "We, the naturalists of the present day, regretting that we know nothing of the extinction of the crane as a British bird two centuries ago—or of the Capercailly, in Scotland, one hundred years since, are, I think, bound to search out all the legends of the Bustard before it is too late, in order to prevent our successor's from reproaching us as we do those who lived at the times I speak of and we shall be the more blameable, for

we ought to have profited by their bad example. I need not say that this remark does not apply solely to the bustard's case, but all birds whose existence in this country has already become, or is becoming, a matter of history and there are, I am sorry to say, many of them deserve the same attention, and I am sure that however humble our efforts may be to effect this, they will not be thought despicable."[48] Arthur Patterson states, "The most-wicked of barbarians were those who remorselessly exterminated the Norfolk race of Great Bustards."[49]

Egg collecting also contributed to the extinction of the bustard and other birds including the great auk which became extinct in 1844 but a major factor in the bird's demise was changing habitat, especially in other parts of the country where land cultivation increased and wasteland was reclaimed and drained. Howard Saunders states, "The enclosure of wastes, the planting of trees, and the increase of population contributed to the gradual diminution of its numbers."[50] Henry Stevenson explains the demise of the bird, "Its chief destroyer was most assuredly the agriculturist. He found his crops wanted shelter, and planted long belts of trees to keep the wind from carrying his soil to the next parish, and removing his own or his neighbour's landmark. This intersecting of the open country was intolerable to the Bustard, which could not bear to be within reach of anything that might conceal an enemy. Its favourite haunts were, therefore, year by year restricted."[51] Great bustards had the habit of deposited their eggs in young corn which was traditionally broadcast by hand and lay undisturbed until it was cut. However, the introduction of the seed drill and horse-hoe lead to the destruction of the eggs. Any eggs that were missed by the machinery were often picked up by the farm hands. The eggs were protected in England by Section 24 of the Game Act, and "trespass in pursuit of" was an offence under the Game Act of 1831. Wild Bird Protection laws came too late for the bird—a species which Henry VIII committed to legislation in 1534 protecting the bird and its eggs (for the nobility). In, 1880, the bird became specially protected, and a close time ordered in England between 1 March and 1 September. An article in the *Eastern Daily Press* in 1897 regarding another programme to encourage reintroduction of the bird on the Yorkshire Wolds, contained this tragic line, "A Great Bustard is now a quaint and curious object in museums."[52]

Historic Rare Birds reveals that in 1900 fifteen individual great bustards from Spain were released in Thetford. This refers to the attempt to re-introduce the great bustard into East Anglia, as this article in the *Eastern Daily Press* in that year states, "Sixteen birds have been liberated, and that they have been allowed a run of 400 acres, which will soon be increased to 800 acres. Lord Walsingham added, "I don't propose to give the exact locality." Lord Walsingham's proposal to reintroduce the great bustard was playfully mocked during the luncheon at the Wayland Agricultural Show in 1900, which was presided over by his Lordship. Proposing a toast to Lord Walsingham, the Rev. J. G. K Mackenzie said that his Lordship was an authority on agriculture, natural history, and sport, his tastes in natural history ranging from lepidoptera to the great bustard. He hoped, "that at some future luncheon in connection with the show they would see Lord Walsingham carving a great bustard (Laughter)." Lord Walsingham, on rising, said that if Mr Mackenzie went out and shot that bustard he should feel more inclined to carve him than the bustard (Laughter)."[53]

In writing an obituary for Colonel Henry Wemyss Feilden (Arctic explorer and naturalist), Dr Sydney Long states, "[Feilden] later contributed many communications to the *Transactions*, the most interesting of which, from the ornithological point of view, is his account of his finding, in 1888, a stuffed great bustard, in a cottage in Peterstone, near Holkham, which had been "used as a plaything by the children both indoors and in the garden." This bird had been shot in Norfolk, and in the opinion of Feilden was almost certainly one of the aboriginal race. It is now in the Earl of Leicester's collection at Holkham."[54] A taxidermy specimen of a preserved great bustard mounted on a wooden plinth sold at Rowley's Antiques and Fine Art Auctions, Ely, Cambridgeshire on 9 April 2022 for £1,400. The estimate was £350-£450. The Watatunga Wildlife Reserve in West Norfolk currently run a breeding programme for the great bustard, in the hope of re-introducing the species back into Norfolk.

ଓଏ

Breckland has five market towns: Dereham, Thetford, Swaffham, Watton and Attleborough and the region comprises an area roughly 300 square miles. Examples of birds in the Lysaght Collection were taken in Brandon (Heath and Parva), Castle Acre, Lexham, Swaffham, Thetford and Mattishall. William Knatchbull Dillistone traded as a naturalist, taxidermist and tobacconist on Market Place, Swaffham. Trade publications list him working in the town between 1904 and 1916. A taxidermist called Dillistone moved from Royston, Hertfordshire to Swaffham where he practiced his trade, before moving to Battle in Sussex where he died in 1930. He was also listed at the address at a hairdresser in 1883. Christopher Frost states, "I have seen a pair of Pheasants in a box-type case by him with a suggestion of clouds on the back. The general style was similar to that of Ellis (also from Swaffham, but rather earlier, who occasionally painted clouds on his case backings), so he quite possibly trained under Ellis and later set up on his own."[55] On 7 September 1906, the *Diss Express* contained a short article relating the story of a group of labourers, working near Beeston, having discovered a severely injured large foreign bird. They tried to keep the bird alive by feeding it but it soon died from its injuries. The bird ended up at Dillistone's workshop where he identified it as a red-winged flamingo that had evidently escaped from captivity.[56] Thomas, W. Ellis was trading as a naturalist, bird preserver and victualler at the White Swan Inn, Castle Acre Street in 1877.[57] He preserved the misidentified 1871 Suffolk black-winged stilt, the 1876 Norfolk white-tailed eagle and the 1876 Norfolk snowy owl.[58] Frost maintains that most specimens he has seen were from the 1860s and of a good standard. His small trade label appears inside his cases.

Another taxidermist, presumably an amateur, is revealed by an obituary in the *Diss Express* in November 1908, "The late Mr. Beverley Leeds, of Wicken Farm, Castle Acre, was Church Warden some twenty years ago. He was a good shot and an excellent taxidermist, as the many beautiful specimens of his work show."[59] An edition of the *Norfolk Chronicle* (1881) has a William Driver working in Diss as a taxidermist and hairdresser.

Taxidermists in Thetford are mentioned several times in the *Transactions* of the Norfolk and Norwich Naturalists' Society in the Victorian and Edwardian period. Although retaining part of its heathland, the majority of the landscape was very different to the heavily forested areas of pine trees which we see today. In the middle of the 19th century the market town was encompassed on the south and west by extensive sandy heaths abounding in rabbit warrens in an almost steppe-like landscape. Reverend Forby's (1830) explanation for the Norfolk dialect phrase 'Coney-Land' was, "a land so light and sandy as to be fit for nothing but the breeding and feeding of rabbits."[60]

Three prominent taxidermists worked in Thetford. John Reynolds was a basket maker, bird and animal preserver at Well Street. Robert Reynolds was a bird, animal and fish preserver on the same street (1856).[61] John Reynolds is advertised as a "Basket and sieve maker and bird and feather preserver" trading on White Hart Street in 1877.[62] An earlier directory (Pigott's, 1839), states that John and Robert Reynolds were in business together on Earle's Lane. John preserved the 1843 Norfolk White-tailed Eagle, preserved and owned the 1843 Suffolk rose-coloured starling [63] and also preserved the two 1846 Suffolk two-barrelled crossbills.[64] David Newby traded at Guildhall Street in 1869,[65] before moving to Magdellen Street in 1890.[66] He preserved the 1873 Norfolk common crane.[67] In *Transactions* for 1896 William Clarke [68] writes of his excursions in the Thetford area. He mentions Newby (presumably at his shop) who had a stuffed Redwing that was shot near Thetford, two stuffed hobbies, one shot at Rushford in 1893 and also several Hawfinch from the Thetford area.[69] Christopher Frost amusingly states, "David Newby … produced cases which are excellent examples of how not to do it. The birds and mammals are always poorly mounted, and the arrangement of the décor inartistic in the extreme. His cases turn up from time to time in this part of the world, and are immediately recognisable through their consistent lack of redeeming features. He was in business during the final three decades of the century."[70] Taxidermists were sometimes paid to remount badly stuffed specimens and there are examples in the ledger of Walter Lowne. When Newby died his widow posted in the *Norwich Mercury* requesting for people to collect their taxidermy pieces from Newby's shop. Anything remaining was to be sold. A good specimen of a white-tailed eagle, set up by Newby around 1870, can be found in Ancient House, Museum of Thetford Life. The interpretation panel under the case states, "We know this was one of his earlier works because it was prepared at his first premises in Guildhall Street." F. Rix is also recorded as trading as a taxidermist in the town. There is one reference made to Rix in the *Transactions* for 1903 on the occurrence of the sooty tern in Suffolk:

> The Sooty Tern (*Sterna fuliginosa*) which I have the pleasure of exhibiting this evening, was found on Santon Downham Heath in the early part of April 1900, by Mr. J. Nunn, of Little Lodge Farm, Santon Downham. He was rabbiting with a companion when they saw the bird lying dead on some bracken about a quarter-of a-mile from Thetford Warren, which is in the administrative county of Norfolk, and half-a-mile from the Thetford to Brandon highway and the river Little Ouse. The weather was fine and the bird quite dry when picked up. It was taken to Mr. F. J. Rix, Abbey Green, Thetford, to be stuffed, who found it very much decomposed and it must have been dead five or six days at least. It was in very poor condition, with nothing in the crop or bowels but dark, clayey moisture. There were no marks of shot or any wound upon the skin. When mounted the bird was returned to Mr. Nunn.[71]

The *Thetford and Watton Times*, 2 March 1885, mentions J. Rolph, "Mr. J Rolph, taxidermist of Bridge Street, has had the following rarities sent for preservation: a white-breasted blackbird, from Elvedon; a pure-white mallard from Wilton; and five crossbills from Lakenheath; also from Lakenheath, two of the very rare scarlet grosbeaks (*Pyrrhula erythrina*), of which less than six species are recorded for the British Isles."[72]

Trade publications mention one taxidermist working in Dereham. This was the gloriously named Robert Goshawk on Cowper (possibly Cooper) Road, Dereham (1890). History presents little about the man, only debt and brawling. Goshawk came to blows with a butcher called Henry Brunton in the Rose pub in Dereham in 1875. Thirty years later he may have moved to Harleston where he owed half a year's rent on a premises. The *Norwich Mercury* recorded a taxidermist in Dereham called Hubbard setting up a deformed 'double-barrelled pig' for the landlord of the Green Man inn.[73] The *Norwich Mercury* reports a fine stuffed otter, having been caught in East Dereham, "preserved and in view at Mr. A. Hubbert's, Quebec Street."[74] Henry Stevenson mentions an unnamed taxidermist in New Buckenham receiving an Alpine Swift in 1831. *Transactions* for 1919 reveal a taxidermist named Edward Clough Newcome living at Feltwell Hall, near Brandon where he had a collection of taxidermy birds. Newcome died at the Hall in 1871, aged sixty-one, "Newcome the falconer was well-known to Henry Stevenson, who was proud of some birds mounted by this clever amateur taxidermist. The keeper of Newcome's hawks was John Madden who, one day when on Southacre Heath in the spring of 1850, had the luck to obtain a totally unknown species of Petrel."[75] It is worth noting that the Stag Inn at West Acre has an interesting selection of antique taxidermy cases inset in the walls of the bar. Perhaps the most interesting is a case of two cirl buntings. In his book,

Manual of British Birds (1899) Howard Saunders states that the bird is fairly common, though very local, but in East Anglia it is rare with only five examples being recorded for Norfolk.[76] B.B. Riviere noted few occurrences, the last being in 1904, with no confirmed instances of breeding in Norfolk to date.

Case Study—The Eurasian Stone-curlew, Burhinus oedicnemus

Victorian taxidermy study of a stone-curlew.
Author.

Lloyd's Encyclopaedic Dictionary, 1895, describes the stone-curlew as "having its headquarters in the open warrens of Norfolk and Suffolk." It remains an elusive and mysterious bird and one of many monikers: Norfolk plover, stone plover and thick-knee. Lubbock reveals that, in India, the bird was known as the goggle-eyed florican.[77] A lesser-known name was 'Culoo,' (Stevenson) which, presumably, was a mispronunciation of curlew, or perhaps a name handed down in Norfolk pronunciation by oral tradition. The birds are known as thick-knees due to the swellings at the joints, less apparent in the young birds—an abbreviation of the naturalist Thomas Pennant's 1776 coinage, 'Thick-kneed Bustard'. Gilbert White, in *The Natural History of Selbourne*, described the racket they made at night and also commented on their legs, 'Swoln like those of a gouty man.' People used to think that staring into its large yellow 'google' could cure jaundice. Their huge eyes help them to see at night as they seek insects, earthworm and occasionally small rodents. Writing in the mid-17th century, Thomas Browne records the presence of the bird in Norfolk, "There is also an handsome tall bird remarkably eyed and with a bill not aboue 2 inches long commonly calld a stone curlewe butt the note thereof more resembleth that of a green plouer [it *crossed out*] & breeds about Thetford about the stones & shingle of the Riuers."[78] The birds were originally placed close to bustards in the systematic list, but Browne's notes reflect that the bird is now known to be closely related to plovers. The bird has a loud wailing call reminiscent of curlews. Browne (who kept four of the birds in cages) described its 'note' as "one of the most charming sounds uttered on the wild trackless heath on a summer's night." Thomas Southwell gives a similar description, "On the extensive heath near Harling on a fine moonlight summer's night, I have several times heard the wild whistle of these birds in every direction, till the air seemed alive with the strange music."[79] The behaviour of this avian oddball is also dramatic, "Their courtship displays include bowing and touching bills, and the birds have been seen running about excitedly, picking up straws, flints or other small objects and tossing them over their shoulders."[80]

Writing in 1879, Thomas Southwell thought that stone-curlews were rapidly increasing in numbers in Norfolk. However, it is a widely-held belief that the eventual destruction of heathland contributed to a rapid decline in numbers of stone-curlew in their original strongholds. W.G. Hale mentions that the populations of stone-curlew was falling due to reclaiming heathland for agricultural use.[81] Michael Seago states, "At the time of Riviere's *History [of the Birds of Norfolk,* 1930] the Stone-curlew was still breeding abundantly throughout Breckland … Although the greater part of Breckland has since been afforested, fears that the Stone-curlews would be forced to depart have happily not proved correct."[82] Henry Stevenson noticed the decline in stone-curlews in their usual haunts in the Swaffham area with a few breeding pairs seen at Lexham, Congham and West Acre. However, Stevenson maintained that the birds were not diminished in the Thetford area (described by Stevenson as "their great stronghold") and also numerous in Feltwell. Encouraged by this, Stevenson states, "there is little fear that as regards the southern and western portions, its presence in summer will still enliven the waste for many generations to come."[83] The birds often move on to other areas if vegetation becomes too dense and tall. Lubbock provides a good description of the birds' favoured habitat, "The greatest allurement to them is an extensive new plantation, made in the open country, and on the improved plan of double-trenching the soil. The loosened ground affords better means of obtaining worms and beetles, their usual food; and the birds appear particularly to delight in the partial concealment which the young trees afford in the first year or two. As soon as the trees attain any size, all attraction ceases."[84]

A diorama in the Norfolk Room at Norwich Castle Museum shows the stone-curlew in a 1930s Breckland landscape. The legend on a postcard from the era, published by Jarrold & Sons Ltd, states, "Typical grass-heath, mere and pine-belts, with Norfolk Plover, Lapwing, Woodlark, Stonechat, Wheatear, and Nightjar." Although a 'Breckland Special,' the taxidermist Henry Pashley noted stone-curlews were nesting at Kelling in North Norfolk. He wrote in his diary

Case of stone-curlews by H.N. Pashley of Cley.
Author with permission from R. Ellis.

on 5 July 1906, "Went to Kelling Hall and over the estate to the parts where the Norfolk Plovers were nesting. I saw 2 pairs, but in the evening as I was leaving, there must have been 4 or 5 pairs on the wing circling about."[85] In his 'List of Birds' Pashley states, "I have seen 3 breeding birds within view on Kelling estate ([the] keeper there knew of 7 pairs). In my young time, I have seen many nests on Holt 'Lowes' and 'Kings Hill', Holt."[86] The Lowes are a mixture of dry sandy heath and bog close to the River Glaven, a habitat for many heathland birds.

Moss Taylor records the occurrence of the stone-curlew on the North Norfolk coast, "Kelling Heath, which was an ancient stronghold for the species was temporarily deserted in 1901, although four or five pairs returned to breed in 1906. Although none bred between 1914 and 1925, at least one pair were once more observed on Kelling Heath, for the last time, in the breeding season. The three specimens of Stone-curlew in the Lysaght Collection were all shot on Kelling Heath (1881—3). Another traditional breeding site was Beeston Regis, where up to two pairs bred until 1866."[87] Writing in 1870, Henry Stevenson states, "Once or twice, within the last four or five years, I have seen small numbers of Stone-curlews between Sheringham and Salthouse, during the months of June and July, and Mr. T. W. Cremer, of Beeston, near Cromer, informs me that a pair or two have hitherto bred, yearly, on some furze-covered [88] hills at the back of his residence, where the poor of the parish have rights of commonage, but having neither heard nor seen them during the past summer (1867)."[89]

Inevitably, Stevenson's account of the stone-curlew in his volumes contains examples of dates and locations of birds shot (between 1851 and 1870). However, in his address in 1893, the president of the Norfolk and Norwich Naturalists' Society wrote, "Only a few weeks ago a friend told me that a neighbour of his in the country sent a message to him to the effect that he knew he was "fond of birds," would he come and shoot some Stone-curlews that had, after an absence of many years, returned to his farm. My friend, who has killed big game and little from the Equator to nearly the Pole, fortunately is "fond of birds" and the news that this fine species had returned to one of its old haunts, long deserted, delighted him as much as their destruction would have caused him regret, and I trust that we may all have the strength of mind to follow his example, and never to molest bird or beast without a good and sufficient reason."[90]

F. M. Ogilvie's collection of cased British birds contains an adult pair of stone-curlews with nestlings and two immature specimens. In his book on Ogilvie's collection, all set up by T.E. Gunn, Christopher Frost states that Ogilvie published a paper on the species in the *Zoologist* in 1891 regarding it as one of the most interesting of British Birds. Frost reveals an article that Ogilvie wrote in *Field Observations* in 1909, "It has always been our endeavour to protect these birds in every possible way; they are never shot intentionally, either by ourselves or our guests, and, in consequence, only six birds have passed through my hands in the last thirty years."[91] As stone-curlews are distinctive (the white horizontal wing bar is very obvious, especially when the bird is in flight), it is hard to believe they could be mistaken for another species. Taxidermy examples appear in the stored collections of Lynn Museum and on display in Norwich Castle Museum. One specimen was shot on Kelling Heath and set up by Walter Lowne. Not afforded any protection by the 1880 Wild Bird Protection Act, the amendments to the Act the next year gave a general close time for the species between 1 March and 1 August and their eggs protected in Norfolk. There are areas of Breckland today where the birds breed and can be seen between March and late September. Perhaps the best place in Norfolk is Weeting Heath. No doubt the establishment of a large number of military training camps assisted the Stone-curlew in maintaining its 'private' habitat in Breckland and the area remains one of the chief localities where this bird breeds in the British Isles. One farm has a breeding pair of birds that have returned every year for the last decade. The Stone-curlew is included in the 2020 publication, *Norfolk's Wonderful 150*, a collection of species from Norfolk to celebrate the 150th anniversary of The Norfolk & Norwich Naturalists' Society.

THE LYSAGHT COLLECTION

Philip Watson's 2010 research paper, *The Birmingham Ornithological Collections, Part 2, The W.R. Lysaght Collection of Birds*, provides a fascinating insight into the Norfolk provenance of specimens in the museum's collection. William Royse Lysaght (1858—1945) acquired an extensive collection from E.M. Connop of Wroxham in 1912—1913. The majority of the collection was acquired by Birmingham Museum in 1954 when a new natural history display was being developed.[92] Watson states, "It is well known that Connop was a local, Norfolk collector, but despite this the bias towards specimens from that county is quite staggering at some 73% of the whole collection. Furthermore it is quite likely that a fair number of the 310 specimens (17%) which are given no provenance also came from that county. The final 10% of the collection includes specimens from the rest of the British Isles and the rest of the world (almost half of them)".[93]

Watson reveals more detailed provenance of the specimens from Norfolk, revealing a marked concentration of collection in certain areas. Watson states, "Of the 1,360 specimens from Norfolk some 785 have a more detailed provenance ... The high numbers respectively from Breydon, Cley, Blakeney, Yarmouth and Hickling hardly need comment."[94] In his foreword to Pashley's notes and lists, B.B. Riviere makes comment that the "wonderful collection" contained many birds "of Pashley's stuffing." Birds were collected mainly from Cley and the areas around Breydon Water. There were 90 specimens collected from Blakeney, 143 from Breydon Broad, 15 from Caister, 85 from Great Yarmouth, 77 from Hickling, 27 from Rollesby Broad, 12 from Salthouse, 101 from Cley and 23 from Yaxham. For the remaining 97 places mentioned, specimens remain collected in single figures.[95] Other useful information to come out of Watson's research are records of the taxidermists who set up the birds. Norfolk taxidermists include: Robert Clarke, J.A. Cole, Walter Lowne, Henry Pashley, W. Pycraft, E. Saunders, John Sayer and George Smith. The only taxidermists used out of the county were Howard Bunn of Lowestoft, Heinrich Gätke, and Griffin of Cambridge.[96] Pashley mentions in his diary setting up specimens for the collection. He preserved a yellow-browed warbler and what he described in December 1895 as, "a goose with head and bill like a Pinkfoot but with bright orange legs."[97] The Lysaght collection includes many Norfolk rarities including Pallas's leaf warbler (Cley-next-Sea, 1896), the greater spotted cuckoo (Caister, 1896), and the desert wheatear (Blakeney Point, 1907).

The Booth Collection in Brighton also contains Norfolk rarities. This collection must have created a considerable impression at the time of conception: a collection of 308 British birds set in dioramas which simulated their various habitats. Indeed, Edward Thomas Booth (1840–90), was a pioneer of the large diorama in modern museums where specimens are portrayed in their natural habitats. The collections remain relatively unaltered today although many of the specimens are faded. In his biography of Maurice Bird, James Parry states that Booth was "one of the leading collectors of his day and who shot regularly at Hickling in the 1870s and 80s..." His prodigious knowledge of birds commanded widespread respect, with MCH noting in a later entry (28 August 1896) how Booth, "used to be able to identify every species of British Bird by handling it behind his back, i.e. by feeling, without seeing the specimen."[98]

Watson also documents some of the private collections in Norfolk that were bought or acquired and added to the collection. Taxidermy was purchased at auction, including Stevens' Auction Rooms, established c.1831 in Covent Garden, London and from other private sales outside of Norfolk. Other cases were obtained from Norfolk including the collection of Mr. W.W. Spelman in Brundall, the collection of the Rev. S.N. Micklethwaite of Hickling (sold on 21 March 1889), the collection of J.G. Overend of Great Yarmouth (sold on 16 June 1876), the collection of Henry Doubleday, J.H. Gurney's collection, the collection of Captain Richard Glasspoole of Norwich (sold in 1846), the collection of Richard Ashby of Egham, Surrey (sold on 6 December 1897), the collection of Rev. H.T. Frere of Burston Rectory, Norfolk (sold on 12 March 1891), the collection of Miss Jary of Burlingham House [99] (sold on 19 September 1892), Colonel H.W. Feilden's collection (presented to E.M. Connop by Henry Pashley on 12 August 1897), the collection of George Barker of Holt (sold on 15 May 1873),[100] and the collection of Robert Rising of Horsey Hall (sold on 17 September 1885), which realised £72 19s 6d, including birds which, according to *The Field* were originally sold "to enrich the fine collection of local birds in the Norwich Museum."[101] Many of the birds in the collection were authenticated Norfolk specimens, but Arthur Patterson noted his dismay at most of the cases realising low prices.

Henry Pashley's diary entry for 21 July 1911 states, "Went out 'foraging' with Mr. Connop to Kelling Heath and Holt Lowes." On 15 September, he wrote, "Mr. E.M. Connop died to-day at 7.30 a.m. and was buried at Rollesby on the 19th".[102]

Notes

1. https://www.taxidermy4cash.com/ (accessed 12 September 2024), Norfolk taxidermy (Charles Dack).
2. K.A. Naylor and M.S. Pollitt, *Historical Rare Birds (List of Taxidermists)*, 2021, https://www.historicalrarebirds.info (accessed 12 September 2024).
3. C. Frost, *A History of British Taxidermy*, (Lavenham, The Lavenham Press, 1987), p. 72
4. *Eastern Daily Press*, 23 September 1896.
5. *Norfolk News* 21 February 1902.
6. *Eastern Daily Press*, 22 October 1904.
7. *Eastern Daily Press*, 27 October 1904.
8. *Norwich Mercury*, 30 August 1882.
9. https://sammymiller.co.uk/ (accessed 12 September 2024)
10. W. White, *History, Gazetteer and Directory of Norfolk*, (London, Simpkin, Marshall & Co., 1890).
11. Commercial Directory of the County of Norfolk (Craven & Co, 1856).
12. *Norfolk News*, 14 April 1877
13. Ibid. 3, p. 73.
14. *Norwich Mercury*, 15 February 1902.
15. H. Stevenson, 'Memoir of the Late Rev. Richard Lubbock,' printed in Rev. Richard Lubbock, *Observations on the Fauna of Norfolk and more particularly on the District of the Broads*. First published in 1845, (Norwich, Jarrold & Sons, 1879), xiv.
16. Ibid. 11.
17. Ibid. 2.
18. Ibid.
19. Ibid. 3, p. 73.
20. *Norwich Mercury*, 11 August 1911.
21. *Lynn News & County Press*, 24 January 1914.
22. Ibid. 3, p. 73.
23. Ibid. 2.

24. John Ray, *A Collection of Words not generally used, with their Significations and Original Meanings*, (1674).
25. S. Toulson, *East Anglia. Walking the ley lines and ancient tracks*, (London, Wild Wood House Ltd, 1979), p. 85.
26. K. Sussams, *the Breckland Archaeological Survey 1994-96*, Suffolk Archaeological Service (Ipswich, Suffolk County Council, 1996), p. 103.
27. T. Browne, *Notes and Letters on the Natural History of Norfolk (1605-1682) more especially on the Birds and Fishes*, with notes by Thomas Southwell, (Norwich, Jarrold & Sons, 1902), pp. 18-19.
28. David and Robert Yaxley, 'Birds in the Stiffkey Hall Accounts,' *Bird and Mammal Report*, Norfolk and Norwich Naturalists' Society, (Lavenham, Lavenham Press, 2013), p. 11.
29. Ibid. 15. Footnote, T. Southwell, p. 68.
30. *Norfolk News*, 21 February 1903.
31. Ibid. 16, p. 66.
32. P. and M. Clarke, *Where to Watch Birds in East Anglia*, (London, Christopher Helm, 1987), p. 110.
33. H. Stevenson, *The Birds of Norfolk, Remarks on their habits, migration and local Distribution*, Vol II, (London, John Van Horst, 1870), p. 8.
34. The Reverend Robert Hamond of High House, Westacre, was an amateur but skilful taxidermist. A short obituary appeared in the 1878-9 *Transactions* of the Norfolk and Norwich Naturalist's Society, "Robert Hamond was born at Kings Lynn, and was the third son of Anthony Hamond, of Westacre, and great uncle to the present owner of that estate. He was rector of Harpley, Gaytonthorpe, and Walton, and occupied much of his time in ornithological pursuits, his accurate knowledge, as a sportsman and naturalist combined, enabling him, an amateur bird stuffer, to give in form and attitude a most life-like character to his specimens, enhanced by the appropriate accessories with which his cases were fitted up. As a taxidermist he was a pupil of the late Rev. Henry Dugmore, of Beachamwell, whose style of "mounting" he even excelled in the points above referred to; and both in the collecting and stuffing of his own birds he received frequent and able assistance from his friend, Mr. Scales, of Beachamwell. At Mr. Hamond's death, which took place on 14 of June, 1831, his ornithological collection passed into the possession of his sister, the late Miss Sarah Hamond, of Swaffham, at whose decease, it became the property, by her bequest, of the late Mr. Robert Elwes, of Congham (Stevenson's *Birds of Norfolk*, vol. ii. p. 33)." *Transactions*, Norfolk and Norwich Naturalists' Society, (Norwich, Fletcher and Son, 1878-9), pp. 389-90.
35. H. Stevenson, H and T. Southwell, *The Birds of Norfolk, Remarks on their habits, migration and local Distribution*, Vol III, (London, John Van Horst, 1890), Appendix B., p. 399.
36. Ibid. 33, p. 12 (footnote).
37. Ibid. p. 12.
38. M. Seago, *Birds of Norfolk*, (Norwich, Jarrold, 1977), p. 63.
39. H.M. Upcher, the *Zoologist*, 2nd Series, Vol. XI, (1876), p. 4882.
40. J.H. Gurney, the *Zoologist*, 3rd Series, Vol XIX, (1895) pp. 95-96.
41. Ibid. 2.
42. This must be the same female bird that Henry Stevenson (1870) said was shot off the sea at Horsey.

43. Ibid. 33, pp. 15-16.
44. J. Wentworth Day, *Marshland Adventure on Norfolk Broads and Rivers*, (London, George G. Harrap and Co. Ltd, 1950), p. 129.
45. Ibid. 33, p. 33.
46. H. Stevenson, H (1866-1890), *The Birds of Norfolk, Remarks on their habits, migration and local Distribution*, Vol I, (London, John Van Horst, 1866-1890), lii.
47. T. Southwell, *Official Guide to the Norwich Castle Museum*, (Norwich, 1895), p. 26.
48. T. Southwell, 'On the Ornithological Archaeology of Norfolk,' *Transactions*, Norfolk and Norwich Naturalist's Society, (Norwich, Fletcher and Son, 1870), p. 22-23.
49. B. Tooley, 'Introduction,' *Scribblings of a Yarmouth Naturalist. An edited selection from the Writings of Arthur Henry Patterson, A.L.S., (John Knowlittle)*, (self-published, 2004), p. 39.
50. H. Saunders, *Manual of British Birds*, (London, Gurney and Jackson, 1899), p. 523.
51. Ibid. 33, p. li.
52. *Eastern Daily Press*, 9 December 1897.
53. *Norwich Mercury*, 15 September 1900.
54. S.H. Long, 'Obit. The Late Colonel Feilden,' *Transactions*, Norfolk and Norwich Naturalists' Society, (Norwich, A.E. Soman & Co., 1921), p. 71.
55. Ibid. 3, p. 73.
56. *Diss Express*, 7 September, 1906.
57. *Directory of Norfolk and Lowestoft* (London, Harrod & Co., 1877).
58. Ibid. 2.
59. *Diss Express*, 6 November 1908.
60. Rabbits were known as coneys or conies. In his article, 'A Rabbit Warren at Swainsthorpe' in the *Norfolk Research Committee Bulletin*, March 1980, Paul Rutledge reveals evidence for former warrens in Norfolk, "This document indicates the sort of evidence on the ground that warrens may have left. They leave frequent traces in maps and estate documents, not only by the word warren but by such names as Coney Close or the Conyger." (p.8).
61. Jarrod & Co.'s *Directory of Norfolk and Lowestoft* (1877).
62. Ibid.
63. Various hand-written notes in fountain pen appear in my copy of Howard Saunder's book, *Manual of British Birds* (1899). The book has plenty of blank pages at the back, presumably for the jottings of keen ornithologists. One paragraph reveals a rose-coloured starling being shot in Suffolk in 1899, "the third [specimen] on the 5/99 was shot by James A. Knox, at Belgriff House, near Yoxford, as it was feeding itself on the lawn." T.E. Gunn preserved the 1871 Norfolk rose-coloured starling and Knight of Norwich preserved the 1867 Norfolk specimen.
64. Ibid. 2.
65. The Post Office *Directory of Cambridgeshire, Norfolk and Suffolk* (London, Ed. Kelly, E.R. and Co., 1869).
66. W. White, *History, Gazetteer and Directory of Norfolk*, (London, Simpkin, Marshall & Co, 1890).
67. Ibid. 2.
68. One of the most well-known naturalists in East Anglia (1877-1923).
69. *Transactions*, Norfolk and Norwich Naturalists' Society, (Norwich, Fletcher and Son, 1896), pp. 306-9.

70. Ibid. 3, p. 73.
71. *Transactions* Norfolk and Norwich Naturalists' Society, (Norwich, A.E. Soman & Co., 1903), p. 752.
72. *Thetford and Watton Times*, 2 March 1885.
73. *Norwich Mercury*, 25 March 1903.
74. *Norwich Mercury*, 25 March 1907.
75. *Transactions*, Norfolk and Norwich Naturalists' Society, (Norwich, A.E. Soman & Co., 1919), p. 14-15.
76. H. Saunders, *Manual of British Birds*, (London, Gurney and Jackson, 1899), p. 211.
77. Ibid. 15, p. 74.
78. Ibid. 27, pp. 23-4.
79. Ibid. 15, footnote, T. Southwell, p. 72.
80. Various authors, *The Reader's Digest Book of British Birds*. (London, Drive Publications ltd, 1969), p. 94.
81. W.G. Hale, *Waders. The New Naturalist.* (London, Collins, 1982), p. 261.
82. Ibid. 37, p. 84.
83. Ibid. 33, pp. 56-7.
84. Ibid. 15, p. 74
85. H.N. Pashley, *Notes on the Birds of Cley, Norfolk*, 1925, New Edition privately published by Christopher Frost, (Lavenham, Lavenham Press, 1992), p. 62.
86. Ibid. p. 120.
87. M. Taylor, *The Birds of Sheringham*. (North Walsham, Poppyland Publishing, 1987), p. 25.
88. Furze = Gorse.
89. Ibid. 33, p. 55.
90. C.B. Plowright, 'Address at Great Yarmouth,' *Transactions*, Norfolk and Norwich Naturalists' Society, (Norwich, Fletcher and Son., 1893), p. 545.
91. Ibid. 3, p.87.
92. P. Watson, *Birmingham Ornithology Collections. Part 2, The W.R. Lysaght Collection of Birds*, (Birmingham Museums and Art Gallery, 2010), p.2.
93. Ibid. p.2.
94. Ibid.
95. Ibid. pp. 2-3.
96. Ibid. pp. 4-5.
97. Ibid. 85, p. 35.
98. J. Parry, *Maurice Bird. The Gilbert White of the Broads.* Norfolk and Norwich Naturalists' Society, (Lavenham, Lavenham Pres, 2024), p. 60.
99. Currently a care home.
100. Ibid. 92, p. 124-5.
101. *Norfolk News*, 3 October 1885.
102. Ibid. 85, p. 76.

The Wild Bird Protection Acts

The Decline in Taxidermy

'What's hit is history. What's missed is mystery.'

Henry Seebohm, ornithologist (1832-1895).

That this Act has been the cause of much adverse criticism is well known; but it has usually been condemned by those who do not understand its provisions, and who are forgetful of the fact that it was drawn up with great care by most of the best naturalists of the day, assisted by practical sportsmen, with a view to protecting our wild birds generally, and to save our songsters and rare visitors from the extinction that previously threatened them.[1]

Sir Ralph Payne-Gallwey, 1889

Introduced by successive Bills of Parliament, the Wild Bird Protection Acts had a marked impact on the trade in taxidermy. The new laws saw a gradual decline in stuffed birds and mammals, especially the rare birds and migrants previously unprotected by a close season or shooting prohibition and so sought after by the affluent collector. Today the laws surrounding the sale and exchange of animals are detailed in the Wildlife and Countryside Act (1981). The Act is based upon schedules of species which are given varying degrees of protection.

The general decline in wildlife in the Victorian and Edwardian eras is attributed to shooting and collecting. Changes in agricultural practice and increased cultivation are contributing factors (the Stone-curlew, for instance). There could be minor changes to the habits of birds. For instance, in the late 19th century members of the Norfolk and Norwich Naturalists' Society noted that a great number of conifer trees were appearing in coastal dune areas. This change appeared to decrease the number of terns nesting in areas where there were most young trees. That is not to say that species did not adapt to changes to the landscape. Lapwing populations increased after the depletion of oak forests that took place during World War One. Redshank and snipe, once limited to coastal wetlands, now also appear inland on agricultural fields. Perhaps rising numbers of 'urban oystercatchers' inland are in part due to the relative safety of nesting on roofs or yards compared to on the ground in their more natural coastal surroundings. The coast is subject to constant change and this is particularly evident in the geography of Blakeney Point, Scolt Head Island

and Holkham. Longshore Drift changes the landscape over progressive seasons. Dunes deplete and accumulate in different areas and storms affect the shingle ridges. Shingle washes down the beach and mud may be exposed for periods on the foreshore. The great collecting areas of Yarmouth and Broadland were also subject to historical topographical change, as Barbara Cornford states in her article, 'Past Water Levels in Broadland,' "The frequent flooding that occurred deposited silt and gravel, and sometimes shelly deposits, on the Broadland marshes ... the absence of dredging in the past meant that tidal activity was less. R.N. Bacon records that about 1840 there was practically no tide at Norwich. River flooding and lack of tidal activity would have important influence on conditions in different locations and at different times."[2] These conditions (and subsequent draining by means of wetland enclosures), impacted on bird and animal habitat. In his 1879 introduction to Lubbock's *Observations on the Fauna of Norfolk*, Thomas Southwell writes, "The changes during the past thirty years have indeed been great, perhaps greater than any like period in the history of our Island. Railways, steam draining mills, and improved cultivation have changed the quaking bogs, where once the Gull placed her procreant cradle, into green pastures where herds feed in safety; the "wavy swell of the soughing reeds" has given place to the bending ears of golden corn; and the boom of the Bittern, the scream of the Godwit, and the graceful flight of the glancing Tern, are sounds and sights altogether of the past."[3]

Birds could also take advantage of 'unforeseen natural events.' For instance the flooding at Salthouse and Cley in 1921, "It augurs well for the future success of our efforts at bird protection that Nature should have come to our assistance, as she has done, on this part of the coast-line. Within the course of a single night (December 31st, 1921), the sea, which man for generations has been striving to keep at bay, by shattering a concrete wall has once again placed under natural conditions acres of reclaimed marshland in this district, which have thus reverted to the ideal breeding-ground they once were when the Avocet, Ruff, and numerous species of seabirds resorted to them as a nesting area ... the Cley marshes similarly flooded, here indeed was a spot such as many birds must have been on the look-out for on their return spring journey to the north. And it was obviously appreciated, because with the advent of spring it very soon became alive with a winged population."[4] Billy Bishop, Warden at Cley, refers to the flooding of the Cley marshes and Glaven Valley as a "period of abundance," compounded by the resting of the breeding grounds during World War Two.[5] Arthur Patterson also reveals positive changes on Breydon Water at the beginning of the Edwardian era. Flats now barely covered at high water were easily sailed over, "Ducks often sit in safety, for the gunner, with all his manoeuvring, fails to get within shooting distance of them."[6]

Expanding on research into habitat loss and changes in habitat is the reserve of ornithological experts. The above examples are included to exemplify other factors in play regarding changes and distribution of bird populations, beyond single explanations for the historical losses sustained by bird species i.e. the discharge of a gun. The above scenarios are by no means apologia for the shooting and stuffing of animals. We will never know with any degree of certainty the exact causes for bird population declines in Norfolk since the early 1800s and the percentage shooting and collecting played in these fluctuations. Incorrect identification may be a contributing factor in distorting recordings of the populations of birds. What could not be identified in flight was invariably shot. As photography, telescopes and field-glasses improved so did the competence in observation.[7] However, some species of birds remain unobtrusive and inconspicuous and thus under-recorded. It is difficult to track and number such birds in an area. Consequently, quantitative evidence for population decline often cannot stand up to critical scrutiny.

The fact remains that it became very clear that species already under threat and common species once abundant and now in decline would both continue to suffer if unregulated shooting continued. Thomas Southwell thought that improvements in guns and boats contributed to the "extinction or banishment" of many birds, a change from Lubbock's era when a gun was invariably a "family piece" passed down from a grandfather.[8] It is also a mistake to assume that all 'common' bird populations in the Victorian era could withstand the onslaught of shooting and collecting under the belief that, 'there was more wildlife around than there is today.' In the Georgian era there were individuals who voiced their concerns about shooting and game dealers, as Benjamin Thompson Lowne recalls, "In the winter of 1829, a bird preserver had brought to him in one market day no less than four hundred wildfowl, five hundred snipe, and a hundred and fifty golden plovers; and at the same time six or seven hundred plovers' eggs were sent to London by one man every week during the season. Now very few birds, in proportion to this, visit our locality."[9] The Norfolk and Norwich Naturalists' Society reveal the inevitable consequences of shooting and collecting, especially among the rarer species of birds in Norfolk. There were a few occasions when birds ended up being stuffed after dying from natural causes: exhausted migrants, birds blown off course during littoral storms, e.g. little auks and skuas. There were also washed-out nests and tidal flooding, e.g. those that affected the redshanks at Cley in 1912. However, storm-blown birds that didn't die of exhaustion were inevitably picked off by the gunners. Dack of Holt and Cole of Norwich received a large number of skuas between October and November 1879. J.H. Gurney states, "I should say that not less than two hundred skuas, mainly *Pomatorhines*, were thus inhospitably treated when driven by adverse gales upon our coast."[10]

History presents revelations which paint a sad picture of the often unrestrained destruction by of bird populations in Norfolk. J.H Gurney and others recognised that species were suffering, and birds once common were becoming scarce or never seen again in the county. Reading through the early annual editions of *Transactions*,[11] it soon becomes clear that the loss of species and breeding patterns in Norfolk was being recognised. By 1874 *Transactions* have the directives of the society printed in the frontispiece. One of the principal objects was, "The discouragement of the practice of destroying the rarer species of birds that occasionally visit the County, and of exterminating rare plants in their native localities." Thomas Southwell writes in the 1870-71 *Transactions*, "In a highly cultivated County like Norfolk, where those animals not actually domesticated, or preserved by the sportsman, are regarded as "vermin" and ruthlessly destroyed whenever opportunity occurs, it is not to be expected that a great number of species will be found."[12] Thomas Southwell continues in similar vein in 1870:

> During a period of 150 years, two species only has ceased to breed in Norfolk, but in the fifty years which have since elapsed, no less than six species have entirely deserted us during the breeding season, viz. the peregrine falcon, kite, common buzzard, bustard, avocet, and black-tailed godwit. Five other species have virtually ceased to breed here, namely: the hen and Montagu's harriers, short-eared owl, bittern, and black tern, only a pair or two of which, from time to time and at uncertain intervals, return to their former homes. Several other species are rapidly disappearing, such as the hobby, marsh harrier, Norfolk plover, ruff, sheldrake,[13] great crested grebe, the common and lesser terns, lapwing, redshank, and ring dotterel. I have myself talked with men who have taken the eggs of the avocet and black-tailed godwit, and who have seen the bustard at large in its last stronghold. The bittern was so common in Feltwell Fen that a keeper there has shot five in one day, and his father used to have one roasted for dinner every Sunday. I have found the eggs of a Montagu's harrier, and know those who remember the time when the hen harrier and short-eared owl bred regularly in Roydon Fen, and who have taken the eggs of the water-rail in what was once Whittlesea Mere. I will not stop to enter upon the causes which have produced this change, nor upon the present condition of some species which are rapidly disappearing, as I should like to avail myself of another opportunity of doing the subject more justice than I could now, but will merely point out what I shall call the moral of this address—let us all strive to follow the example of the good Dr. Brown[e],[14] and of the no less worthy Mr. Lubbock, in preserving for our successors a faithful account of what we see and know in our own time, and in collecting all the information possible from every source respecting those species which are passing away from us, or have been lost within the memory of man.[15]

In his 1879 introduction to Lubbock's *Observations on the Fauna of Norfolk*, Southwell reiterates his objections to shooting and taxidermy,

> With sincere regret I have to confess that it is from a certain class of naturalists, happily I believe few in number, that most mischief is now

to be feared. The passion for *collecting* has in some few cases grown to such an extent that the ardent love of Nature for her own sake, has succumbed to the desire to possess a well-filled cabinet, and rare and local birds are destroyed wholesale … individual specimens or pairs are no longer sufficient for this purpose, but whole series of skins, of both sexes and in all stages of plumage, are sought after … Such persons should remember that they are inducing both the gunners and the bird-stuffers to violate highly beneficial Acts of Parliament without even the excuse of benefitting science, but simply that they may be supplied with an unlimited number of skins, by exchanging which to enrich their private collections.[16]

There is a curious contrast between the Liberalism of the mid-19th century, often in close harmony with religion, and the uncaring and sometimes cruel attitude to wildlife. Ethical concerns centred on promoting social reform which offset the materialism of mid-Victorianism but such worthy motives did not extend to the natural world. This was apparent on many levels. In the 1850s it was estimated that a thousand horses a week died in London. Martin George, author of *Birds in Norfolk and the Law, Past and Present*, states, "In a further expression of their short-sightedness and greed, the Victorians developed an increasing passion for collecting, not just the eggs of the more uncommon species, but their stuffed corpses, what Patterson in his later books described as "the nomenclature-faddists." Moreover, whereas in the past many individuals would have considered it sufficient to take the contents of a single nest of each species, it later became the norm to collect numerous clutches. Similarly, although a single skin might once have been deemed sufficient, it became customary to collect a whole series of both sexes and in all stages of plumage (Southwell, 1879)."[17] 'Collection,' of course, meant preservation by taxidermy. Christopher Frost brings to our attention a passage written in 1840 by William Swainson, the noted 19th century naturalist. Swainson succinctly reveals the attitudes of mid-century Victorianism, "The economy of animals can only be studied when the functions of life are in full activity; their haunts must be explored, their operations watched, and their peculiarities observed in the air. But in order to acquire a more accurate knowledge of their external form, and to investigate their internal structure, it is absolutely necessary to examine them in a dead state. Hence has arisen the art of Taxidermy …"[18] As regards this 'scientific approach' Martin George has this to say, "The status of many species also suffered on account of the absence of well-illustrated field guides, which exist in such numbers today. Any bird not immediately recognisable from a distance was liable to be shot so that it could be taken home and identified at leisure from one of the cumbersome works of reference then available."[19]

NATURALISTS AND TAXIDERMY: SCIENCE AND COMPLICITY

There was a frustrated relationship between the naturalists, gunners and collectors. The desire for sport and ownership of rare species maintained the trade in taxidermy. Many records and observations in the Victorian and Edwardian *Transactions* are from recordings of species that were shot and handed in to a taxidermist. Taxidermists and naturalists were often collectors themselves and were inevitably complicit in the demise of some of the rarer birds. Collectors focused on the extraordinary, not the quotidian. Contributors to the annual *Transactions* often talk of specimens euphemistically "finding their way to the bird-stuffers," or, "being obtained." There is an impression that some naturalists and taxidermists sought to distance themselves from the act of killing, or at least wished to acknowledge their own discomfort. Norfolk naturalists were unanimous and outspoken in their hatred of using feathers for ladies' hats, no doubt driven by the fact that birds and animals were being killed for fashion rather than for any 'necessary' scientific purpose. Henry Pashley was not happy with J.H. Gurney's remarks on the following occasion, "All the Sand-Grouse taken at Cley[20] and the immediate neighbourhood were taken from June 1st to October 17th. The Protection Act came into force on February 1st, 1889, after the birds had all left. I had 33 specimens through my hands, the highest number throughout the Kingdom for any one taxidermist, 'Not that is anything to your credit', says Mr. J.H. Gurney. I did not shoot any of them, so no need for Mr. J.H.G. to make such a remark."[21] In 1886, Henry Stevenson concedes, "I had certainly given up all idea of examining any more sand-grouse during that year, when summoned by the bird-stuffer to inspect the last three; and though sharing with other naturalists and sportsmen a regret that so many of these interesting birds should have been slaughtered during the nesting season, I was glad enough of the opportunity afforded me of observing the autumn plumage of the species, and of comparing the tints of their freshly moulted feathers with those of the earlier specimens."[22] Writing under his pseudonym John Knowlittle, Arthur Patterson submitted a piece to the *Eastern Daily Press* in 1896. He neatly summarises the curious position of the taxidermist, "The taxidermist, in nine times out of ten, is a lover of nature—his very inclination towards it made him a stuffer—he stuffs for love until sometimes necessity makes him stuff for a living ... he knows very well that constant persecution brings him constant work, but it finally destroys itself because nothing remains to be destroyed."[23] A letter to the *Eastern Daily Press* reflects a similar stance, "I was vexed at seeing when in Norwich on Tuesday last in a leading taxidermists' window quite a number of these useful birds, and no doubt their "preserver" was equally sorry, but of course it was not for him to turn work away, much as he might deprecate the slaughter."[24] The "Useful bird" in question was the barn owl. In his book *Notes of an East Coast Naturalist*, Patterson clearly expresses his contempt for indiscriminate shooting while at the same time acknowledging, "The spread of bird literature, and the more systematic formation of private collections of birds, have done much towards the furtherance of our knowledge of the comings and goings of many species, and of the occurrence of others hitherto rarely, or never before, noticed or recorded."[25]

Ornithologists gleaned valuable information from taxidermists for their research and publication. Writing his acknowledgements in the preface to *The Birds of Norfolk, Remarks on their habits, migration and local distribution, Volume I*, Henry Stevenson states, "Nor can I omit testifying at the same time to the unvarying civility and assistance I have received from our provincial taxidermists. To the late Mr. John Sayer, his assistant Mr. Gunn, and Mr. Knights, of Norwich, I owe many opportunities of examining in the flesh the rarer specimens that have passed through their hands for some years past, and in most cases of ascertaining, by dissection, peculiarities of food, or internal construction."[26] In his preface to his second volume Stevenson states, "I am also much indebted to the various bird preservers of the county for notices of scarce species and frequent opportunities of examining rare birds in the flesh; of these my thanks are especially due to Mr. Cole and Mr. Roberts, of Norwich, Mr. Lowne and Mr. Smith, of Yarmouth, Mr. Dack, of Holt, Mr. Pashley, of Cley and Mr. Newby, of Thetford. I am, also, much indebted to the published notes of Mr. T. E. Gunn, which I have acknowledged in the text."[27] Pashley and Gunn recorded the dietary habits across species providing interesting information for ornithologists. Information was *ad hoc* and sporadic and invariably took the form of listing the contents of the stomach before a bird was stuffed. F.M. Ogilvie gives an example, explaining here the assistance he was given by two taxidermists in examining a red-breasted fly-catcher. "Crop, empty. Stomach, containing large quantity of insect remains. These were very kindly examined for me by Mr. James Edwards, F.E.S., of Norwich, and proved to consist mainly of Earwigs; there were also fragments of two species of ground Beetles (Dyochirius globosus, Dichirotriclius obsoletus) and of a homopterous insect, Acoceplialus nerosus. These notes were taken a few hours after death. Mr. T. E. Gunn, E.L.S., dissected the bird before me, and I am also indebted to him for verifying my description and measurements and for other assistance."[28] On describing a little owl,[29] B.B. Riviere states, "It was [Gunn's] habit to make careful notes of the contents of the stomach of every bird which passed through his hands."[30] Thomas Southwell writes in 1871, "The stomachs of some of those [little gulls] dissected contained remains of small fish, shrimps, and sand worms, with sand and gritty substances. In the stomach of one were five sticklebacks, some of which could be identified as the ten-spined species. In another was a small fragment of chalk with seaweed attached, and something very like a minute portion of mutton fat. Examples in the flesh, weighed by Mr. T. E. Gunn, varied from three ounces in immature birds to four and a half ounces in adults."[31] By the 1920s dissections and analysis of feeding habits were still being done, but not haphazardly as specimens appeared on the taxidermist's table. Research became systematic and organised. For instance, in his article written in 1924, 'An Investigation of the food of Terns on

Blakeney Point,' the naturalist Dr. W.E. Collinge states, "As this investigation will necessarily involve the shooting of a limited number of Terns at regular intervals through the coming breeding season for the purpose of having their stomach contents analysed by an expert, it was understood that the National Trust would take immediate steps to inform the Norfolk County Council of the wishes of the conference, so that the Council might release an accredited officer of the Trust for the period of this investigation from the operation of the Wild Birds Protection Order of this body, under which all species of Terns are protected throughout the year in the County of Norfolk."[32] Billy Bishop reveals that reasons for the 'investigation' were as follows"

> With the passing of the Gentlemen Gunners and the mysterious disappearance of the flat fish in the mid-twenties, especially the flounders, in and around Blakeney Harbour, the livelihood of the local wildfowlers and fishermen began to suffer. At the same time, the number of terns breeding in the area was increasing rapidly. Naturally, they were blamed for the shortage of fish. So the Ministry of Agriculture and Fisheries gave permission for a number of terns to be shot and sent to the Yorkshire Museum for analysis of the food found in them ... a total of forty-eight common terns, nine sandwich terns and six little terns were shot and sent off ... the Museum scientists found that the terns were in no way to blame for the shortage of fish and the material loss to the fishermen. It was soon realised that the revenue lost by these men could be regained by taking numbers of visitors over to Blakeney Point to see the tern colonies.[33]

Today, trips to the Point to see the seals and terns are organised by Beans Boats, Bishop's Boats and Temple Seal Trips. In April 2023 three National Trust rangers moved into the old Lifeboat House on the Point until late October, to ward off predators and limit ground disturbance which threatens the colonies of little terns. The little tern is included in the 2020 publication, *Norfolk's Wonderful 150*.

By the late 19th century there appears to be a change in traditional thinking amongst the naturalists. There was a growing sense of the finiteness of native birds, mammals and the vulnerability of their habitats. Arthur Patterson hoped for change. He saw that birds would be safeguarded, "not so much by the Acts of Parliament—for English folk hate compulsion—perhaps, but by teaching our youngsters forbearance, kindliness, and the like towards creatures around them, and setting the example ourselves."[34] The Norfolk naturalists still visited taxidermist's shops (both Southwell and Gurney were regular visitors to Pashley in Cley and Stevenson sourced many rare specimens from Gabriel Pigott, also in Cley),[35] but there was a move to donate collections to displays in public museums and the gradual welcoming in of a new era where birds could be studied in their natural environment and prosecutions handed out to individuals who continued the old ways. The only way to achieve this was by law. Written information accompanying a display of birds' eggs in the natural history collection in Norwich Castle Museum explains, "Today most of the old collections have been given to museums, where they are still used for research. In the 1960s scientists used egg collections to help prove that pesticides could harm birds such as the Peregrine Falcon … However, surveying birds 'in the field' produces the most useful information to aid their conservation."

By 1891, Arthur Patterson had finished with shooting birds. He writes:

> Nowadays, a man or a boy can derive much joy from bird watching without the desire to kill … I only regret that so many incidents in my books should relate to slaughter and sport. I believe I am a naturalist now, for I can admire nature without the slightest desire to destroy."[36] Patterson clearly regrets his shooting days and he is keen to impress this upon the reader and returns to the subject many times in his books. In his prefatory note to *Notes of an East Coast Naturalist* in 1904 he wrote, "It may not be out of place to add that, since 1891, I have, I have entirely discarded the gun as a 'help' to observation, and have derived incomparably more real pleasure and interest in the pursuit of wild life with a filed-glass than I ever did with the fowling-piece.[37]

The Wild Birds Protection Acts

Thomas Southwell writes:

> The wild cliffs and headlands which protect our island home from the ravages of the ocean are no longer the remote regions they formerly were, the railway brought them close to the great centres of "civilization," and man, the destroyer, soon found fresh material for the exercise of his avocation. Until the recent passing of the "Sea-birds Protection Bill" put a stop to such practices, excursion trains were run to certain parts of our coast, where during the breeding season multitudes of gulls and auks are known to congregate, conveying large numbers of so-called "sportsmen," who, thoughtless of the cruelty and mischief they were perpetrating, slaughtered them without mercy, leaving their callow young to die of starvation! Every humane man, even though he have not the love for those harmless and beautiful birds, which a study of their habits is certain to inspire, must rejoice that a stop has been put to this wasteful destruction of God's creatures.[38]

The passing of the Sea Birds Protection Act in 1869 was a result of the efforts of Professor Alfred Newton, founder member of the British Ornithologists' Union. He brought to the attention of Parliament the cruelty of the battues at Flamborough Head where sportsmen hired steamers to sound their sirens to lift sea birds from their nests in the cliffs. The Preservation Act ordered a close season from 1 April to 1 August, protecting 33 species of birds.[39] The '33' birds also generalised, i.e. the Act afforded protection to all species listed simply as 'Gull,' or 'Tern.' The repealed Acts of 1869, 1872 and 1876 culminated in the passing of the Wild Birds Protection Act in 1880 which included Bitterns and Norfolk Plovers. A weakness of the legislation, especially in a county like Norfolk where large areas were divided up between landowners, was that owners and occupiers of land were exempt from prosecution for killing or taking a non-scheduled species. J.R.V. Marchant writes:

> ... it makes no difference for the purpose of this Act whether the owner or occupier had or had not the right to take or kill wild birds or to give permission to others so to do."[40] A letter in the *Eastern Daily Press* in February 1892, entitled 'Cruelty to Birds at Cromer and Elsewhere,' expressed this deficiency, "The absurdity of the Protection Act is its one-sidedness. Why are the landowners or landholders allowed to use their discretion with reference to protecting or persecuting birds on their own land, as they may see fit, and even have power to allow birdcatchers and hedgepoppers all through the close season to catch or slay whatsoever is unfortunate enough to wing over or walk on the said holdings.[41]

Birds of prey were omitted from the species listed in the schedule of the 1880 Wild Bird Protection Act. Henry Pashley's recollections towards the end of his life gives us an insight into owl (all revealed as 'common' or 'very common') and raptor numbers:

> Peregrine Falcon—several seen, 2 or 3 taken, nearly every year ... Hobby—first for Cley taken by a gamekeeper at Cley Watering in May 1913 ... Merlin—had not seen one till 1895 ... Of late years has been commonest Falcon in autumn, also winter, while Kestrels have become scarcer ... Rough-legged Buzzard—visits us nearly every autumn ... Common Buzzard—had four specimens from this district in 25 years ... White-Tailed Eagle [42]—female taken at Holt in November 1889 (now in the Connop collection) ... Marsh Harrier—had 3 in 25 years ... Montague's Harrier—used to breed on Kelling and Salthouse heaths ... I received a female and 3 full-grown young; crops contained young chickens. They had eaten most of the spring chickens of the man who brought them to me, so he shot them (Connop collection) ... Hen-Harrier—uncertain visitor, formerly more plentiful, 12 specimens in 25 years ... Goshawk—Only one taken ... Sparrow-hawk—not very common, used to be tolerably plentiful ... Honey Buzzard—very rare. Had three in 25 years ... Osprey—rare visitor.[43]

In his memoir of Richard Lubbock in *Transactions* for 1876-77, Henry Stevenson focusses on Lubbock's notes on birds of prey:

> His warnings as to the senseless persecution of the hawk tribe in general for the preservation of game, apply still more forcibly at the present

day, for he points to the enormous increase of ground vermin, in rats and mice, as the nemesis of the wholesale destruction of their natural enemies owls, kestrels, weasels and stoats. His theory over the fate of the nobler falcons was also aroused by his deep interest in all that related to hawks and hawking, and, as he happily puts it, the very sight of one nowadays is 'like that of the rusty nail or the monument of a departed hero, for the memories of the past crowd upon the mind when these birds, now proscribed and almost annihilated amongst us, were the favourites of ladies and the companions of princes.'[44]

CASE STUDY—THE RED KITE, MILVUS MILVUS

The red kite, or often simply referred to as the kite in the Victorian era, is abundantly familiar to us today, its distinctive forked tail seen over by roads and motorways. In 1903 W. Swaysland wrote, "Perhaps no British bird of Prey has suffered more from the hostility of the farmer and gamekeeper than the kite, or Glead[45] ... every man's land has been against it, and the warfare so persistently carried on has almost led to its extinction."[46] Although the bird predates on rabbits, moles and frogs, the prejudice against the bird was due to its notoriety in taking juvenile ground game: the young of pheasants, partridges, hens etc. before they can fly. Swaysland continues, "As already intimated, it is an assiduous visitor to the poultry yard, but does not exhibit the audacity or courage of the Sparrowhawk. It pounces unexpectedly upon its prey, but its character seems wanting in spirit, as numerous instances are recorded of the maternal hen attacking the intruder."[47] As Swaysland was writing in an age when the expression 'road-kill' had yet to be coined, he makes no note of the bird's preference for carrion, so often seen on busy roads and 'easy-pickings' for the kite who have adapted to the modern world as scavengers. They are 'social raptors.' One bird will indicate to another where another carcass lays. This behaviour is not the reserve of the kite. Other raptors, the white-tailed eagle for instance, are scavengers and klepto-parasites (stealing food from other predators). A friend of mine shot a pheasant while rough shooting in Beeston, Breckland. He decided to leave it in a 'scrape' and collect it later. An hour or so later he returned to the bird and noticed a 'fed-up'[48] buzzard languidly flying up from the pheasant having enjoyed a meal, free of effort.

There is one red kite in the Ogilvie Bird Collection and is thought to be one of the last records of the species for Suffolk at the time the collection was

Red kite.
Sam Owen Photography.

put together. T.E. Gunn, who set up the bird, published details in the *Zoologist* in January 1884, "An adult specimen of this species was picked up dead on the sea beach at Aldeburgh, Suffolk on 23 September 1881: evidently exhausted in its migration to the coast, it had dropped into the sea and was drowned. It was washed ashore in a particularly fresh condition, and I found no marks on its body to indicate its having received any injury to account for death. The plumage was in perfect condition, and the body rather fat."[49]

Martin George reveals that the kite was also the quarry of other raptors, "Perhaps the most surprising quarry species was the red kite. In the early 19th century this was, according to Newton,[50] very common throughout England, and especially abundant in the (Breckland) district, so rich in rabbits."[51] Writing in the mid-17th century Thomas Browne mentions the presence of the bird in Norfolk, "Aldrovanus takes particular notice of the great number of kites about London & about the Thames. Wee are not without them heare though not in such numbers."[52] Swaysland also mentions the bird "as a quarry for other birds to be flown at," this being, "corroborative of the cowardice of its nature." Henry Pashley makes no mention of a kite in his list of birds and the kite does not appear in Walter Lowne's ledger and workbook amongst the 213 birds of prey that he preserved during his lifetime. J.H. Gurney donated kites to the natural history collection at Norwich Castle Museum, some specimens which may have come from his father. A good example can be seen at the museum in The Bird Room (catalogue no.145). Another specimen was set up by Roberts having been shot at Woodbastwick. I have seen only one taxidermy specimen for sale at an auction in Newmarket. The bird was in poor condition, its delightful background depicted a woody landscape leading to open fields. All things pointed to it being a case by Peter Spicer.

Kites were regarded as vermin in the Victorian era and a threat to pheasant populations which led to their extinction in England and Scotland in the 1870s, hence the omission from taxidermists' books after this date. The kite remains the national bird of Wales. In the Victorian era the bird was thought to have ceased nesting in Norfolk about 1830. An apparent anomaly, J.H. Gurney records a kite being spotted in Norfolk in 1880, "Many years ago a kite was killed in the "Hungry-Hills" woods at Northrepps (exactly the same locality which produced the specimen in 1880). I have a pencil sketch by some unknown hand, apparently taken after it was stuffed, and a note to the effect that it was shot whilst in the net of devouring a rabbit, and the skin preserved."[53] One bird was killed at Winterton on 7 October 1881, eventually given to the Norwich Castle Museum. The sale of Robert Rising's collection of birds in 1885 included "a very fine pair of kites shot in Staffordshire. The lot realised three-and-a-half guineas."[54]

The kite was not covered in the Act of 1880, with its eggs only protected in Devon and Brecon. It was to be a rare visitor in North Norfolk (the coastal areas between Weybourne and East Runton), for many decades to come, as Moss Taylor revealed in 1987, "A rare visitor recorded on four occasions. Singles at Kelling Heath on 22 March 1958, Weybourne on 15 April 1959 and 12 December 1978 and Sheringham on 27 March 1981."[55] It was not until the 1990s that the kite soared in numbers again over the skies of Norfolk. In the summer of 1990, thirteen red kites were brought from Spain and released in the Chilterns. The bird remains today as one of the most successful stories in bird conservation in the UK and gradually became abundant in Breckland and some of the old shooting grounds at Winterton and Snettisham.

༄༅༅

In 1900, a further Act was passed which included a clause relating to the sale or sales that occurred before a specimen came into the possession of a taxidermist:

> "A person shall not be liable to be convicted under section three of the Wild Birds Protection Act, 1880, of exposing or offering for sale, or having the control or possession of, any wild bird recently killed, if he satisfies the court before whom he is charged either (1) That the killing of such wild bird, if in a place to which the said Act extends, was lawful at the time when and by the person by whom it was killed; or (2) That the wild bird was killed in some place to which the said Act does not extend, and the fact that the wild bird was imported from some place to which the said Act does not extend shall, until the contrary is proved, be evidence that the bird was killed in some place to which the said Act does not extend.[56]

J.H. Gurney was offered various specimens whose provenance he knew to be dubious, i.e. birds which could not be presented with the prefix 'Norfolk' as they were caught or shot elsewhere. Such birds were given the prefix 'Rejected.' Unscrupulous dealers could offer up this excuse in their defence, especially in areas like Breydon Water where orders within the Acts and close seasons for specific birds were not always consistent across county borders.

Describing May in Broadland, Arthur Patterson reveals the changes met by a closed season and the impact on the taxidermists, "Many a rarer bird, attired in its springtime best, mingles with the commoner herd. But close-time has thrown its protecting clauses around them, and they remain unmolested by the gunner who envies them their jackets. The bird-stuffer now loses his richest plumaged specimens. There was no close season until well into the 70s."[57] There were objections. An application was made in April 1885 to move the close season to alleviate the hardship the blanket regulations put upon the gunners on the Norfolk Coast. The Norfolk and Norwich Naturalists' Society agreed that certain species of wildfowl could be shot outside of the season, a motion approved by J.H. Gurney, H.M. Upcher and others. The resolution brought before the Court lost by twenty-eight to eight votes.[58]

Amendments to the Acts

There was much debate regarding the efficacy of the Seabird, Wild Bird and Wildfowl protection acts: primarily what birds to include and also the practise of egg collecting as being one of the main causes of species extermination.[59] However, egg collecting persisted well into the 1920s especially targeting the rarer species. In his book, *Countryman's Memoirs*, Ted Eales talks about the "crafty" egg collectors on Blakeney Point in the early 1950s. Naturalists suggested further additions and changes when certain birds were not covered in the Acts, including Pallas's Sandgrouse. On 28 May, 1907, a letter was read from the Wild Birds' Protection Society to Mr. G. F. Buxton, pointing out that goldfinches and owls were not sufficiently protected in Norfolk, and a sub-committee was formed to enquire into the matter. The question was brought before the Norfolk County Council, and in consequence of this and the representations of other bodies, the necessary protection was obtained.

Highlighting the areas of Norfolk where intense nesting populations were situated, Thomas Southwell opined for a more nuanced and localised approach, targeting the professional dealer whose sole aim was profit from egg collecting. The Acts of 1880 and 1881 failed to protect the eggs of any species. Eggs were also collected for food and Southwell differentiates between small and large-scale thievery:

> As I stated last year, my opinion has always been that no Wild Fowl Protection Act will prove effectual without some provision for preserving eggs ... although I regard any Act to protect small birds in this country during the nesting season (with some few exceptions) as wholly uncalled for, the permitted robbery of their eggs, as hitherto, seems to me an anomaly, since, unquestionably, the hedge-sparrow, thrush, blackbird, and others, suffer infinitely more from the egger than the gunner at that time of year; nevertheless, in such cases, I should regret indeed to see the law set in force for the arrest of every thoughtless bird-nesting urchin in our rural districts, whose depredations should be checked by other influences. Not so, however, on our broads and marshes, where the egg stealers are a very different class. Men, who either trespass in search of eggs, or take advantage of their occupation, in likely localities, to hunt for and secure them, well knowing their market value, and where best to dispose of them. With the prices now offered by dealers for the eggs of the Bearded Tit, how can we look for an increase in that species by protecting the birds alone? Or if the nesting bittern escapes the gun, what marshman could resist the temptation (no penalty attaching to the act), of securing its literally golden eggs.[60]

Arthur Patterson was astonished to read the following letter, dated 6 April 1892, "Dear Sir, Could you get me Bearded Tits in the flesh? Can give you 3s, 6d. each. Also nests and eggs of the same. If at any time you can offer pied or albino birds, shall be glad to hear from you."[61] The Bearded Tit is included in the Norfolk & Norwich Naturalists' Society's publication, *Norfolk's Wonderful 150*.

Henry Pashley also disapproved of blanket enforcement of the Acts. He writes in his diary in January 1897, "The case against the lad, C. Long,[62] who shot the Roseate Tern came before the 'Bench' to-day (just six months after the affair). The Chairman made it pretty warm for the Inspector, S.P.C.A., who prosecuted, as the Chairman put it, 'for letting the affair hang over the boy's head for six months,' ending with, 'It may be law but it's not justice.'"[63] Billy Bishop said that the boy was fined 23s 6d and Pashley paid the fine to save the boy from going to prison for seven days.[64]

When the Bill came up for its second hearing, Auberon Herbert, MP, successfully proposed that the Bill should also provide protection for "small birds generally." This was criticised by Stevenson who said it prevented 'pest' species like crows being controlled.[65] In 1894 an amendment was made to the 1880 Act which gave local councils, on application to the Secretary of State, permission to make it an offence to collect the eggs of rare species and to establish areas where all birds and their eggs could be protected. These were the beginnings of the protected bird sanctuaries today. However, it was not an offence to be in possession of wild bird's eggs, unless the wardens of local bird protection societies could catch the thieves red-handed. Further responsibility was given over to local councils in 1886 when they could apply to the Home Office for protection orders banning the taking or killing of any bird at risk.

On 8 April 1895 an Order of the Secretary of State applied provisions relating specifically to Norfolk under the Wild Birds Protection Act 1894. The Order prohibited the taking or destroying of eggs of specific species throughout the entire county. These were the bearded tit (a bird of great concern amongst Norfolk naturalists as the Acts were being honed), crossbills, barn owls, wild ducks and teal of all species, norfolk plovers, the ruff and reeve, ring dotterel, ring plover, oystercatcher, terns and great crested grebe.[66] The bearded tit (mouse) and crossbill were applied to the original 1880 Act. J.H. Gurney was delighted that the barn owl was on the schedule list. He wrote:

> There is one bird now rapidly becoming scarce with us, owing to constant persecution, for which we would especially plead, we refer to the Barn Owl, than which the farmer and game-preserver does not possess a greater friend, and yet there is scarcely a gamekeeper's gibbet on which it is not found, and very many are annually brought to the Norwich bird-stuffers. Mr. Frank Norgate counted twenty-six good-sized rats in the nest of a single Barn Owl, which were quite fresh, and as the weather was very hot at the time, he is convinced they must all have been killed the previous night: let those who know the destruction committed by rats when they have young ones, which is almost all the year round,

try to realise the service performed by this pair of birds, and then judge of the wisdom of allowing them to be destroyed. Both the Long-eared and Brown Owls are scarcely less serviceable, and would increase rapidly if not so often killed.[67]

The records of Walter Lowne reveal that he preserved at least 173 barn owls. The bird is also included in *Norfolk's Wonderful 150*.

A Wild Birds Protection Committee was set up by the Norfolk County Council in 1895. The committee invited the Secretary of State to afford protection to the eggs of all birds in two large areas. Consequently, for a period of one year from 1 May 1897 the taking or destroying of eggs of any species of wild birds was prohibited in the warrens, maram and sand-hills at Winterton, all the marshes and low-lying and uncultivated lands, fens, reed grounds, warrens, marram or sand hills, and sea shore, to the line of high water mark, in the several parishes of Waxham, Horsey, Potter, Heigham, and Hickling. The law also covered Hickling, Ormesby, Rollesby, Hemsby, Filby and Burgh broads. Hickling broad is the largest stretch of open water in Broadland, comprising extensive sedge and reed beds. Like Breydon, it would have been a difficult area to oversee and police. The foreshore from the Estuary Sluice at North Wootton to the eastern boundary of the Parish of Cley-next-the Sea marked the second area.[68] The dunes at Winterton (re-named Winterton-on-Sea in the 1950s), extend for more than 250 acres and are probably the second largest dunes in the country. It was a major 'picking ground' for egg collectors and shooting alike. Today the stretches of shingle are one of the most important areas for the little tern.

There is a lovely description of Ormesby, Filby and Rollesby Broads in Alfred Dutt's *The Norfolk Broads* (1906). Dutt (1870–1939) wrote many books on East Anglia. He states:

> The scenery of these Broads is pleasantly varied. The shores are well-wooded, there are quiet creeks not unlike those of Barton, islets fringed with fen sedge, willow herbs, and purple and yellow loosestrife, underwoods garlanded with honeysuckle, white bells of the great convolvulus, gardens with handsome peacocks and butterflies flutter among Canterbury bells and hollyhocks, and bays beautiful with white water-lilies. The reed and rush beds are many acres in extent; their varied green in summer and amber and tawny hues in winter are among the most striking effects visible from the open water. Coots and grebes are abundant on Filby and Rollesby; the woods are full of crooning pigeons, and during the summer months the reeds are musical with warblers. In winter, large numbers of wild fowl visit the Broads, especially Filby, but the shooting is preserved.[69]

It is also worth mentioning the deployment of decoys, a subject of particular interest to Henry Stevenson, who incorporated a paper called 'Decoys in Norfolk' in Volume III of his *Birds of Norfolk*. Richard Lubbock in his *Observations on the Fauna of Norfolk* also devoted a lengthy appendix on the subject. Although an invention to lure wildfowl into areas so birds could be shot, they were also used for conservation purposes, "Sir Thomas Browne was right when he attributed the abundance of wild-fowl in Norfolk to the very many decoys, especially between Norwich and the sea … decoys are being revived both in Norfolk and Suffolk. The main requirement for success is proximity to the coast, and absolute quiet, with, if possible, a thick plantation around the pool."[70] The first decoy 'used for good' was Horsey Mere. The extensive tract was constructed by 'Old' George Skelton and was described as a "veritable paradise" for wild fowl.

Six further Bird Protection Acts were passed between 1902 and 1925. The Acts prohibited employing birds as lures, using 'bird lime' (a sticky substance, often made from boiled holly bark, used to trap small birds) and the use of pole traps, hooks or thread 'teagle' traps. The Acts also made it illegal to confine any bird (except poultry) in a cage so small that it could not stretch its wings. Martin George states the later Acts, "provide evidence of a growing revulsion against cruel practices, the passing of the Protection of Animals Act in 1911 being another example."[71] Thomas Southwell wrote about otters in Norfolk in 1870–71, "In Mr. Stevenson's notes, kindly placed at my disposal, I find mention of no less than forty otters sent up to Norwich for preservation, between the years 1852 and 1867, and a bird-stuffer in this city told me that in one year sixteen passed through his hands alone."[72] Walter Lowne alone stuffed 48 otters during his career.

The Norfolk Wild Birds Protection Committee continued to enhance the Acts by steering the Secretary of State towards a longer close season, banning eggs on all foreshores in Norfolk and extending the number of birds whose eggs were protected.

A Cautious Approach

Members of the Norfolk and Norwich Naturalists' Society were enthusiastic about the passing of the original 1880 act, "The Wild Birds Act is of incalculable service in saving the lives of thousands of the feathered creation on our southern shores, by putting a stop to the bird-catchers' nets, at the time when they are just about to breed. I should not wonder if the Linnet soon vanished as completely as the Goldfinch seems to have done. At one place alone I found at least 200 Linnets' wings, which would mean 100 birds killed. This Act has now been repealed, and replaced by the Wild Birds Protection Act, passed September 7, 1880."[73] However, the Act had yet to be tested. It appears that the efficacy of the Wild Bird Protection Acts varied across the county. For instance this report is from just after the first Act was passed, "A Green Sandpiper was observed in the neighbourhood of Holt, on the 5th of June; and on the 6th, three Spoonbills were seen near the lifeboat house at Blakeney, feeding by the water's edge; and the fact is worthy of record that, although discovered and watched for some time through a glass by two local birdstuffers, the birds remained unmolested, and the recent Act respected. At Yarmouth, the inducements held out to the gunners to secure all rarities would have insured their destruction. The man who breaks the law gets the best of it, at present."[74] Yarmouth taxidermist E.C. Saunders referred to the first Act as "feeble." Martin George states that eight years previously the 1872 Bill for the Preservation of Wild Fowl was also greeted with reservation, "The penalties prescribed for shooting these birds[75] in the designated close season were so derisory, being a reprimand for a first offender, and a fine of 5 shillings for a second offence, that Stevenson (1873) and others pointed out that wildfowlers would ignore the legislation."[76] The inevitable chain of events that led from the gunner, to the taxidermist, to the collector, continued for the moment. A Select Committee reviewed the situation, one of those giving evidence to it being Henry Stevenson. An Act for the Preservation of Wild Fowl was passed in 1876, extending the close season and amending the penalty of up to £1 per bird shot within this period. It can be said that these precursors to the 1880 act also suffered because they originally made notice only in the pages of the *London Gazette*. Christopher Frost describes the events surrounding T.E. Gunn's prosecution in 1881. After a day's shooting the taxidermist moored up alongside the Bowling Green pub near Breydon Water when the local 'weights and measures' officer demanded to see the birds he had obtained:

> Such Acts were in their infancy during Gunn's early days, and were not rigorously enforced. Prosecutions did occur, however: Gunn himself was taken to court in June 1881 for being found in possession of five Dotterel and two Turnstones on his return from a shooting trip in a punt on Breydon Water. (The latter were referred to as 'Plovers' on the summons.) He pleaded guilty to six charges but not guilty to the two concerning the 'plovers', which he contended were not Plovers but Turnstones, and as such were not included in the Schedule of the 1880 Act. He was doubtless assuming that those passing judgement on him would not be ornithologists, for Turnstones were at the time classified as members of the Plover family (though nowadays they are usually placed among the Sandpipers.) He got away with this, but was fined 'five shillings' for each of the other six birds. In his defence he tried to persuade the Bench that he was ignorant of the new Act, and that the birds in question had very little marketable value. (Dotterel were uncommon birds which would probably, in fact, have been readily saleable, especially in summer plumage.) Many collectors—including Ogilvie—similarly ignored the protection laws when it suited them.[77]

Frost describes how a newspaper report was read out to an assembled party of wildfowlers and taxidermists in 1888, seven years after the prosecution. The reaction was recorded by Arthur Patterson in his book, *Wildfowlers and Poachers*. Frost states, quoting Patterson, "One of those present that evening was Ben Dye, himself a taxidermist, "Good old Tom Gunn," he interjected at one point, and the general feeling of the gathering was strongly with Gunn and against the new protection laws, which were making life harder for those who earned their living from shooting wild birds."[78] "The Good old Days" refer to the age when there was no restriction placed upon taking birds, animals and fish. William Alfred Dutt states, "At the time when the Rev. R. Lubbock wrote his descriptions of a typical Broadsman, the Acts of Parliament existing for the protection of wild birds were seldom enforced, and through Norfolk and Yarmouth claimed jurisdiction over parts of the rivers ... the gunner could shoot and the fishermen net,[79] whenever and almost wherever they chose."[80] However, this apparent disregard for the law, gradually resulted in many people being deprived of their chief means of livelihood. Some of the wildfowlers adapted, becoming wherrymen, eel-catchers and rush cutters. Dutt talks of the age of the wildfowler becoming "practically extinct," apt words indeed. Nicholas Everitt, writing a chapter on wildfowling in Dutt's book states, "Speaking generally, it is not correct to say that wild-fowling in Broadland is practically a thing of the past; it is better to describe it as being more or less confined to private individuals. The rights of the public are being gradually curtailed to the narrowest possible limits, and so jealous is the game preserver, the Broad-owner, and the riparian proprietor, that the time when such rights will no longer exist seems to be drawing very near."[81] Perhaps Everitt was predicting the dawn of the era of private shooting for those with 'big purses.'

Henry Stevenson evidently thought that old thinking would not change overnight. In *Ornithological Notes* for 1882, Henry Stevenson writes, "In the course of the summer I had ocular demonstration of the abundant breeding of wild-fowl on a Norfolk estate, where the strict preservation of game proves a sure safeguard. Here, on extensive waters, were seen many pairs, with their young, not only of the Common Wild Duck and Teal, but of Shovellers, Garganey, Pochards, Tufted Ducks, and Gadwalls, as well as Great Crested and Little Grebes. Further details as to locality, site of nests found, &c., are carefully preserved in my journal and, in the interest of our rarer indigenous species of fowl and, not to gratify the curiosity of roving birdstuffers, whole "clutch" egg-collectors, or the ubiquitous excursionist (beguiled by the flashy articles of popular writers on local natural history), will remain further unused till time may render it safe to do so."[82] In his biography of Maurice Bird, James Parry reveals a diary entry from 26 March 1912, "Letter from Bird Protection Society re killing of Bitterns, Kingfishers, Bearded Tits and Nightingales and Norfolk Plover. A. Nudd said re protection of birds at Hickling, "Call it a sanctuary, I call it a cemetery." Parry states that the "letter referred to by 'MCH' was from the Royal Society for the Protection of Birds, regarding complaints it had received about 'the way in which rare and interesting birds are slaughtered in Norfolk notwithstanding the Bird Protection Order ..."[83] The nature of Bird's reply is unknown. Parry goes on to reveal Bird's diary for 15 May 1919 which shows an excerpt from a letter from the Yarmouth taxidermist Saunders in which he lets Bird know that he was working on two little owls, a black redstart and a pied flycatcher. Parry states, "Despite legislation designed to protect birds during the 'closed' season (1 March to 31 July) and greater awareness of the impact of collecting on vulnerable populations, it is clear from this letter that the taxidermists' trade in scarce species was still thriving."[84] Parry makes the point that for some collectors it was difficult to shake the zeal of possessing taxidermy specimens (whatever the strictness of the law) and at the same time publically demonstrating conservation, "MCH was an avid collector, and we know from his diaries and letters that he shot birds himself, received birds killed or found by others, and acquired already mounted specimens from taxidermists and fellow collectors. The fact that he was still adding to his collection as late as 1906 (and even later, it seems), raises the rather unsavoury prospect that he was continuing to collude in the shooting of rare species while also apparently making the case for their protection. How else can one explain the presence of the 1906 Marsh Harriers in his collection …"[85]

In 1984, Peter and Margaret Clarke wrote about where to watch birds in Norfolk. They stated, "There are two extremely rare breeding species, the Goshawk and the Golden Oriole, which have deliberately been omitted for the sake of security. The Goshawk has nested, or attempted to nest, in the Breckland area; sadly, some have been shot and eggs were taken from another."[86] Today, a reluctance to disclose locations of rare birds is perhaps put in jeopardy by the lightning-speed of social media.

From 1900, the contributions and reports made by taxidermists in *Transactions* begins to diminish until it fades out completely by the 1920s, replaced by lengthy reports by Norfolk bird protection societies, especially in the old hunting grounds of Cley and Breydon. This also coincides with the first inclusion in 1921 of a section of photographic plates within each publication. Take this small passage from the *Transactions* of the same year, "Arctic Tern there were many opportunities for observing the parent bird at close quarters. By the courtesy of Mr. Nash we are able to reproduce photographs of a nest of each of these species taken by him on Blakeney Point this year." Taxidermy had perhaps achieved its apotheosis. In his biography of the naturalist Maurice Bird, James Parry reveals an undated entry in Bird's diary for April 1907, "Undated clipping of an NNNS event at Castle Museum in Norwich, recounting how Arthur Patterson had "exhibited a series of lantern slides of bird-life, taken by Dr Heatherley, and alluding to the growing interest shown in photographing wild birds in their native haunts, stating that it had not only given a sport to observation, but was tending to the protection of many rare species. The shooting of a rare bird with a camera is becoming quite as fashionable as knocking it over with a fowling-piece." Parry continues, "Times were changing, as this newspaper excerpt makes clear. The advent of photography as a means of recording birds—and 'proving' their occurrence—was ushering in new ideas and attitudes."[87] Richard Kearton (1862-1928) and his brother Cherry (1871-1940) were leading exponents of the new discipline of wildlife photography.[88]

William White's *History, Gazetteer and Directory of Norfolk*, cites thirteen bird and animal preservers working in the county in 1883. The same directory lists just five in its 1922 edition. It appears that most naturalists did not mourn the days when collecting was at its peak, indeed, many had for years been calling for changes to be made. In 1925, B.B. Riviere describes Henry Pashley winning five prizes for taxidermy, "in the days when many more collections of cased and mounted birds were made than is the case today—a change which few perhaps will regret"[89] Michael Seago writes, "When Henry Pashley died it was the close of a way of life. The heyday of the collectors had ended. Effective wild bird protection legislation meant the cessation of indiscriminate shooting of exotics. Taxidermy declined. Bird-watching became fashionable."[90] Arthur Patterson shows the marked difference in pricing between Overend's sale of uncased local birds on 16 June 1876 and a sale of mostly cased birds in 1885. For instance a spoonbill specimen from the first sale fetched £1 and 6s. A pair of cased spoonbills realised £10 10s nine years later. 180 uncased specimens were disposed of in the first sale. By 1930, however, Patterson maintains that private collections were being sold for next to nothing, "on the death of their owners dispersal ensued in most cases and interest died with them. In some cases they hardly covered the expenses of cartage to the sale-room."[91]

Punt guns had allowed large-scale killing from a single burst. In the winter of 1889 Henry Pashley stated, "in three shots with a small punt-gun, a gunner at Blakeney got: 1st shot 120 Knot, 2nd shot 8 Sheld-Drake, 3rd shot 27 Brent Geese."[92] Those days were also coming to an end. However, the use of the punt-gun did not stop straight away. H.S. Davenport, in his essay, 'Protection of British Birds' (1901), gives a picture of the changing circumstances on Breydon Water and its environs:

> On the 1st of March, 1901, died "Lucky" John Thomas, better known amongst the fraternity of local sportsmen as "Pintail," the last of a long line of Breydon wild-fowlers, and the third bearing that Christian name. How many predecessors in the family of similar occupation there were it is impossible to say, but certain it is that he was the last of his race, and it may also be said that with his demise passes into oblivion the last of the professional punt-gunners who have, like Othello, found their occupation gone, for what the drainage of the surrounding lowlands, the "growing up" of Breydon, the increased traffic, and other altered conditions did not effect, the Close Season and the Bird Protection Acts have effectually accomplished. It must be remembered that prior to protection being afforded to the spring migrants, shooting went on all the year round, and many of our rarest birds were obtained at a season, to take advantage of which to-day would be judged a misdemeanour. What a number of Spoonbills might, even of late years, have been slain but for protection! So it will be seen that even with the enhanced value of rare specimens, it is impossible to gain a livelihood to-day with punt and

shoulder-gun. Yet an occasional hard winter makes shooting profitable while the severity of the weather lasts, and something like the old times reminds us of those palmy days of wild-fowling, and the poulterer's stalls again creak with the weight of the slain. There are still a few punt-guns, but these are used more for pleasure than for profit.[93]

Billy Bishop states that the expert wildfowlers worked the coast at Cley until the 1930s. There were at least fifty punt-gunners still operating on the north Norfolk coast up until that time. Some wildfowlers made the crafts themselves. Some of the punts were less than safe and sat poorly in the water and not particularly adapted to the recoil of a muzzle-loaded 4-bore weighing over 125lb, especially as there was often only ten-inches between man and water.

Christopher Stoate states, "By the First World War fashions as well as attitudes had changed. Increased motorised transport and other social changes demanded less elaborate and more practical headgear and the demand for stuffed birds for hats rapidly diminished. All kinds of traditions, social and political had been superseded as a result of the War. Displays of exotic birds in the home became unfashionable as new contemporary designs favoured clear cut lines over cluttered interiors. However, the demand for native animals and interest in British rarities persisted in some traditional quarters."[94] The interbellum years were still an age of enchantment to many people. Traditional tastes for those that could afford it took a long while to change. However, life after World War One reflected a country that was riven and socially ill at ease, forever changed by war. There was certainly no sudden cut-off point when the popularity for casing up new specimens ceased. Established taxidermy firms that continued to trade after the First World War were even aiming to restock their shelves. The well-known Scottish firm, H.M. Murray & Son of Carnforth (1872–1961) wrote to Henry Pashley requesting bird skins and stuffed specimens. The letter is dated 21 July 1918:[95]

Dear Sir,

Excuse the liberty I am taking but I was at my old friend [ ] at
Birmingham a week ago. He recommended to write to you. He said you
had a quantity of bird skins and stuffed specimens and that you would
be pleased to sell me some if you had any I wanted and he thought the
prices would be right. I would be glad to hear what you have either
in British specimens or from the Continent representing our British
species. I am not particular about specimens being [ ] taken in England.

    Waiting your kind reply
    Yours Faithfully,
    H. Murray & Son

The Norfolk Wild Bird Protection Societies and a Positive Future

At the start of the Edwardian era the Norfolk naturalists were beginning to notice that their efforts were having a positive effect. In 1903 Thomas Southwell wrote:

> Those who have read in the *Birds of Norfolk* the sad story of the persecution suffered by the shore-breeding birds on the Norfolk Coast, even so late as the year 1890, and regretted the rapid process of extermination which then seemed to threaten these interesting visitors, will rejoice in the beneficent change which has been brought about by the strict enforcement of the enactments for the protection of Wild Birds. Certain species, such as the Bittern, Black Tern, Godwit, Avocet, and Ruff were lost to us beyond recall, and the Common and Lesser Terns, with the Great Crested Grebe and Shelduck, were rapidly following; but now, happily, all the latter are as steadily increasing in numbers, and even the Bearded Tit is more than holding its own, whilst the former long death roll of slaughtered passing summer migrants is annually replaced by a list of rare species observed. It is no longer needful to speak with bated breath of the precise nesting resorts of the gregarious shore-breeding birds.[96]

One of the most important objectives set out by the Norfolk and Norwich Naturalists' Society was maintaining the breeding habitats of birds extending along Norfolk's coastline of dunes and salt marsh. By the turn of the 20th century the creation of local societies and the posting of wardens helped a great deal to protect breeding sites and secure the well-known collecting areas in the county. Areas set out by local councils as 'protected' needed policing and by people knowledgeable in the field. As Martin George states, "In his report, published in 1919, the Montague Committee[97] observed that, 'as long as the law remains as varied and difficult to understand as at present, it can hardly be expected to secure any satisfactory degree of observance,' it went on to note that the police, 'labour under certain grave disadvantages: the average constable has no great knowledge of birds, and would probably not know a protected species when he saw it.'"[98] A closed shooting season and protection by law were no hindrance to some of the sportsmen, collectors and the so-called oologists who saw it as their right to carry on with their practices. Other methods were employed to capture birds when the noise of a shotgun might attract the attention of the wardens. In January 1903, The *Illustrated London News* printed full-page steel engravings depicting bird-snarers at work under the title, 'The violation of the Wild Birds Protection Act.' Snaring was a familiar method of trapping long before the Protection Acts were in place. Christopher Frost states that Arthur Patterson often referred to the activities of a group of bird catchers who used snares and clap nets on the dunes north of Yarmouth to catch migrant birds for the London market.

Wild Birds' Protection Societies in Norfolk were set up next to the Sandringham Estate at Wolferton, Blakeney and Cley, Wells and Breydon. Thomas Southwell reveals the important place the Societies have in the history of conservation in Norfolk:

> The societies sought funds to employ 'watchers' during the nesting season … and the excellent results of the Society's operations may be judged from the fact that the usual spring "trips" of land Dotterels, Whimbrels, two Black-winged Stilts, Spoonbills and Avocets, with many other less rare birds, have passed on their way unmolested, and the watcher has made notes of all the more noteworthy migrants. The benefits conferred by these inadequately supported Societies can hardly be too highly estimated; so far as Norfolk is concerned the supply of material for the hateful plume trade is effectually cut off, at least, during the breeding season when the birds are most easily obtained. The interest evinced by the King in their protection, added to the gracious letter to the Royal Society for the Protection of Birds from the Queen, whose kindness and humanity to all living creatures is so well known, may at length have the effect of emphasising the disgust long felt by all right-minded people at the horrid displays of mutilated birds, which are supposed to add to the attractiveness of feminine adornment.—T. S.[99]

Southwell's attitude towards the 'plume hunters' is clear. Arthur Patterson wrote an angry piece about killing birds for feathers, entitled 'A Protest by a Masculine Naturalist, The Goura Mount' (published in *Croydon: Society for the Protection of Birds* in 1906). Goura refers to Victoria-crowned Pigeon. He writes, "Oh! That the women of England would pity the poor birds, and eschew feathers and crests and aigrettes."[100] The Society for the Protection of Birds (later to become the RSPB) was founded in 1891 by Eliza Phillips, Etta Lemon, Catherine Hall and Hannah Poland. They campaigned against the use of feathers in fashion and killing game birds for sport. It was established in response to the dissatisfaction over the 1872 Bird Protection Act. The society gained its Royal Charter in 1904. In 1913, following pressure from the RSPB, the Home Office set up an enquiry into the legislation relating to bird protection. Despite various amendments in the intervening years a comprehensive Bill was not passed until 1954, its late realization no doubt due to the passing of two world wars.

WOLFERTON WILD BIRDS' PROTECTION SOCIETY.

The Wolferton Wild Birds' Protection Society was set up by Colonel George Cresswell (1852-1926), in 1905. His son Francis followed in his father's footsteps, serving in the Norfolk Regiment. He died at Mons in 1914, one of the earliest casualties of the war. George Creswell also became the Honourable Secretary of the Norfolk and Norwich Naturalists' Society. The land protected was next to the Sandringham Estate and comprised the nesting-ground, a flat shingle area on the edge of the Wash, at the back of which were reclaimed marshes with the higher grounds of Sandringham further inland. The Society secured the active co-operation of His Majesty the King as a subscribing member. Cresswell writes in 1903, "(Patron) His Majesty [Edward VII] took a personal interest in the matter, as the protected breeding ground is on the shore of the Wash abutting on the Sandringham Estate. We put on a watcher during the nesting season, from the middle of April to the middle of July ... Perhaps the most noticeable increase of all is in the Ringed Plover, which, owing to protection, is now becoming numerous and nests freely. Many more ducks nested on the ground protected by the Society than have ever done before. These comprised Wild Duck, Teal, Shoveller, and Shelduck, and I am glad to be able to report that a Gadwall nested for the first time. Owing to the exertions of the watcher (W. Pooley) very few of the early Green Plover and Ringed Plovers' eggs were carried off by Grey Crows this year."[101] The Royal patronage increased when H.R.H. the Prince of Wales became Vice-Patron. Cresswell states:

> The season of 1906 has been the best yet recorded; all the birds showing a marked increase. The Common Terns have nested in large numbers, and the colony of Lesser Terns has largely increased. These beautiful birds being in much greater numbers than heretofore. The Ring Dotterels have not only increased in numbers on the protected ground, but have spread to other parts. The Sheld-ducks have increased in number, and Wild Ducks, and Shovellers have also nested in numbers. When we compare this state of things with the melancholy account of the devastation to which the two species of Terns and the Sheld-duck were formerly subjected in this district as set forth in the 'Birds of Norfolk,' one cannot but rejoice at the rescue of these beautiful birds from the destruction then impending.[102]

With royal funding and a secure hut for the watcher, the Wolferton Wild Birds' Protection Society was a great success (in 1921 it was the only one of the Societies that showed a credit balance in its accounts). By 1921 the area protected little terns, common terns, ringed plovers, shelduck, bitterns (at least ten pairs 'hatched-off' in 1920), ruffs and reeves, bearded tits, great-crested grebes and lapwing. Six pairs of Montagu's harriers reared their young, two pairs of marsh harriers were present and two pairs of short-eared owls nested in the area. As Sydney Long had it, "The fruits of the rigid protection to which this district has been subjected during the past few years are now becoming apparent."

Blakeney and Cley Wild Birds' Protection Society

In the early spring of 1901 the Blakeney and Cley Wild Birds' Protection Society was formed. Lord Calthorpe, the principal owner of the fore-shore, was the chief supporter of the Society. Major Quintin Gurney was appointed the honorary secretary and treasurer. Mr. R. J. (Bob) Pinchen was engaged as the watcher on the Point during the breeding season. His first report, issued at the end of 1901, mentioned that there were about 140 nests of the common tern and about

60 of the little tern. There were also nests of the ringed plover, redshank and shelduck. The number of terns' nests trebled or quadrupled, and since 1906 a pair of oystercatchers was seen nesting there regularly, while other species also benefited. Up to the year 1900, no provision existed for the protection of nests. On two occasions the Society successfully instituted proceedings for taking eggs, and on a third occasion a man was prosecuted for shooting a tern out of season. *Transactions* for 1906 reveals, "Mr. Quinton E. Gurney reports that the season of 1906 was on the whole a very satisfactory one, notwithstanding spells of very unfavourable weather. The Terns' nests, especially those of the lesser tern, again increased, not only in number but in the extent of ground they covered."[103] In 1907, Thomas Southwell reported, "It was found necessary to institute one prosecution, which fell heavily on the scanty funds of the Society, resulting in leaving a balance due to the Treasurer; [104] but it is interesting to learn that two of the Oyster-catcher's eggs which had been stolen, but recovered by the watcher, duly hatched off." Blakeney Point was acquired from Lord Calthorpe's trustees by Charles Rothschild in 1912 as a result of the efforts of Professor F.W. Oliver of the University College London, who led a public appeal for its purchase. In the same year, the Point was handed over to the National Trust.

There was relief for the bird populations in Cley during the First World War as Henry Pashley reveals in his diary for 1914:

> The notes for this year are very scanty, as from August until the war ended the whole of the shooting ground, beach, marshes and estuary, was occupied by the Military. No one was allowed on the beach, not even children, and no person carrying a gun was allowed anywhere. The officers had the shooting all to themselves. A few officers were good shots, but the majority "couldn't hit a hayrick." It was not until sometime after the Armistice that anyone was allowed to shoot, but a few individuals were granted permits now and again from the C.O. The first six months were not very prolific. There were very few wild-fowl, but a few birds out of the ordinary were taken. [105]

Pashley was concerned about the fate of the marshes at Cley and Salthouse. He wrote to Adeline Marie Russell, Duchess of Bedford, expressing his views. The Duchess visited him on occasion and Pashley greatly respected her knowledge of birds and love of the landscape on the Norfolk coast. In his diary entry for 3 September 1919 he writes, "Her Grace the Duchess of Bedford has taken Wiveton Hall for two months. Her Grace called on me several times and we had several 'birdy' talks. I found Her Grace to be one of the keenest observers I have ever met."[106] It was Pashley's wish that the area could be protected as a sanctuary under the aegis of the Duchess. She wrote to him from her home at Woburn Abbey on 8 October 1919:

> Thank you for writing to me about the Salthouse Marsh. I am making

enquires as to whether the Council would entertain the idea of letting it in its present condition with a view to it being preserved as a sanctuary.

I am afraid however, there is very little chance of their doing so, as I believe the keeping in repair of the sea wall is a very expensive business and I could not undertake to be responsible for this. Any very high sea might break it down altogether and the expense would probably be enormous.

I think too that there would be an outcry nowadays if one attempted to keep out possible cultivation. I am sorry as it would be a great loss to your part of the world if it were drained and indeed to England generally as few such places are left for birds.

I am hoping to get back to you again in a week next Saturday and shall come and see you. I wonder whether there has been much migration since I left.

Yours Faith—[107]

On 23 October the Duchess wrote to Pashley to tell him that the council had accepted her offer of shooting rights over Salthouse marshes and if he knew of "a little house" that she could stay in for a few days at a time. The missive also requested if Pashley could buy "two pretty postcards of Cley and Blakeney for her notebook." The shooting rights ran into complications regarding exactly what area would be under her aegis. Various other missives continued, including her praise for "the genius" of Arthur Patterson. The Duchess died of a heart attack six months later in April 1920, six years before Dr Sydney Long played an important role in the acquisition of the land which now comprises the Cley and Salthouse reserve. Long founded the Norfolk Naturalists' Trust (now the Norfolk Wildlife Trust).

After the First World War tern populations increased on the North Norfolk coast. In 1920 a few common terns (about twenty pairs), nested

Dr Sydney H. Long. Honorary secretary of the Norfolk and Norwich Naturalists' Society for 24 years and its president in 1907-8. Long was a pioneering conservationist, responsible for the creation of the country's earliest nature reserves on the North Norfolk Coast.

Image courtesy of the Norfolk County Council Library and Information Service at www.picture.norfolk.gov.uk.

on Salthouse Broad, and although the nests and young suffered considerable molestation at the hands of boys and others, the birds returned to breed in considerably increased numbers in 1921. That year, on one of the islands, (presumably Scolt Head), it was estimated that there were from 500 to 600 nests of the common tern. In 1913 the Society issued permits to those that wished to shoot birds for food, a traditional activity they saw going back to time immemorial. In order to keep track of shooting, permits were issued in the 'open season.' The Society concluded, "This system makes it possible to locate any misdemeanour and, if necessary, to refuse access in serious cases in future years. It will also be possible from time to time, on expert advice, to schedule such species of birds as it is desired to protect completely. The system of permits has been generally taken up—seventy-two having been issued up to the end of the year."[108]

Author's father (right) recording terns on Blakeney Point, North Norfolk, late 1960s
Author.

The Wild Birds' Protections Committee overseeing Blakeney and Cley sought to extend its field of operations. There were calls to have an additional warden on Scolt Head Island. Members of the Norfolk and Norwich Naturalists' Society visited Bob Pinchen on Blakeney Point in the summer of 1920 (Pinchen's position as watcher was by now all year round. He held the post until he retired in 1930). Their report states, "On Blakeney Point, as those of our members who visited this reserve on May 29 will know, there is a strong and flourishing colony of Common and Little Terns with an increasing number of Sheld-ducks. It is interesting to note that Sandwich and Roseate Terns are also making an attempt to colonise on this area, where two nests of each species with eggs were found this year. We visited the Point on August 28, when there were still 200–300 Terns in residence. Amongst these we were able to identify a number of Sandwich Terns and a few Roseate Terns. There were also a few quite young chicks on the nesting ground."[109]

In 1923 the Committee provided 'a watcher' on Scolt Head, "We have set an example this year to other bird protection societies by appointing to this post one of the best-known bird photographers, Miss E.L. Turner. We hold the opinion that the post of watcher on such a highly interesting and undeveloped area as is Scolt Head Island should be held, if possible, by an educated, scientifically-trained naturalist, and in the person of Miss Turner we have such a one."[110] Dr. Sydney Long explains Turner's accommodation, "The hut erected on this island last year has been furnished out of the "Scolt Head Fund," raised by Mr. R. J. Colman, and has been occupied during the past nesting season by Miss E. L. Turner, who offered her services as watcher. It may now be described as a well-found, water-tight hut, with sleeping accommodation for four people, and commanding from the plateau on Scolt Head, on which it stands, one of the most glorious views to be obtained in Norfolk. Although egg-collecting on the island has for long been looked upon as one of the local "industries," it is the more satisfactory to be able to report that during the past season no attempt has been made to molest the breeding birds or their eggs. Signed (on behalf of the Norfolk W.B.P. Committee), Sydney H. Long, Hon. Sec."[111]

Emma Louise Turner (1867–1940) was an ornithologist and pioneering bird photographer. Like many naturalists, Turner was drawn to the Norfolk coast and spent part of each year in Norfolk. In 1911 her photograph of a nesting bittern was the first evidence of the species breeding in the country since the latter part of the 19th century. Turner volunteered for the role as "protector of the Tern colonies." At the age of 57 she lived on the island in the hut which had no electricity or running water. She wrote a book about her experiences entitled, *Birdwatching on Scolt Head*. Scolt Head itself has remained of great interest to botanists and ornithologists. The island is famous for its ternery at the western end, especially breeding colonies of common and sandwich terns. Scolt Head was acquired in 1923 through the efforts of Dr Long and Professor Oliver. The extreme eastern edge of the island was retained by the owner Lord Leicester. The island was bought by public subscription on behalf of the Norfolk and Norwich Naturalists' Society and was handed over to the National Trust. J.P. Morley and Hilary Allison state, "With foresight remarkable for the period, Professor Oliver and Dr. Long worked between 1910 and 1925 to secure first Blakeney Point and then Scolt Head Island into the care of the National Trust, thus protecting these two areas in perpetuity for scientific study and public enjoyment. In 1926, Dr Long, who was born in 1870 at Wells-next-Sea, founded the Norfolk Naturalists' Trust with the acquisition of Cley Marshes as its first nature reserve … Many others have helped to protect Blakeney Point and Scolt Head Island including local fishermen, wildfowlers, common right holders, members of harbour committees and villagers at Brancaster Staithe, Overy Staithe, Stiffkey, Morston and Blakeney. Without their support the conservation of these areas would have presented greater difficulties."[112]

By 1925 it appears that many species, once depleted in number, were increasing in the Cley region. In describing Henry Pashley's notes and diary, B.B. Riviere states:

> In this diary, again, representing as it does a continuous ornithological record for one locality over a period of some forty years, there will be found evidence of considerable changes in the status of various birds during this time, which are of very great interest, and it is gratifying to find that in so many cases this change has been in the nature of an increase. To give but a few instances: The Shorelark and Lapland Bunting, which in the [eighteen] sixties and eighties respectfully were regarded as very great rarities, are now regular winter visitors to Cley, the former in considerable numbers. The Black-tailed Godwit, no specimen of which appears to have found its way into Pashley's shop until the year 1917, has since then occurred regularly as an autumn, and occasional spring, migrant; whilst the Sandwich Tern, a rare passer-by of the eighties, now breeds in hundreds, almost within sight of Pashley's windows.[113]

WELLS WILD BIRDS' PROTECTION SOCIETY

A report in *Transactions* from 1906 reveals, "The return of the Black-headed Gulls to their old grounds is most interesting, they are nesting in the very piece of marsh which is known as 'Mow Creek' by the old Wells gunners [c.f. *Birds of Norfolk*, vol. iii. p. 331), after having been dislodged as a breeding species for nearly 70 years."[114] The Wells Wild Birds' Protection Society was formed in 1888 by Charles Annesley Hamond (1856-1914) and Colonel Henry Wemyss Feilden (1838-1921) and greatly supported by Lord Leicester, who was applauded for his 'sanctuary' at Holkham Mere, "where Lord Leicester has for many years refused to allow a shot to be fired, it is a concrete instance of the success attained by protecting given area of sea-water and birds unmolested," an article in *Norwich Mercury* in 1896 reported.[115] Charles Annesley Hamond lived at Twyford Hall, East Dereham and was a botanist and ornithologist. Feilden was a British Army officer, Arctic explorer and naturalist. After an illustrious career he settled in Wells in 1880 where he lived for over twenty years before moving to Sussex. He became President of the Norfolk and Norwich Naturalists' Society in 1885. The Wells Wild Birds' Protection Society oversaw the large ternery at Wells [116] and sufficient funds bore the expense of a watcher on this section of the coast. The watcher continued in his post until a year or so before his death (in 1914), when the protection of the birds was taken over by the Holkham Estate. *Transactions* for 1920 reveals, "The present watcher is Tom Cringle, who reports that the birds have had a good season ... the Black-headed Gulls, which until recently confined their nesting sites to the neighbourhood of the Mow Creek, have this year nested all over the marshes as far as Stiffkey Marsh." Cringle laments that many eggs at Wells are "robbed by boys and others."[117]

BREYDON WILD BIRDS' PROTECTION SOCIETY

In 1888 the Breydon Wild Birds' Protection Society was formed with the object of stopping the indiscriminate shooting of the rare birds known to visit this tidal estuary during the summer months. *Transactions* for 1901 mentions the Caspian Tern, "Mr. Patterson, on more than one occasion on July 21st and 22nd 1901, watched one of these birds fishing on Breydon. It passed on, thanks to the Wild-birds protection. Another was seen on 24th July, 1902."[118] *Transactions* for 1906 reported on the progress of the Breydon Wild Birds Protection Society, "Mr. Henry P. Frederick, the Hon. Sec. is to be congratulated upon having sufficient funds to enable him to employ a watcher on Breydon during the whole of the close time, and the Society has done excellent work in securing the safety of many rare birds which visited that favourite resort during the summer of 1906; it is quite refreshing to read of the rare birds seen instead of SHOT, and as the watcher is a very experienced man, there is no doubt as to the accuracy of his identification of the various species ... seeing that the whole area of the Broads is a " protected District," there is still hope that if perfectly undisturbed, Mr. Hamond's anticipation maybe realised and that like the Black-headed Gulls at "Mow Creek," they may once more return to their former nesting sites. The above are some of the more important entries in the watcher's diary, and it may be taken for granted that the safety of all these birds, so far as Breydon was concerned, was due to the presence of the Society's watcher."[119] Breydon was perhaps the most difficult area to secure. Arthur Patterson states, " ... it is for its bird life that Breydon is chiefly famous, for there is not another spot of its size in the British Isles where a large variety of birds has been seen or so many rare species have been taken."[120] This is certainly born-out by the large numbers of birds shot on Breydon and in Broadland in general that now exist in the Lysaght Collection in Birmingham. The watcher, George Jary, was on duty, living in the Society's house-boat on Breydon Water, from the middle of March to the end of August, "His presence undoubtedly acts as a deterrent to the indiscriminate shooting that formerly took place on this tidal estuary during the closed season." [121] Arthur Patterson states that the first watcher employed was 'Ducker' Chambers in 1880, "He met with a very hostile reception, because the Close Season was to affect Breydon, and the crowd that then carried guns afloat, or onshore. Not that he cared, for he had been a noted boxer, of big bodily build, he was bluff and a little boisterous, and not by any means officious ... But just think what a task it was to police the whole area of many hundreds of acres of mudflats and crinkling drains."[122] Patterson describes how some of the wildfowlers would ply Ducker with beer at the Cobham Tavern. It appears he didn't need much persuading being a "very droughty old fellow." Leaving the watcher in a drowsy state the gunners would conduct a bit of illicit shooting, "effecting a remunerative sale from rival stuffers and collectors ... Bird-folks who were egg collectors, dealers in birds and eggs and collectors, were always on the alert and were not unlike competitive "bookies" at the racecourse that did their best to outwit anybody else."[123] Patterson writes about his experiences with George Jary in *Wildlife on a Norfolk Estuary* (1907), "There is not a gunner afloat today," Patterson said, "Jary the watchman is Jary the *preventative* man, as with a policeman, it is not so much for the crimes he detects as for the infringements of the law he prevents that he is employed here."[124]

In 1906 it was reported to George Cresswell, "I am informed that not a gun was fired on Breydon during the close season, notwithstanding the visits of many rare birds."[125] However, in the Badlands of Breydon, there were still gunners who broke the law, even in the 1920s as this report reveals, "George Jary is the watcher, a position he has held for twenty years. He is familiar with the different species of birds that visit this estuary and has a knowledge of most of the local gunners. He was on duty for five months, from the beginning of April to the end of August, living in the Society's houseboat moored in the Ship-Drain. It was necessary to renew the boat this year, as the old boat (second-hand when purchased twenty years ago), could no longer be rendered watertight … It was reported to the Secretary that indiscriminate shooting from the walls of Breydon had been going on during the month of August, especially in the early morning on Sundays. It is therefore satisfactory to record that at the Great Yarmouth police-court on September 11th the Society successfully prosecuted one of these gunners for shooting a Ringed Plover on Sunday, August 27th." The Society fully accepted that it was very difficult on a wide area like Breydon to "get in touch' with these law-breakers." Arthur Patterson knew George Jary well. He was known as "Newcome" and appointed watcher in the Spring of 1900, his reception being a mixture of jeers and insults. Patterson spent a fortnight with Jary on his houseboat, The Pickletub, describing his experiences in a series of articles in the *Norwich Mercury*. When Jary died in 1934, Patterson wrote about him in the *Eastern Daily Press*. He described him as altogether more alert than his predecessor, "the sly visits of the more daring defiers of the law ceased … He had on two or three occasion fallen overboard. He could not swim, so he rolled over, and floated on the tide until some observer came to help him … Jary's deafness had greatly spoiled his later life; and he developed into insanity. He ended his days in the Fisherman's Hospital, just off Yarmouth market place."[126]

By the 1930s the employment of wardens to protect birds was being questioned but not without reservation. This passage from the *Transactions* of 1933 reveals, "For many years the committee has put a watcher in its houseboat on Breydon Water during the summer months with the object of preventing the shooting of rare visitors during the closed season. On the other hand, the demand for stuffed specimens has now practically died out, and in view of the expense of maintaining such a watcher and the increased expenditure that has arisen for providing watchers on other parts of the coast-line of Norfolk which are important nesting areas, the question of continuing the Breydon watcher will have to be carefully considered by the committee before next year. It is hoped that an increase in the subscription list will allow the Committee not to make this change."[127]

Arthur Patterson wrote in 1930, "Competitive methods of obtaining rare specimens (methods not always worthy of commendation) made for exultation, chagrin, or disappointment among rival collector. To-day very few in East Anglia, and I am bold to say in the country, pile up cases of glass-eyed birds; these are not now fashionable. But these private collections had quite a halo of romance and of reminiscences attached to them that even the non-collector shared in, whilst scribbling bird-folk made these household museums, or mausoleums, historic."[128] Modern collectors have been replaced by a phalanx of birdwatching 'twitchers,' equally keen to tick off the next rarity.

Notes

1. Lord Walsingham, Lord and B.T. Payne-Gallwey, *Shooting: Moor and Marsh*, (London, The Badminton Library, Logmans, Green & Co., 1889), p. 327.
2. B. Cornford, *Past Water Levels in Broadland*, Norfolk Research Committee Bulletin, No. 28, September 1982, pp. 15-16.
3. Rev. Richard Lubbock, (1845) *Observations on the Fauna of Norfolk and more particularly on the District of the Broads*, 1845, (Norwich, Jarrold & Sons, 1879), Introduction by Thomas Southwell, p. iii.
4. *Transactions*, Norfolk and Norwich Naturalists' Society, (Norwich, A.E. Soman & Co., 1921), p. (?).
5. B. Bishop, *Cley Marsh and its Birds*, (Woodbridge, The Boydell Press, 1983), p. 31.
6. W.A. Dutt, *The Norfolk Broads*, (London, Macmillan, 1906), p. 257.
7. A footnote written by Thomas Southwell in Richard Lubbock's *Observations on the Fauna of Norfolk* reveals a rare instance of recording birds in the mid-19th century, in this case the woodcock, by means of photography. Southwell states, "So tame has this bird been known to become when incubating, that Mr. Gurney Buxton was able to photograph one on her nest near Cromer in 1859. In 1868, Mr. John Gurney succeeded in photographing another at Bixley, near Norwich. Both birds eventually brought off their young." (p. 113, footnote).
8. Ibid. 3, p. v.
9. Benjamin Thompson Lowne, *A Popular Natural History of Great Yarmouth and its Neighbourhood*, (London, George Hall, King's Street, 1863).
10. H. Stevenson, *Transactions* (1880), 'The Abundance of Domatorhine and smaller Skuas on the Norfolk Coast in October and November 1879,' (Norwich, Fletcher and Son, 1879), p. 103-4.
11. *Transactions* for 1875-76 includes correspondence between Robert Marsham of Stratton Strawless, Fellow of the Royal Society, and Reverend Gilbert White of Selbourne, Fellow of Oriel College Oxford and author of *The Natural History of Selbourne*.
12. T. Southwell, 'Pt. 1, Mammalia and Reptilia, '*Transactions*, Norfolk & Norwich Naturalists' Society, (Norwich, Fletcher and Son, 1871), p. 72.
13. Shelduck.
14. Sir Thomas Browne, doctor, polymath, naturalist, philosopher and writer.
15. T. Southwell, 'On the Ornithological Archaeology of Norfolk, '*Transactions*, Norfolk

and Norwich Naturalist's Society, (Norwich, Fletcher and Son, 1870), p. 22-23.
16. Ibid. 3. ix.
17. M. George, *Birds in Norfolk and the Law, Past and Present*. Occasional publication No. 6. Norfolk and Norwich Naturalist's Society, (Lavenham, Lavenham Press, 2000), pp. 12-3.
18. C. Frost, *A History of British Taxidermy*, (Lavenham, The Lavenham Press, 1987), p. 8.
19. Ibid. 17, p. 13.
20. 10 taken, 1 to 2 July, 1889.
21. H.N. Pashley, *Notes on the Birds of Cley, Norfolk*, 1925, (Lavenham, Lavenham Press, 1992), p. 18.
22. H. Stevenson, *The Birds of Norfolk, Remarks on their habits, migration and local Distribution*, Vol I, (London, John Van Horst, 1866), p. 391.
23. *Eastern Daily Press*, 26 June 1896.
24. *Eastern Daily Press*, 26 February 1892.
25. Arthur Patterson, *Notes of an East Coast Naturalist*, (London, Methuen & Co, 1904), p. 45.
26. Ibid. 22.
27. H. Stevenson, *The Birds of Norfolk, Remarks on their habits, migration and local Distribution*, Vol II, (London, John Van Horst, 1866), p. vii.
28. *Transactions*, Norfolk and Norwich Naturalists' Society, (Norwich, Fletcher and Son, 1890), p. 198.
29. Thomas Littleton Powys, 4th Baron Lilford (1883-1896), one of the eight founders of the British Ornithologists' Union in 1858, avid naturalist and collector of taxidermy, was responsible for the introduction of the little owl into England in the 1880s. Christopher Frost states that it was Charles Waterton, the well-known naturalist who first attempted to introduce the species to Britain, releasing five birds, acquired in Italy, in the grounds of his Yorkshire home in 1843 (Frost, 1989, *The Ogilvie Bird Collection*, p. 27). Pat Morris (*Transactions*, 1988) states that Walter Lowne preserved his first little owl in 1900. Morris states that the reason for this was that it was recently introduced species (introduced to Norfolk c.1910). One wonders whether its rarity remained due to persecution only gradually curtailed by successive Protection Acts and their various amendments by 'Orders of the Secretary of State.' By the 1920s the bird had increased in number. (I regularly see little owls in Breckland, for instance at Castle Acre Priory). Henry Pashley states, "Becoming very common here. I believe it has bred at Kelling: in June 1910 I received a very young bird and a brooding female. Now (1924) very plentiful in North Norfolk." In 1922, B.B. Riviere said that the little owl was in almost every instance harmless to game. Between January 1913 and December 1916, 40 little owls passed through the hands of T.E. Gunn. Every one contained the remains of beetles, not one contained any 'game.' The Dor Beetle seems to be the staple and favourite food of the bird. (*Birds of Norfolk*, p. 257). Other naturalists were not so enthusiastic about the owl. F.M. Ogilvie held strong views about introducing non-indigenous species. He had thirty-five skins of the little owl but did not have any of them set up by a taxidermist as he saw the owl as an unwelcome addition to the British Isles List, " ... courageous and bold, even to the point of impudence, and, in addition, exceedingly prolific ... increasing very rapidly in many parts of England, and likely to prove exceedingly harmful."
30. B.B. Riviere, *Ornithological Notes from Norfolk. Annual Report*, 1922, p.257.
31. T. Southwell, *Transactions*, Norfolk and Norwich Naturalists' Society, (Norwich, A.E.

The Wild Bird Protection Acts

Soman & Co, 1871).
32. W.E. Collinge, 'An Investigation of the food of Terns on Blakeney Point,' *Transactions*, (Norwich, A.E. Soman & Co, 1924), p. 46.
33. Ibid. 5, pp. 29-30.
34. *Eastern Daily Press*, 26 June 1896.
35. Ibid. 21, p. 10.
36. B. Tooley, 'Introduction,' *Scribblings of a Yarmouth Naturalist. An edited selection from the Writings of Arthur Henry Patterson, A.L.S., (John Knowlittle)*, (self-published, 2004), pp. 33-4.
37. Ibid. 25, vii.
38. T. Southwell, 'On the Ornithological Archaeology of Norfolk,' *Transactions*. The Norfolk and Norwich Naturalists' Society, (Norwich, Fletcher and Son, 1870-71, p.22.
39. Ibid. 17, p.13.
40. J.R.V Marchant and W. Watkins, W (1897), *Wild Birds Protection Acts 1880-1896*, (London, R.H. Porter, 1897, reprinted by Forgotten Books, F.B. & c. Ltd), p. 43.
41. *Eastern Daily Press*, 26 February 1892.
42. 16 February 2024, I saw a white-tailed eagle flying over low-lying boggy meadows on in Breckland. I wondered what had sent the greylag geese up! Although an occasional winter visitor to the county, the species is of high conservation concern. The bird that I saw was presumably one of a number of birds originating from the Isle of Wight reintroduction project. The scale of the bird can be appreciated by seeing the Victorian example in the Bird Room at Norwich Castle Museum.
43. Ibid. 21, pp. 113-4.
44. H. Stevenson, 'Memoir of the Late Rev Richard Lubbock. By Henry Stevenson, 1877,' *Transactions*, Norfolk and Norwich Naturalists' Society (Norwich, Fletcher and Son, 1876-77) p. 301.
45. From the Anglo-Saxon, *glida*, to glide.
46. W. Swaysland, *Familiar Wild Birds*, (London, Cassell & Company, 1903), p.279.
47. Ibid. p. 110-1.
48. The expression in modern parlance comes from falconry, when a trained hawk has had its fill and is unwilling to fly.
49. C. Frost, *The Ogilvie Bird Collection*, (Lavenham, The Lavenham Press, 1989), p. 75.
50. A. Newton wrote '*Hawking in Norfolk*' (1879).
51. Ibid. 17, p. 3.
52. T. Browne, *Notes and Letters on the Natural History of Norfolk, more especially on the Birds and Fishes, with notes by Thomas Southwell*, (Norwich, Jarrold & Sons, 1902), p 4.
53. J.H. Gurney, J.H., Transcript of address held at 13th annual meeting, *Transactions*. Norfolk and Norwich Naturalists' Society, (A.E. Soman & Co, 1881), p.274.
54. *Norfolk News*, 3 October 1885.
55. M. Taylor, *Birds of Sheringham*, (North Walsham, Poppyland Press, 1987), p. 21.
56. Ibid. 40, p. 44.
57. A.H. Patterson, *Man and Nature on the Broads*, (London, Thomas Mitchell, 1895), p. 54.
58. *Norwich Mercury*, 18 April 1885.
59. Egg collecting still occurs despite stringent laws. On 3 May 2024 the BBC reported that a man was handed a suspended jail sentence for amassing a collection of almost

3,000 wild birds' eggs. He was caught on camera taking nightjar eggs from a nature reserve near Holt in Norfolk. He had previously served two prison sentences for illegal egg collecting in 2005 and 2018.

60. T. Southwell, 'Remarks on the 'Wild Birds' Protection Act of 1872,' *Transactions, Norfolk and Norwich Naturalists' Society*, (Norwich, Fletcher and Son, 1872-73), p (?).
61. A. Patterson, *Wildlife on a Norfolk Estuary*, (London, Methuen & Co., 1907), p. 247.
62. Billy Bishop states that Stratton Long was the eldest son of the boy that was prosecuted for shooting roseate terns in 1896. When Bishop was writing, Stratton Long was the last punt-gunner left on that area of the Norfolk coast. I presume this is the same Stratton who owned a chandlers in Blakeney and who knew my father. We would visit him on regular occasions for bits of tackle or bait. I remember him having a very wicked sense of humour.
63. Ibid. 21, p. 37.
64. Ibid. 5, p. 14.
65. Ibid. 17, p.14.
66. Many birds were known by different names in Norfolk, which sometimes lead to confusion (or advantage to be had by obfuscation) regarding the Wild Bird Protection Acts: Kentish Plover = Alexander Plover (Breydon gunners), Bullfinch = Bloodruff, Nightingale = Barley bird, Great Tit =Bee Bird, Bittern = Bottle Rump, Long-tailed Tit = Bottle Tom, Shelduck = Burrow Duck (J.H. Gurney), Whinchat = Fuzhacker, Yellow hammer = Guler. Determining classification was a problem for Thomas Browne two hundred years previously when he was writing *Notes and Letters on the Natural History of Norfolk, more especially on the Birds and Fishes*. In his introduction to Browne's work, Thomas Southwell wrote about the pioneering naturalists of the era, "they had to depend on the vague descriptions of fowlers and others; the same bird would probably be known in half a dozen different localities by as many names, and since no satisfactory mode of preserving specimens had then be discovered, examples for comparison were not available." (xv) Browne refers to the great crested grebe as the 'Loone.' Thomas Southwell also brings to our attention Richard Lubbock's writing on terns. He says terns are known on the Broads by the name of 'Dars,' the common tern was 'the Dar,' the lesser the 'Little dar,' and the black tern as the 'Blue Dar.' Waters were muddied further as terns were also known locally as Sea Swallows, Starns and Pearls. (Lubbock, *Observations on the Fauna of Norfolk and more particularly on the District of the Broads*, p. 168, footnote). In the Norfolk and Norwich Naturalists' Society publication, *Maurice Bird. The Gilbert White of the Broads*, the author, James Parry, includes as an appendix a list of local names for birds reproduced from *Broad Norfolk*, published in 1893 by the Norfolk News Company and reprinted from the *Eastern Daily Press*.
67. J.H. Gurney and T. Southwell, 'Fauna and Flora of Norfolk, Part XI, Birds. Section II,' *Transactions*, Norfolk and Norwich Naturalists' Society, (Norwich, Fletcher and Son, 1886), p. 430.
68. Ibid. 40, p. 127-8.
69. Ibid. 6, p. 431.
70. *Norwich Mercury* 29 January 1896.
71. Ibid. 17, p.20.
72. Ibid. 12, p 75.
73. *Transactions*, Norfolk and Norwich Naturalists' Society (Norwich, Fletcher and Son, 1880), p. (?).

74. *Transactions*, Norfolk and Norwich Naturalists' Society, (Norwich, Fletcher and Son, 1879-80), p. 136.
75. Mallard, pochard, shoveler, teal, widgeon, avocet, curlew, dunlin, greenshank, 'godwit,' lapwing, 'phalarope,' 'plover,' redshank, ruff, 'sandpiper,' snipe, whimbrel and woodcock.
76. Ibid. 17, p.15.
77. Ibid. 49, p. 19.
78. Ibid. 18, p. 47.
79. Certain restrictions were placed on fishermen under 'The City of Norwich Act of 1867.'
80. Ibid 6, p. 89.
81. Ibid. N. Everett, 'Wildfowling,' p. 370.
82. *Transactions*, Norfolk and Norwich Naturalists' Society (Norwich, Fletcher and Son, 1883), p. 782.
83. J. Parry, *Maurice Bird. The Gilbert White of the Broads*. Norfolk and Norwich Naturalists' Society, (Norwich, Lavenham Press, 2024), p. 87. N.B. A. Nudd refers to Alfred Nudd (1858-1937), 'marshman,' gamekeeper and companion of Bird.
84. Ibid. p. 95.
85. Ibid. p. 121.
86. P. and M. Clarke, *Where to Watch Birds in East Anglia*, (London, Christopher Helm, 1987), p. 118.
87. Ibid. 83, p. 81. The article was published in the *Eastern Evening News* and *Eastern Daily Press* on 6 May 1907.
88. Ibid. 83, p. 105.
89. Ibid. 21, introduction.
90. M. Seago, 'An Occasional Series on notable Norfolk Naturalists. Henry Nash Pashley.' Published in the *Eastern Daily Press*, 1992.
91. A.H. Patterson, *A Norfolk Naturalist. Observations on Birds, Mammals and Fishes*, London, Methuen & Co., 1930), p. 8.
92. Ibid. 21, p. 20.
93. H.S. Davenport, 'Protection of British Birds,' *Transactions*, Norfolk and Norwich Naturalists' Society, (A. E. Soman & Co, Norwich, 1901).
94. C. Stoate, *Taxidermy. The Revival of a Natural Art*, (London, Sportsman's Press,1987), p. 16.
95. Letters to Pashley concerning birds and taxidermy. MC 3565/2 Norfolk Record Office
96. T. Southwell, 'Wild Bird Protection on the Norfolk Coast,' *Transactions*, Norfolk and Norwich Naturalists' Society, (Norwich, A.E. Soman & Co, 1903), p. 323-5.
97. The Hon Edwin Montagu. The committee of enquiry was set up to address the legislation surrounding bird protection.
98. Ibid. 17, pp. 24-5.
99. Ibid. 96, p. 323-5.
100. Ibid. 36, p. 37.
101. G. Cresswell, *Transactions*, Norfolk and Norwich Naturalists' Society, (Norwich, A.E. Soman & Co, 1906).
102. Ibid.
103. Ibid.

104. The societies suffered with a paucity of funding. For instance, the Wells Society's funds for 1906 were depleted due to the money spent on poisoning rats which were having a devastating effect on nesting gulls. "Thanks to the public-spirited manner in which the Earl of Leicester has taken over the responsibilities of the Wells Wild Birds' Protection Society, several subscribers to this Society have transferred their subscriptions to the Breydon Society. We hope that others will do likewise, and so help to wipe out the deficit which the latter Society had to face at the commencement of this season." (Transactions, 1909).
105. Ibid. 21, p. 80.
106. Ibid. pp. 87-8.
107. 'Letters to H.N. Pashley from the Duchess of Bedford,' 1919. MC 3565/3 Norfolk Record Office
108. Transactions, Norfolk and Norwich Naturalists' Society, (Norwich, A.E. Soman & Co, 1913), p. 13
109. Transactions, Norfolk and Norwich Naturalists' Society, (Norwich, A.E. Soman & Co, 1920).
110. Transactions, Norfolk and Norwich Naturalists' Society, (A.E. Soman & Co, 1923), p. 487-8.
111. Ibid.
112. H. Allison and J. Morley, *Blakeney Point and Scolt Head Island*, (The National Trust, Norfolk, 1989), pp. 9-10.
113. Ibid. 21, p. 8.
114. Transactions, Norfolk and Norwich Naturalists' Society, (Norwich, A.E. Soman & Co. 1906), p. 497.
115. *Norwich Mercury* (from an article in the Spectator, 29 January 1896.
116. In 1956 the Wells Urban District Council voted to adopt the name Wells-next-Sea.
117. Transactions, Norfolk and Norwich Naturalists' Society, (Norwich, A.E. Soman & Co. 1920),
118. Transactions, Norfolk and Norwich Naturalists' Society, (Norwich, A.E. Soman & Co. 1901), p. 738.
119. Transactions, 'Miscellaneous Notes and Observations,' Norfolk and Norwich Naturalists' Society, (Norwich, A.E. Soman & Co, 1906), p. 496.
120. Ibid. 6, p. 263.
121. Transactions, Norfolk and Norwich Naturalists' Society, (Norwich, A.E. Soman & Co. 1923)
122. Ibid. 36, p. 40.
123. Ibid. p. 41.
124. Ibid. 61, p. 177.
125. Transactions, Norfolk and Norwich Naturalists' Society, (Norwich, A.E. Soman & Co. 1906)
126. Ibid. 36, pp. 48-9.
127. Transactions, Norfolk and Norwich Naturalists' Society, (A.E. Soman & Co, 1934). 'Wild Bird Protection in Norfolk.' Norfolk and Norwich Naturalists' Society p. 471-2.
128. Ibid. 91.

Norwich Castle Museum and Modern Interpretation

Any study of East Anglian taxidermy would be incomplete without looking at the collection in Norwich Castle Museum. This is the finest natural history collection to be found in Norfolk and of great importance, both nationally and internationally. Most of the early exhibits were private collections donated by its founders in 1825. The museum appointed its first paid curator the following year. The Bird Gallery was created in 1894 when the castle first opened as a museum and has changed very little since. It contains 318 different specimens of birds.

The museum includes the collections formed by B.B. Riviere, J.H. Gurney (over 400 specimens) and E.C. Arnold. Maurice Bird's collection was also bequeathed to the museum on his death in 1924. Billy Bishop describes his experiences with E.C. Arnold at Cley after he had taken up post of Warden, "The gunner who will always be remembered as the most successful and scientific of the collectors was the late E.C. Arnold. For more than fifty years, he spent every September at Cley and eventually became the owner of an area east of the north end of the East Bank which now bears his name—Arnold's Marsh ... When I first became Warden of Cley, E.C. Arnold used to sit in a boat in the middle of this area and shoot at every uncommon wader that passed."[1]

'Diorama of the North Norfolk Coast; common terns with young.'
Ted Ellis Norfolk Wildlife Room, Norwich Castle Museum & Art Gallery.

J. Wentworth Day vividly praises Norwich Castle Museum in his 1950 book, *Marshland Adventure*, focusing on the six dioramas in The Norfolk Room. Renamed the Ted Ellis Norfolk Room in 1987, "to commemorate all that Ted did for the Museum and Natural History in Norfolk," the dioramas and artwork in the room still have a marked impact today, although much of the Norfolk countryside has changed since the 1930s. When they were first opened to the public they were considered the finest in Europe. Modern information boards explain how the dioramas were created and the tricks involved in creating a sense of depth and space. Ernest Whatley (1874-1952) painted four of the backgrounds: Yare Valley, Breydon Water, North Norfolk Coast and Breckland. Whatley was a regular exhibitor at the Royal Academy. His skills were used in creating a panoramic diorama of his painting 'The vineyards of Cyprus,' which was displayed as part of the Festival of Britain in 1951, shortly before his death. Other backdrops including 'Norfolk Loke' were painted by Horace W. Tuck (1876-1951) who was the former Vice-Principal of the Norwich School of Art. Wentworth Day describes the North Norfolk Coast diorama as a "superb piece of landscape and bird display, which is no less than twenty-six feet in length."[2] He quotes Dr Frank Leney's description of the case (Leney was curator of the museum at the time):

> It depicts the inland view from the terneries looking over the salt-marshes with their carpet of purple sea-lavender interspersed with the bright green of the glasswort and more sombre tones of the sueda,[3] the sunlight gleaming on the many channels and pools. The tide-line in the foreground with its flotsam and jetson of seaweed, skate eggs, clusters of whelk eggs, shells, and many other things, forms a happy hunting-ground for the gay little ringed plover. Oyster-catchers move off their scarlet legs to the left and a shelducks diving into its nest in a rabbit's burrow on the right. Three pieces of sea-lavender are shown—viz., *Statice limonsium. S. reticulate,* and *S. binervosa*
>
> On the other side of the sand-hill is seen a glimpse of the North Sea, and in the foreground is a group of common terns in the middle of the breeding season, with eggs and chicks of all sizes, some of which are hardly distinguishable from the pebbles on the beach. A few little terns are coming in over a sand-dune on the right. The dunes are covered with marram grass and the pink flowered sea-bindweed, making a most realistic setting for the birds.[4]

Praise for the Museum is revealed ninety years earlier by Benjamin Thompson Lowne, "The specimen of the Western Duck, shot here [in Great Yarmouth], is now in the collection of birds at the Norwich Museum, with many other rare birds from our district. This collection is one of the finest in England, and no naturalist should visit the county without seeing it."[5] Thomas Southwell was closely connected to the museum. He served on the committee from 1893, when the old museum was transferred to Norwich Castle. In his *Official guide to the Norwich Castle Museum*, 1895, Thomas Southwell reveals the origins of the Lombe Collection in the museum, "There are here some of the most beautiful as well as the rarest of British birds, most of which possess the additional attraction of local origin. We will first speak of the Lombe collection, which was formed by the late Edward Lombe, of Melton near Norwich, and presented to the Norwich Museum by his daughter, the late Mrs. E. P. Clarke, of Wymondham. At the time it was made, early in the present century, it must have been one of the most complete private collections in this country. It was removed to the old Museum, and opened to the public."[6] Southwell goes on to reveal Gurney's contribution to the museum, "We enter the noble room in which are displayed the bulk of the specimens forming the splendid collection of Raptorial Birds, which form a lasting memorial of the energy, liberality, and profound acquaintance with this branch of Ornithology possessed by the late Mr. J. H. Gurney, who, in 1853, stated his intention to form as complete a collection as possible of the Birds of Prey, and the beautiful series here exhibited, as well as a large number of skins reposing in the cabinets in The Skin Room, testify to the success which has attended his untiring efforts ... the visitor cannot fail to regard the extensive series of beautifully-mounted specimens, many of them from very remote parts of the world, and some of great rarity, but for scientific study the visitor must be referred to the unmounted collection to be found in the cabinets of The Skin Room."[7]

'Raptorial Bird Room,' Norwich Castle Museum.
Image courtesy of the Norfolk County Council Library and Information Service at www.picture.norfolk.gov.uk.

The collections of Gurney, and, in part, Stevenson, went into the public domain. A few of Gurney's cases ended up at the Lysaght Collection and reflected his travels over his lifetime, (see his book, *Rambles of a Naturalist in Egypt & other Countries*, 1876) for example, two Red-footed Falcons from Palestine and a Tawny Pipit from France.[8] In his Preface to *The Birds of Norfolk, Remarks on their habits, migration and local distribution*, Volume I, Henry Stevenson clearly values both collector and naturalist, "I feel no little pride in having interested so many zealous naturalists and collectors in the occupation of my leisure hours."[9] Stevenson's taxidermy collection of Norfolk-taken birds was auctioned off in Norwich and included bee-eaters, a pectoral sandpiper and a pair of black terns which were the last pair ever to have nested in Norfolk, "One cannot but regret that the magnificent collection of stuffed birds, over which he spent much money and spared no pains, was not secured intact for the [Castle] Museum collections, but the friends of that institution did their best to raise money for that purpose, and with the fund, at all events some of the choicest rarities were secured."[10] Whilst the museum comprises the large collections of Messrs Riviere, Lombe, Gurney and Arnold, Arthur Patterson reveals that other specimens came from various sources, "The adventures attendant on a 'stranger's' capture are sometimes interesting. A Caspian plover (*Aegialitis asiatica*) was knocked over on the North Denes, and its murderer left it at a house, where the mistress threw it on top of the clock, to be out of the way of the cat. It was taken down, dusty enough, and shortly after identified, and has since been permanently lodged in Norwich Museum."[11] The oldest specimen in the museum is a red-legged partridge shot by H.C. Collison and set up by Thomas Hall of London in 1790.

The museum also stores thousands of 'cabinet' study skins for study and research and 10,000 specimens of eggs including those of the now extinct Great Auk. There are 300 fishes from the collection of Arthur Patterson and an interesting interpretation board detailing his life and significance as a naturalist. Dr David Waterhouse, former senior curator of Natural History and Geology, Norfolk Museums Collections, is keen to stress the emphasis on local material and that the collection contains examples from all the major East Anglian taxidermists from 1790 to the present day. In a video that accompanies the Norfolk Museums Collections website and online resources, Dr Waterhouse says that natural history collections, "provide a valuable resource for helping us understand the world in which we live … natural history collections play a vital role in our understanding of biodiversity, evolution, population genetics and the environmental impacts of climate change."

Interpreting Public Collections

For the keepers of collections under the care of the organisations such as the National Trust and English Heritage, the question of interpretation is an interesting one. Dr Peter Moore, English Heritage's curator of collections and interiors at Audley End House reflects that, "While individual specimens are well documented in physical lists and catalogues, additional interpretation is largely provided through digital media and online content. For those wanting more information during their visit, room stewards are on hand to contextualise and interpret the collections. The historic house environment is not analogous to a museum and its presentation is necessarily different. Preserving the character of a place which was once a family home is important; however, the cultural associations of that historic context, and its aristocratic associations, can lead to natural history collections in country houses being perceived in a very different way from those displayed in a museum environment."[12] For wealthy Victorian collectors, their natural history collections and the frenetic desire to collect species were often a matter of ownership, partly born of competitive ambition with other contemporary collectors and also how they stood in the hallmarks of natural history achievements.

The history of taxidermy is integral to the wider history of natural history. Many people quite expect to see collections of Victorian taxidermy as they walk around a country house. It is part of the 'package' that includes oak-clad galleries, servant's quarters and kitchens. Natural history collections are inherently linked to the dynastic collections of books and manuscripts in the country house library. For the latter, think of Blickling Hall and the illuminated manuscripts in Holkham Hall. However, free-standing specimens categorised and displayed in museums exist in an academic or scientific veneer, whereas tableaux collections, once private, now in the public domain can be freighted with negative significance, impelled, no doubt, with a connection to the rich big-game hunters who wished to preserve their trophies which were shot for sport in one of the colonies, a time when British Officers and civil servants enjoyed 'bagging' a tiger. Contemporary museums with 19th century roots have been criticised as complicit with colonialism and seen as 'Imperial archives.' The National Trust's Colonial Countryside project attempted to address the Colonial angle via children-led narrations which explored the Tiger Carpet at Kedleston Hall. This may help in part to readdress taxidermy, which in the context of animal welfare, became tainted by association. Natural history has perhaps lost its didactic meaning. There is a disparity between Victorian fashionable decoration and necessary instruction and education. Prioritisation can be a reason why collections are sold or housed in stored museum archives where people can view specimens on request. For instance, in February 2011 Sworders Fine Art auctioneers sold a collection of taxidermy housed in the Northampton Museum. For the museum it was a matter of prioritisation, "The Museum, unable to display all but a few cases for many years, has been through the formal de-accessioning process for these items and is giving some cases to other museums, however, the majority are to be sold. The proceeds are being ring-fenced for the conservation of important watercolours and artefacts in their collection."[13]

Taxidermy is seen by many as a cultural relic of another age, one that is superseded by modern technologies in an age where concerns of species and habitat loss are paramount. Taxidermy's mimetic value has faded. These collections and individual mounts were crucial in disseminating anatomical, zoological and taxonomic knowledge. Museums and private collections often contained specimens from voyages of discovery and by the latter part of the 18th century, Bécoeur had developed his arsenic paste allowing specimens to arrive in Britain in a reasonable condition. Today, voyages of discovery are taken place in our living rooms via large HD television screens. However, there are obvious limits to experiences with the natural world as mediated through a screen. Christopher Stoate states, "The viewer remains remote from the viewed and only in the presence of the actual animal can the size, texture and three-dimensional shape be fully appreciated ... Mounted animals have also been used with great success to give the blind some knowledge of animals' size, structure and texture. There is an important role for taxidermy in education in helping people to relate directly to wild animals and providing some background information on which to base a knowledge of the interactions between them."[14] In 2019 the Breckland team of Natural England came across a stone-curlew in an antiques shop. Taxidermist, Krysten Newby restored the bird which Natural England took with them on educational and training talks.

The 'fixed' aspect of taxidermy displays means that they cannot be changed since their original conception, but modern interpretation is important for our understanding of historical collections. The natural history collection in Norwich Castle Museum is a fine example of this approach. An interpretation board entitled 'Modern Collecting' accompanies the natural history collection in the museum, "Although most of the Natural History specimens in the museum were acquired many years ago, we are still adding to the collections. These are specimens which are found dead, or killed by cars or cats … Some of the equipment we use is 'high-tech,' but traditional techniques are still important." Another display case shows the tools and accoutrements of the taxidermists, "As a craftsman, artist and naturalist, a good taxidermist took years to develop the skills necessary for his job … demand for their skills declined sharply after the Second World War."

Taxidermy specimens are still powerful objects and represent various historical narratives. They have historical and epistemological depth and are coded with *sitz em leben*, the context and time in which an object has been created. That is to say, their significance within a certain era which used taxidermy to expand natural knowledge. Taxidermy collections are enigmatic and paradoxical and difficult to decipher. They accrue other meanings as time moves on. Taxidermy in itself requires a sound grasp of anatomy and at the same time great artistic skill. It is perhaps an irony that the interest in collecting taxidermy today often focuses on possessing an uncommon or rare species that would be unlikely to be seen in the wild except in the form of a taxidermy mount, a process that contributed to its rarity in the first place. While there might be an international drive to reinvent

Records of the Azorean natural history collection in the Museu Carlos Machado, founded 1876, Ponta Delgada, Azores.
Author.

the museum and address the challenges that modern museums face, there is hopefully still space for learning about how our ancestors lived and interpreted the world as our museums evolve. I have visited many public collections of taxidermy, both in this country and abroad. In 2018, I went to see the natural history collection in the Museu Carlos Machado in Ponta Delgada on the island of São Miguel in the Azores. I had the museum to myself walked around eight large exhibition rooms while a mini-hurricane raged outside. It made for an interesting, but unnerving experience.

Notes

1. B. Bishop, *Cley Marsh and its Birds*, (Woodbridge, The Boydell Press, 1983), p. 13.
2. J. Wentworth Day, *Marshland Adventure on Norfolk Broads and Rivers*, (London, George G. Harrap and Co., 1950), p. 130.
3. An old word for 'suede.' More likely, however, Wentworth Day is referring to *Suaeda vera*, or Shrubby Sea Blight.
4. Ibid. 2, pp. 127-130.
5. B.T. Lowne, *A Popular Natural History of Great Yarmouth and its Neighbourhood*, (London, George Hall, 1863), p. 37.
6. T. Southwell, *The Official Guide to the Norwich Castle Museum*, (Norwich, Jarrolds, 1895), p.16.
7. Ibid. p. 31-2.
8. P. Watson, *The Birmingham Ornithological Collections, Part 2—The W.R. Lysaght Collection of Birds*, (Birmingham Museums and Art Gallery, 2010), p. 14.
9. H. Stevenson, *The Birds of Norfolk, Remarks on their habits, migration and local Distribution*, Vol I, (London, John Van Horst, 1866), xi.
10. *Transactions*, Norfolk and Norwich Naturalists' Society, (Norwich, Fletcher and Son, 1888), p.560.
11. A.H. Patterson, *Notes of an East Coast Naturalist*, (London, Methuen & Co, 1904), p. 48.
12. Correspondence with author.
13. Sworders Fine Art Auctioneers, *The February Country House Sale* catalogue, Tuesday 22 February 2011, p. 92.
14. C. Stoate, *Taxidermy. The Revival of a Natural Art*, (London, Sportsman's Press, 1987), pp. 28-29.

Notes for the Collector

In the middle of the 19th century, over a hundred Norfolk families owned estates greater than 2,000 acres in size. There were also numerous smaller landowners in the county. After 1875, a long depression in English agriculture and industry set in, which reduced estate incomes and put severe pressure on their owners. The situation was often made worse by the accumulation of debts from family settlements, extravagant expenditure (often sustained over generations), and the introduction of death duties in 1894. Landowners were forced to sell their possessions, let their estates for shooting, reduce staff levels or take up residence elsewhere. Estates became neglected as their owners strived to save money and many estates disappeared as farms, parks and woodland were sold off and halls were left to decay. Kate Sussams states, "The agricultural depression from the 1870s and the effects of two world wars took a heavy toll on the Breckland estates and a large percentage were broken up and the houses demolished (Barnes 1993). Great houses were demolished at West Tofts, Didlington, Weeting, Fornham St. Genevieve, Santon Downham and Cavenham—all between the 1920s and 1950s. Some still survive, although often in other forms ... only a few are still occupied as residences such as Oxburgh Hall (occupied by the Bedingfield family since it was built over 500 years ago, now owned by the National Trust."[1] Two world wars had a catastrophic effect on many owners of country houses. In 1921, *Estates Gazette* revealed that a quarter of all English land had changed hands in the previous three years. During the Second World War the government requisitioned hundreds of houses. The land could be used as a training ground and the houses occupied by troops. After the War many landowners sold their houses, or gave them to the National Trust.[2]

Christopher Frost states that the 1930s marked a decade when many collections were split up or destroyed, "Many large collections, formed when taxidermy was at its most fashionable, came onto the market in the 1930s as their original owners passed away. By this time, interest in them had dwindled to such an extent that in some cases the prices realised hardly covered the expense of cartage to the saleroom. I have heard of countless collections that were just thrown onto a bonfire or rubbish heap because nobody wanted them. If only people could have known then that one day they would be of as much interest and relevance to natural history historians and collectors as they had once been to their original owners."[3] Perhaps this decline is partly responsible for the spread of taxidermy cases into public houses and private ownership via auction and estate sales. Natural history collections were sometimes split up and specimens that once resided in large tableaux boxed-in cabinets, were remounted on bases and sold separately. This has resulted in problems with provenance and the age of specimens, especially when a specimen is endangered or protected. There are still private collections in Norfolk today, often passed down from generations. The existence of these collections in their entirety maintains historic and local importance. Their integrity and the stories surrounding them would be lost forever if cases were sold and split up, which has been the fate of many other collections. Custodians of these collections often wish to remain anonymous.

There is much to admire in a taxidermy case: its preservation going back over a hundred years or more, the skills of the taxidermist and the realistic foliage and groundwork created for the diorama. The latter can be appreciated in much the same way as the delightful world created by a detailed model railway. Societal proclivities may change but antique taxidermy has remained popular with collectors, despite the modern ethical climate weathering its appeal in some quarters (taxidermy cases are a prominent part of the décor in the Jugged Hare pub on Chiswell Street in London). There are serious collectors wishing to add to their collections and cases at auction have sold for a lot of money. In 2019 Keys Fine Art Auctioneers sold a collection of Norfolk-based taxidermy cases in their 'Ornithology, Wildlife and Sporting Art' sale. The 300 lots included work by Gunn, Lowne and Lockwood.

The first thing to think about when purchasing a piece of taxidermy is that we have probably reached a stage where antique specimens, once resplendent in their original colours and preservation 150 years ago can only depreciate with age, especially if they been kept in direct sunlight or have succumbed to insect attack. Is it old? The dealers or auctioneers may not know themselves, as a piece of taxidermy may have already moved around several times before reaching them. Cased taxidermy is more likely to have stood the test of time than free-standing mounts. Free-standing (uncased) studies can be particularly difficult to date without provenance. Examples might have come from large cabinets in country houses when tableaux were split up and specimens sold separately. Specimens could have been 'rehoused' on more than one occasion and displayed in different formats as Pat Morris reveals in *The Braybrooke Taxidermy Collection at Audley End*, "In 1858, Richard Neville (by now having become the 4th Lord Braybrooke), began a full-scale rearrangement of the collection … His assortment of old cases of British and European birds were emptied and the specimens were remounted and installed in big new cabinets among simulated natural surroundings. The species were now grouped, with the owls together, all the ducks, all the seabirds and so on, as was often the fashion in many of these grand collections."[4]

Other examples can be more recent than 1947 and the buyer should be wary, especially if the specimens are on the endangered list. A lot of taxidermy was brought into the UK from France in the early 2000s, including buzzards and other birds of prey with no provenance. Auction houses are now aware of the laws surrounding taxidermy. Years ago, the proprietor of an auction house in Cambridgeshire was fined £6,000 after offering wild bird's eggs for sale. The

Cambridgeshire Police and RSPB attended the auction on the day of the sale. A dealer I know said that the arrests were made the moment the gavel went down. I think they were making a point. The obsessive collector is still a dangerous beast. I have been offered birds eggs with a nudge and a wink. Don't go near them. I have also seen cases of taxidermy for sale with eggs in the case. This may seem a grey area as the eggs are part of the diorama but it would still be illegal to sell, and effectively, own, the case.

Some taxidermists, i.e. the famous fish preserver Cooper, had small labels inside their cases. When 'correct' this greatly helps with provenance. The passing of the years has meant that labels fixed to the back of cases may have faded, fallen off or have been painted over. In the same way that new labels are put inside old leather gun cases to raise their value, very occasionally labels inside or to verso are faked. I have only seen this with cases of fish, which were not Coopers, despite the promise of the label in the top right-hand corner of the case. If a label appears overly 'distressed' or the paper is too thick then you may be onto something. An unscrupulous vendor is only likely to try this tactic when the taxidermist is known to attract high prices. Some auctioneers and dealers inflate reserve prices and price tags by attributing cases without labels to well-known taxidermists. Words like 'in the style of,' 'attributed to,' or 'after' may occasionally be used. 'Attributed to' will generally realise less money than 'by.' Victorian and Edwardian taxidermists often followed each other in style. Attributing a case to the renowned Norwich taxidermist T.E. Gunn increases the reserve price. The attribution often goes unquestioned and is sometimes very hard to tell due to the 'Norwich circle' being so similar.

Graham Austen has occasionally been asked to help an auction house identify cases of birds coming up for sale. Sometimes identification is tricky when the birds have faded and/or are in their winter plumage. Juvenile birds, first and second winters, can also be difficult. The number of juvenile birds in cases might in part be due to the naiveté of the young bird around humans and thus being easier to catch. Conversely, I have never understood why many auction houses and antiques dealers take little if any time to correctly identify what they are selling. I have a cased pair of Sandwich terns by the Norfolk taxidermist Henry Pashley which have been nicely restored by Graham as the birds had completely faded and the tail-feathers had dropped. They were originally sold at auction in Norfolk as "a cased pair of gulls in naturalistic setting." They maintained their nom de plumes when I discovered them in an antiques shop in Holt. Often general dealers want to turnover their stock quickly, move their pieces on and don't seek time on identification. This, of course, is advantageous to the collector. The quality of taxidermy is often dictated by the quality and condition of the skin before work was started, or the presence of insects when the cases were sealed ready for display. Felicity Bolton, Natural History Conservator at the National Trust's Royal Oak Foundation Conservation Studio states, "Materials used in taxidermy often dictate how long they will last. Taxidermy techniques that were used in the 18th–19th Centuries changed over the years, although there are taxidermists still practising traditional techniques. Most modern day materials such as polyurethane plastics and foams, which are sometimes used by taxidermists, may not last. This may present challenges for collectors and curatorial staff in the future. Labels associated with specimens often contain important species and locality information, as well as inherent information such as handwriting and label style about the collector or collection."[5]

Christopher Stoate's *Taxidermy. The Revival of a Natural Art* gives detailed information on collections and their care. Cracks and holes in cases present the most potential for damage caused by insects which may not always be seen when purchasing a case. Stoate states, "Two groups are involved, moths (Lepidoptera) and beetles (Coleoptera) and of the latter *Anthrenus verbasci* is probably the most often encountered. The adult beetles, like the closely related *Anthrenus museorum*, are small, normally black and white or brown and yellow and most often seen in summer … While feeding, the larvae produce 'frass,' a mass of fine powdered droppings, which can usually be seen on the groundwork beneath the point on the skin where the animals are feeding."[6] A few years ago I was looking around an outdoor stall at Costessey Showground Antiques Fair in Norwich. Seeing that I was taking interest in the taxidermy on offer, the dealer drew my attention to a case of mallard ducks. He took great delight in explaining to me that, "the top of the case comes off so you can get inside." You could see daylight through gaps in the lid. I noticed a few tiny feathers in the bottom of the case and knew something was working on the birds. Some species of birds are much more likely to be affected than others. Gulls, ducks and geese seem to be particularly immune. This may well be due to the thickness and oily nature of the plumage (if a yellow stain is apparent on the plumage on the underside of a seabird, this is the fat seeping through and a product of poor preparation by the taxidermist when the bird was set up. If a taxidermist does not clean the fat from the underside of the skin, the fat will rot and cause a yellow stain.). The soft, delicate plumage of the jay, on the other hand, makes them particularly susceptible to attack. The woodcock is also fragile. Graham Austen said, "Sneeze and their feather's come off".

Beware of online auctions. I have come a cropper on a few occasions. I purchased a rainbow trout online only to discover that the fish was a cast. A 'cast' is a replica. As the name suggests, a mould is made over the fish, usually in silicone rubber and then covered with a layer of fibreglass and painted. Some of these casts can be very attractive. My rubber fish wasn't particularly attractive in its MDF case. Graham called it "the Waitrose trout." Carriage can be a large problem when buying online. Glass in the cases can break despite the best efforts of the person packaging it up. Cases can be turned upside down, thrown about and generally you will be fortunate if the taxidermy arrives unscathed. Fish are the least risky specimens to transport, but mounts, especially the very old ones, are prone to split. Again, I have seen real eggs for sale by online auction (replica eggs these days are often superb). I would avoid taxidermy from Europe. Specimens from Italy and Malta seem to occur most frequently.

Notes

1. K. Sussams, *The Breckland Archaeological Survey 1994-96*, Suffolk Archaeological Service (Ipswich, Suffolk County Council, 1996), p. 103.
2. Some collections were destroyed by bombing during the Second World War, for instance the Tolhouse collection in Great Yarmouth. Some of the case illustrations in Gunn's catalogue of his own collection, have the word 'blitzed' alongside them in his son's handwriting, indicating those which were destroyed by German bombs during the Second World War (C Frost, *The Ogilvie Bird Collection*, p. 18).
3. C. Frost, *A History of British Taxidermy*, (Lavenham, The Lavenham Press, 1987), p. 15.
4. P. Morris, *The Braybrooke Collection at Audley End*, (Ascot, MPM Publishing, 2019), pp. 2-3.
5. Correspondence with author.
6. C. Stoate, *Taxidermy. The Revival of a Natural Art.* (London, Sportsman's Press, 1987), p. 36.

Appendix

WILD BIRDS PROTECTION IN NORFOLK, 1914.

TRANSACTIONS OF THE NORFOLK AND NORWICH NATURALISTS' SOCIETY, PP. 765–9 (LINNAEAN CLASSIFICATION OMITTED)

It has long been recognised by those interested in the protection of wild birds in the County that the Schedule to the Act of 1880 is a very confused list, as it gives in alphabetical order a number of local names without mention of the scientific name of the bird indicated. From a careful collation of the various Acts with the Bye-laws of the Norfolk County Council and of the Norwich Town Council, it would appear that the Regulations now in force, shorn of their legal language, can be thus condensed. The following birds are protected between the first day of March and the first day of September: Auk, Little, Avocet, Bee-eater, Chough, Colin or Virginian Quail, Crossbill, Cuckoo, Curlew, Diver (all species) Dotterel, Dunlin, Fulmar, Gannet or Solan Goose, Godwit (all species) Grebe or Loon (all species) Greenshank, Guillemot or Willock, Black Guillemot or Tystey, Gull or Seamew (all species except Black-backed) Kittiwake or Tarrock, Lapwing or Peewit, Lark, Merganser (all species) Nightingale, Nightjar (Fern-owl, Goatsucker, or Nighthawk), Oyster-catcher, Petrel (all species) Phalarope (all species) Plover (all species) Puffin (or Sea Parrot), Quail, Californian, Shaw Razorbill (Marrot or Murre), Redshank, Ringed Plover (Ringed Dotterel, Stone Runner, or Stonehatch), Roller, Ruff or Reeve, Sanderling, Sandpiper or Summer-Snipe, Sand-Martin, Shag or Scout, Shearwater (all species) Skua (all species) Smew, Spoonbill, Stone-Curlew or Thicknee, Whimbrel, Woodcock are protected between the first day of February and the 13th day of August. Snipe, Teal and all species of Duck are protected between the first day of March and the first day of August.

The following birds are protected throughout the year: Avocet, (In County of Norfolk only.) Bittern, Common, Bittern, Little, Bustard, Great, Goldfinch, Grebe, Great Crested, Harrier (all species) Hobby, Hoopoe, Kingfisher, Oriole, Golden, Owl (all species except the Little Owl, Redpoll (all species) Sandgrouse, Pallas. Siskin, Spoonbill, (In County of Norfolk only) Stilt, Black-winged, Tern (all species) Tit, Bearded (Reedling or Reed-Pheasant), Woodpecker (all species). At Blakeney Point all Wild Birds are protected between 1 March and 1 September. All Wild Birds are protected on Sundays between the first day of September and the first day of March in the following areas, to which is now added Blakeney Point, and the Eggs of all Wild Birds are protected in the same areas until the last day of February, 1919: "(a) Hickling Broad, Whitesley and Heigham Sounds, Blackfleet Broad, Horsey Mere, Martham and Somerton Broads, and the Rands, Skirts, and Walls thereof, and Fens and Reed

Grounds appertaining thereto respectively, and the Islands therein, and Dykes communicating therewith, including the Hundred Stream or Thurne River and Ancient Bed and the Rands and Walls thereof from Heigham Bridge to the Sea at Winterton, and all the Marshes and low-lying and uncultivated Lands, Fens, Reed Grounds, Warrens, Marram or Sand Hills and Sea Shore, to the line of high water mark in the several Parishes of Waxham, Horsey, Potter Heigham, and Hickling, and such part of the Parish of Catfield as lies to the East of the Midland and Great Northern Joint Railway. 11 (b) The Warrens, Marram or Sand Hills, and Sea Shore, to the line of high water mark in the Parish of Winterton. "(c) Such parts of the Rivers Yare and Wensum as are within the administrative County of Norfolk, and the Streams communicating therewith; the River Bure and the Streams communicating therewith; and Rockland and Surlingham Broads, and the Rands, Skirts, and Walls of each such River and Broad, and Fens and Reed Grounds appertaining thereto respectively, and the Islands therein, and the Dykes communicating therewith. "(d) The series of Broads known as Ormesby, Rollesby, Hemsby, Filby, and Burgh Broads, and the Rands, Skirts, and Walls thereof, and the Dykes communicating therewith; and the Fens, Reed Grounds, and low-lying Lands, Marshes, and Pastures adjacent thereto, including Lady Broad or Hard Fen Water in the Parish of Filby, Brandyke Broad in the Parish of Burgh St. Margaret, and Muckfleet Dyke, and the Marshes and low-lying Lands and Pastures near or adjacent thereto respectively. "(e) The whole of the Foreshore of the County of Norfolk, including the Shingle, Sand Hills, Salt Marshes, Creeks, and other unenclosed Lands extending from high water mark to the first boundary of enclosed or cultivated land separating the Foreshore from them."

The eggs of the following birds are protected throughout the County: Bittern, Common, Bittern, Little, Bustard, Great, Crossbill, Grebe, Great Crested, Harrier (all species) Hobby, Kingfisher, Owl (all species), Oyster-catcher, Plover, Ringed (Ringed Dotterel, Stone Runner or Stonehatch), Ruff or Reeve, Sand-Martin, Stone-Curlew, Teal (all species) Terns (Sea Swallows, Pearls, or Dip Ears), all species, Tit, Bearded, Wild Duck (all species) Woodcock, Woodlark. Within the County of the City of Norwich, which extends, by river, from Hellesdon Bridge to Hardley Cross and from Trowse Bridge to Earlham Bridge, the taking or destroying of the eggs of any species of Wild Bird except the House Sparrow—is prohibited until the last day of February, 1919. Penalties. £1 for every bird or egg taken or destroyed, and forfeiture of such birds or eggs, as well as forfeiture of any trap-net, snare, or decoy-bird used for taking Wild Birds in contravention of the Acts. Attention is also called to a Bye-law of the Great Yarmouth Port and Haven Commissioners, which prohibits, under a penalty of £5, the use of any firearm or air-gun by persons " while using or while in, or upon, or about the Rivers or the banks or shores thereof " under the control of the Commissioners. As the Rivers under such control extend from Yarmouth to Hellesdon Mill on the Wensum, to Geldeston Lock on the Waveney, to Coltishall Lock on the Bure, to Wayford Bridge on the Ant, and to the whole course of the Thurne, such a Regulation, if properly enforced, would be of great help in the preservation of our Marshland birds.

Index

Acle, 83, 93
Acts of Parliament,
   amendments, 14, 77, 119, 138, 148
   Bill for the Preservation of Wild Fowl, (1872), 142
   Blakeney and Cley Wild Birds' Protection Society, 149
   Breydon Wild Birds' Protection Society, 88, 155
   Game Act, (1831), 112
   Montague Committee, 147
   Preservation of Wild Fowl Act, (1876), 142
   Protection of Animals Act, (1911), 141
   Sandgrouse Protection Act, (1888), 43
   Sea Birds Protection Act, (1869), 133
   Wells Wild Birds' Protection Society, 154
   Wild Bird Protection Acts, 14, 28, 73, 83, 102, 125, 141
   Wild Bird Protection Act, (1880), 76–77, 119, 134
   Wild Bird Protection Act, (1900), 103
   Wildlife and Countryside Act, (1981), 125
   Wolferton Wild Birds' Protection Society, 148–149
All England Ornithological Show, 79
Arnold, E.C., 49, 163, 166
arsenic, 15, 29, 66, 78, 88, 167
Ashton, F., 62, 111
Attleborough, 21, 104, 113
auction, 23, 33, 70, 86, 90–91, 94, 96, 103, 113, 120, 136, 170–173
Audley End, Essex, 59–60, 166, 171
Audubon, J.J., 29
Austen, G., 29, 172–173

Aylmerton, 104
Aylsham, 26, 103

Barclay, J.G., 17
Beechamwell, 109, 111
Beeston Regis, 118
Bird, M.C.H., Rev., (MCH), 15–17, 55, 73, 82, 88, 120, 143–144, 163
Birds
   avocet, 38, 71–72, 126, 128, 147–148, 175
   Baillion's crake, 61
   barn owl, 92, 130, 139–140
   bearded tit, 65, 92, 138–139, 143, 147, 149, 175–176
      see also bearded tit mouse, 73, 139
   bittern, 62, 65–66, 75, 82, 90, 126, 128, 134, 138, 143, 147, 149, 153, 175–176
   bluethroat, 46–49, 55, 80
   capercaillie, 34, 59
   crane, 44, 111, 114
   geese, 33, 145, 173
   glossy ibis, 57, 88, 93
   golden plover, 14, 90, 127
   goshawk, 80, 115, 134, 144
   great bustard, 59, 63, 66, 107–113
   great-crested grebe, 76, 128, 139, 143, 147, 149, 175–176
   green woodpecker, 75–77
   grosbeak, 90–91, 115
   harrier, 14, 83, 88–89, 128, 134, 144, 149, 175–176
   hawfinch, 29, 77, 79, 114
   heron, 56, 64–65, 67, 71, 75, 89, 96
   honey buzzard, 44, 134
   hummingbird, 27, 37, 74
   kingfisher, 59, 63, 75–77, 79, 87, 143, 175–176
   lapwing, 14, 33, 117, 125, 128, 149, 175
   little auk, 80–82, 104–105, 127
   little bustard, 38, 66, 82, 85, 105,

111
little owl, 131, 144, 175
little tern, 38, 132, 140, 149–150, 152, 164
Norfolk plover, 83, 116–118, 128, 134, 139, 143
    see also stone–curlew
Pallas's sandgrouse, 38–43, 49, 138, 175
pectoral sandpiper, 57, 85, 90–91, 95, 165
plover, 38, 40, 82, 88, 90, 95, 104, 117, 127, 139, 142, 149–150, 156, 164, 166, 175–176
    see also golden plover
red kite, 135–137
Sabine's snipe, 61
shelduck, (Sheld–duck) 147, 149–150, 152, 164
skua, 80, 127, 175
snipe, 33, 38, 50, 54, 57, 61, 66, 82–83, 90, 95, 125, 127, 175
    see also Sabine's snipe
spoonbill, 71–72, 93, 141, 145, 148, 175
stone–curlew, 83, 107, 116–119, 125, 168, 175–176
    see also Norfolk plover
tawny owl, 59
tern, 32, 38, 66, 76, 83, 96, 115, 125–126, 128, 131–132, 134, 139–140, 144, 147, 149–155, 164–165, 172, 175–176
water rail, 88
waxwing, 60
white–tailed eagle, 14, 82, 113–114, 134–135
Birkbeck, H.A., Maj., 109–110
Birkin, H.R.S. (Tim), Sir, 35
Bishop, Billy, 25–26, 32, 35–36, 39, 41, 46, 126, 132, 139, 146, 163
Black Dyke Fen, 109
Blakeney, 20, 32, 35, 38, 42–43, 48–50, 55, 60, 64, 81, 120, 132, 141, 145, 148–149. 151–153, 162

Blakeney Point, 32, 37, 120, 125, 132, 138, 144, 150, 152–153, 175
Blickling Hall, 167
Booth, E.T., 16, 59, 120
Borrer, C.D. (Sea–Pie), 17, 49, 55
Brancaster, 38, 41–42, 153
Brandon, 40, 106, 113, 115
Breckland, 14, 83, 102, 106, 113, 117, 119, 135–137, 144, 164, 168, 170
Breydon Water, 14, 21, 32, 57, 70–71, 89, 92–93, 120, 126, 137, 142, 145, 155–156, 164
Breydoners, 73, 92
Briston, 43
British Empire, 24
Browne, T., Sir, 19, 71, 107, 116–117, 136, 141
Brundall, 120
Brunstead, 16
Buckenham, 82, 115
Burgh Castle, 41
Burlingham House, 121
Burnham Overy, 41, 50
Burston Rectory, 78, 121
Buxton, C., 17
Buxton, G.F., 138, 157
Buxton, T.F., 17

Caistor, 95
Calke Abbey, Derbyshire, 59, 62, 82, 88
Calthorpe, Lord, 149–150
Castle Acre, 113–114
Castle Rising, 105, 109
Cavenham, 170
    Cavenham Heath, 111
Chambers, 'Ducker', 155
Chesney, K., 27
Clarke, W.G., 17, 106, 114
Cley–next–the–Sea, 14, 32, 76
Coke, T., 3rd Earl of Leicester, 16, 113, 153–154
Collections,
    Connop Collection, 25, 54, 59, 64, 134
    Lysaght Collection, 37–38, 41, 49, 50, 54, 63, 67, 77, 82, 88, 92, 111, 113, 118–120, 155, 165
    Ogilvie Collection, 41–42, 58–59, 76, 119, 135
    Tolhouse Collection, 174

Colney Hall, 20
Congham House, 111
Connop, E.M., 37, 59, 64, 82, 95, 119, 121
Costessey, 21, 109–110, 173
Cremer, T.W., 60, 108, 118
Creswell, G., Col., 148
Cringle, T., 154
Cromer, 38, 50, 118, 134
Crompton, J., Rev., 17
Currie, F.L., Rev., 39

Dack, C.B., 31, 63, 82, 102, 108, 127, 131
Darwin, C., 24–25
Day, J.W., 71, 73, 103, 110, 164
Dead Man's Wood, nr. Weybourne, 43
Dersingham, 50, 109
Dickens, C., 35
Didlington, 170
diorama, 27, 59, 117, 120, 164, 171–172
Diss, 114
Doubleday, H., 96–97, 120
Downham Market, 105
Duchess of Bedford, 22, 150, 162
Durrant's Game dealers, 15, 80–81
Dutt, A., 21, 140, 143

Eales, W.E.R. (Ted), 32, 138
East Runton, 43, 137
Eaton, 82
Edward VII, King, 106, 149
egg collecting, 73, 112, 138
Eldon, 108
Ellis, R., 41, 44
Elmham, 54
    Elmham Hall, 111
Elvedon, 40, 115
Elwes, H., 111

Fakenham, 79, 82, 103–105
Feilden, H.W., Col., 113, 121, 154
Felbrigg Hall, 41, 59
Feltwell, 95, 115, 117, 128
Fenland, 104
fire screen, 75
First World War, 16, 28, 33, 36, 62, 106, 146, 150–151
Flamborough Head, Yorkshire, 38, 133
Forby, R., Rev., 106, 114
Forestry Commission, 106
Fornham St. Genevieve, 170

Fritton Lake, 73
Frost, C., 13, 28, 37, 46, 50, 55–56, 58–59, 62–67, 80, 88–90, 92–95, 102, 104–105, 113–114, 119, 129, 142, 147, 170

George, M., 40, 42, 129, 136, 141–142, 147
glass dome, 50, 78
golf balls, 70, 74
Great Exhibition (1851), 27
Great Yarmouth, 14–15, 21–22, 26, 39, 49, 57, 59, 67, 70–71, 79–80, 82, 85–92, 94–95, 97, 120, 156, 164, 176
Fuller's Hill, 15, 70, 82, 93
groundwork, 27–28, 41, 50, 78–79, 104, 171, 173
Gunn family
    E.W., 62
    F.E., 62, 82, 131
    T.E., 15–17, 22, 27, 41–42, 44, 48, 54–65, 76–77, 82, 84, 89, 110–111, 119, 131, 136, 142–143, 171–172
Gunton, 62, 109
Gurney family
    Anna, 86
    J.H., Sr., 17
    John Henry, (J.H.), Jr., 16–18, 41, 47–49, 54–56, 59, 65–66, 73, 77, 81–83, 85, 89, 91, 95–96, 104–105, 108–110, 120, 127, 130, 132, 136–137, 139, 163, 165–166
    Quintin, Maj., 149
    Robert, 17–18

hairdressing, 103
Hale, W.G., 117
Hamilton, J.P., 109
Hamond, C.A., 154–155
Hamond, R., Rev., 108–109,
Harleston, 57, 115
Harpur Crewe, V., Sir, 59, 88, 110
Henry VIII, King, 112
Herbert, A., MP, 139
Hevingham, 15, 82
Heydon, 57
Hickling, 18, 38, 42, 83, 89, 95, 120, 140,

143, 175–176
Hillington Hall, 111
HMS Rattlesnake, 24
Hockwold, 61, 109–110
Holkham Hall, 16, 60, 64, 167
Holt, 31, 34, 63, 82, 102–103, 108, 118, 121, 127, 131, 134, 141, 172
Horsey Mere, 109, 141, 175
Hunstanton, 39, 49, 73
Hunt, J., 65, 67

Icklingham, 110

Jary, G., 155–156
Jefferson, R., 26, 44
Jodrell, A., Sir, 50

Kearton family
    Cherry, 144
    Richard, 144
Kelling, 31, 117
    Hall, 118
    Heath, 118–119, 121, 134, 137
Keswick, 21
    Hall, 17, 95
King's Lynn, 19, 26, 39, 41, 50, 63, 73, 104–105, 111
Kingsley, C., 26

Lakenham, 82
Lakenheath, 40, 115
Larling, 109
Lesser Rorqual Whale, 87
Lexham, 108, 113, 117
    Lexham Hall, 109
Lilford, Lord, 16, 34
Lodge, G.E., 16, 29
Lombe, E., 95, 111, 165–166
Long, S.H., Dr., 16–17, 19, 20, 32, 47, 113, 149, 151, 153,
Lowne family
    B.T., 164
    Walter, 15–16, 21, 33, 41, 49, 55, 57, 67, 70–71, 73–77, 79–89, 93–94, 102–103, 114, 119–120, 131, 136, 140–141, 171
Lubbock, J., 24
Lubbock, R., Rev., 16, 19–21, 31, 54, 57,

61, 86, 91, 94, 104, 107–108, 110, 116–117, 126–128, 134, 141, 143,
Lysaght, W.R., 37, 97, 119

Martham, 70, 78, 83, 175
millinery, 75
    plume hunters, 148
Ministry of Agriculture and Fisheries, 132
Montagu, Lord, 16
Morris, P.A., 57, 70–71, 74–76, 78, 80–81, 83–85, 88, 92–93, 171
Morston, 38–41, 49, 109, 153
Mundesley, 50
Museums
    Ancient House, Thetford, 111, 114
    Birmingham Museum and Art Gallery, 37, 64, 119
    Glandford Shell Museum, 50
    Ipswich Museum, 58
    Kings Lynn Museum, 39
    Museu Carlos Machado, 168–169
    Norwich Castle Museum, 18, 24, 39, 41, 43, 48, 56, 58, 62–63, 66–67, 77, 82, 84, 94, 108–111, 117, 119, 133, 136, 144, 163–169
    Time and Tide Museum, Great Yarmouth, 92

Narford, 108
National Fisheries Exhibition, 56
National Trust, 14, 32, 59–61, 82, 132, 150, 153, 166–167, 170, 172
Natural England, 168
Neville, R., 4th Lord Braybrooke, 171
New Buckenham, 115
Newton family
    Alfred, Prof., 23, 133
    Edward, Sir, 23
Norfolk Broads, 16, 94
    Rollesby Broad, 54, 120
Norfolk Naturalists' Trust, 32, 151, 153
Norfolk Wild Birds Protection Committee, 141
Norfolk Wildlife Trust, 20, 32, 151
North Creake, 50
North Walsham, 26, 82, 90, 104
North Wootton, 140
Northrepps Hall, 66

Norwich, 15, 17, 20–22, 25–26, 40, 44, 48–49, 54–57, 62–67, 71, 73, 75, 77, 79, 82–85, 93, 104, 108, 110–111, 120, 126–127, 130–131, 139, 141, 165, 172–173, 175–176
    All Saint's Green, 66
    Grammar School, 20
    Playhouse, 13
    School of Art, 164
    St. Giles Street, 54–55, 62
Nudd, A., 40, 67, 143

Ogilvie, F.M., 41, 58, 76, 119, 131, 142,
Ormesby, 77, 140
ornithologist, 14, 16–17, 20, 22, 29, 32, 34–35, 43, 46, 60–61, 65, 67, 83, 90, 92, 102, 125, 131, 133, 142, 153–154
ornithology, 13, 16, 21, 39, 96, 165, 171
otter, 56, 63, 84, 103, 115, 141
Overend, J.G., 95, 120, 145
Oxburgh Hall, 170

Pallas, P.S., 39
Parry, J., 16, 23, 55, 68, 82, 88, 99, 120, 124, 143–144, 160–161
Pashley family
    Fred, 41, 62–63, 111
    Henry Nash, 13–17, 22, 25, 31, 33–38, 40–41, 43–46, 50, 59, 73, 76, 81–82, 84, 89, 93, 116–118, 120–121, 130–132, 134, 136, 139, 145–146, 150–151, 154, 172
    Hilton Parker, 34
    Nancie Margaret, 34
Patterson, A.H. (John Knowlittle), 15–17, 21–22, 39–41, 43, 67, 70–74, 77, 80–82, 85–88, 90–94, 112, 121, 126, 129–130, 132–133, 137–138, 142, 144–145, 147–148, 151, 155–157, 166
Payne–Gallwey, R., Sir, 125
photography, 16, 26, 29–30, 89, 127, 144–145
Pinchen, R. (Bob), 149, 152
Plowright, C.B., 90, 95
Plumstead Hall, 111
polecat, 57
Power, F.D., 47–49, 134

Pulham Market, 66

rabbit, 29, 57, 106, 114, 135–136, 163
Raffles, S., Sir, 26
Raveningham, 57
Ray, J., 106
Reymerston, 82
Richards, F.I., 36–37
Riddlesworth Hall, 111
Riviere, B.B., 14, 16–17, 22, 34, 40, 48, 116–117, 120, 131, 145, 154, 163, 166
Rothschild, C., 150
Roudham Heath, 109
Royal Natural History Galleries, London, 50
Royal Oak Foundation, 172
Roydon Fen, 128

Salthouse, 38, 47–48, 60, 72, 118, 120, 126, 134, 150–152
Sandringham, 50, 148–149
Santon Downham, 115, 170
Saunders, H., 16, 39–40, 43, 48, 71–72, 75, 81, 112, 116
Savage Club, The, 85
Scolt Head Island, 32, 125, 152–153
Scott, R.F., Capt., 38
Scottow, 82
Sea Palling, 85
Seago, M., 39, 66, 82, 117, 145
Second World War, 32, 63, 92, 168, 170
Seebohm, H., 125
Sheringham, 48, 50, 54, 118, 137
    Sheringham Hall, 61–62
Shooting,
    closed season, 28, 87, 137, 144–145, 155–156
    decoy, 21, 140–141
    dust shot, 25
    game dealers, 15, 63, 90, 127
    Gentlemen Gunner, 26, 36, 74, 90, 132
    gunsmith, 25–26,
    punt gun, 72, 145
    shotgun, 73, 147
    wildfowler, 14–15, 25, 33, 36, 41, 71, 73, 81, 104, 132, 142–143, 146, 153, 155

Index

wildfowling, 21, 33, 143
Singh, F.D., Prince, 111
Sizewell Hall, 58
Skelton, G. (Old), 141
Smith, J.E., Sir, 21–22, 27, 67, 92–93, 108, 120, 131
Snettisham, 49–50, 82, 137
Societies
    Army and Navy Co-operative Society Ltd, 28–29
    East Counties Angler's Society, 85
    Linnean Society, 22, 58
    Norfolk and Norwich Naturalists' Society, 16–17, 19–22, 43, 57–58, 61, 66, 82, 85–86, 89, 95, 102, 114, 118, 125, 127, 137, 141, 147–148, 152–154, 175
    Royal Society for the Protection of Birds (RSPB), 143, 148
    Society for the Protection of Birds, 19, 148
    Zoological Society, 19, 26–27, 44, 58
South Pickenham, 40
South Walsham, 82
Southwell, T., 16–20, 40, 54, 57, 67, 72, 81, 83, 85–86, 91, 107–108, 110–111, 117, 126–129, 131–133, 138, 141, 147–148, 150, 164–165
Stalham, 82
Stevenson, H., 16–21, 31, 39–41, 43, 48–49, 55, 59, 61, 64–66, 75–76, 81, 91, 95, 105, 107–112, 115–118, 130–132, 134, 139–143, 165
Stiffkey, 38, 109, 153–154
Stoate, C., 64, 146, 167, 173
stoat, 17, 57, 83–84, 135
Stratton Strawless, 82
Swaffham, 17, 26, 40, 56, 108, 113, 117
    Swaffham Heath, 111
Swainson, W., 26, 129
Swanton Abbot, 104
Swaysland, W., 75, 77, 81, 135–136

Taxidermists—by area
    Breckland, 106–121
    Great Yarmouth, 70–97
    Kings Lynn, 26, 63, 104–106

North Norfolk, 102–104
North Norfolk Coast, 31–50
Norwich, 54–67
Taxidermy, 13–17, 21, 23, 25–29, 33–34, 48, 50, 57, 59–62, 65, 70, 73, 78, 86, 93–94, 96, 102, 104, 106, 110–111, 113–115, 119–120, 125, 128–130, 136, 144–146, 163, 165, 167–174
    case, 24, 33, 57, 60, 63, 73, 103, 115, 170–171
    shop, 22, 34, 88,
Taylor, M., 43, 118, 137
Thetford, 19, 39–42, 77, 84, 102, 108, 110, 112–115, 117, 131
    forest, 106
Thomas, E., 22
Thomas, (Pintail), 74, 145
Thorburn, A., 29
Tooley, B., 21–22, 93
trade label, 14, 34, 41, 55, 62, 64–65, 78, 103, 114
Tristram, H.B., 61
trophy mount, 13, 24, 29
Tuck, H.W., 164
Turner, E.L., 16–17, 153
Turnrow, G., 87
Twyford Hall, 154

Upcher, H.M., 61–62, 109, 137

Victoria, Queen, 27

Walpole St. Peter, 39
Walsingham, Lord, 112–113
Wangford Warren, Suffolk, 40
Watatunga Wildlife Reserve, 113
Watson, P., 38, 119–120
Waxham, 39, 41, 85, 140, 176
Wayland Agricultural Show, 112
weasel, 57, 63, 83–84, 135
Weeting, 170
    Hall, 111
    Heath, 119
Wells–next–the–Sea, 20, 32, 41, 65, 148, 153–155
West Acre, 108, 110, 115, 117
West Tofts, 170
Weybourne, 17, 43–44, 50, 137

Whatley, E., 164
White, G., Rev., 116
White, W., 21, 34, 35, 53, 56, 63, 67, 70, 71, 75, 102, 145,
Williams, J.E., 37
Winterton, 39, 85, 110, 136–137, 140, 176
Wiveton, 44
      Hall, 150
Woburn Abbey, 150
Woodbastwick, 136
Wretham, 19, 107, 109
Wymondham, 165

Yaxham, 120

Milton Keynes UK
Ingram Content Group UK Ltd.
UKHW020952241024
449966UK00006B/114